CONTENTS

MAKING MIRACLES

Inspiring mind-methods to supercharge your emotions and rejuvenate your health

ARNOLD FOX, MD
BARRY FOX, PhD

THE NAPOLEON HILL FOUNDATION

JAICO PUBLISHING HOUSE
Ahmedabad Bangalore Bhopal Bhubaneswar Chennai
Delhi Hyderabad Kolkata Lucknow Mumbai

Published by Jaico Publishing House
A-2 Jash Chambers, 7-A Sir Phirozshah Mehta Road
Fort, Mumbai - 400 001
jaicopub@jaicobooks.com
www.jaicobooks.com

Published in arrangement with
The Napoleon Hill Foundation
1 College Avenue, Wise
Virginia 24293, USA

MAKING MIRACLES
ISBN 978-81-7992-892-9

First Jaico Impression: 2008
Fourth Jaico Impression: 2012

Printed by
Snehesh Printers
320-A, Shah & Nahar Ind. Est. A-1
Lower Parel, Mumbai - 400 013.

FOREWORD

Great people are ordinary people with extraordinary amounts of determination.

Epictetus

Tough times never last. But when tough times strike, we often wish for miracles. The greatest miracle, of course, is the one that is always with us: our God-given spirit. Many of us have made it through tough times with nothing but spirit. That's all we needed.

I remember the tough times when I was growing up. We scratched our way through the Depression. We lost our home and farm to a tornado. There were tough times building the ministry. We were poor in money. But we were rich in spirit, the greatest wealth of all.

It's great to see that two scientists–a medical doctor and a psychologist–understand the tremendous God-given power of the human spirit. They present a crystal clear message: You hold the key to health and happiness in your hands. And it all starts with the positive thoughts in your mind. They show you how to use that key with a sure blend of science, inspiration, and scripture.

The Drs. Fox–Arnold and Barry, father and son–describe how your words, thoughts, and actions are translated into the things of the body, into chemical and electrical substances and messengers that affect your immune system, your heart, your cholesterol, indeed, your every cell. These two spiritual men have reunited what modern medicine mistakenly tore asunder. In rejoining the human body and spirit, the Foxes make available generous doses of the best medicine one can have: spirit.

Here you have a writing team that brings two exciting perspectives: The father's life was tempered by the privation of the 1930s and the fear, then exuberance, of the 1940s; the son came of age during the great turmoil of the 1960s. From opposite sides of what we once called the generation gap, they join to present their exhilarating science of the human spirit. And it is a science of the spirit they describe, for they show us how mind and body are joined. They teach us that the body cannot be healthy unless the spirit is whole. And they give us their marvelous prescription for joy, belief, love, forgiveness, and prayer.

And what a prescription it is! In readable, inspiring language, they teach how to turn on the power of the spirit. The writing is brisk and sometimes humorous, sometimes touching, always fascinating and profound. The Foxes challenge us to be our best, then tackle the management of our own medical care. They point out that our well-meaning doctors often fail in their efforts to give us good health, because a pill or surgery isn't the best medicine for most of our ills. The best medicine is often a generous dose of Good Spirit.

Strange words coming from doctors? In the past, yes. But the Foxes are helping to lead the medical community into the future. We're headed for a great future, one in which science will serve our spirit, as well as our physical body.

Scripture tells us that a merry heart is like a medicine. The Foxes tell us why, then give us the good words that help make us merry. They are truly, as the Reverend Norman Vincent Peale said, "an amazing father and son team."

How honored I am to add this opening word to a book written by a son and father whom I have known as dear friends for years and years!

DR. ROBERT H. SCHULLER

PREFACE

Making Miracles is a medical doctor's 14-day program for health, happiness, and success in every aspect of life. You will learn how to bolster your spirit, improve your health, strengthen your immune system, brighten your outlook, and open up many new avenues in your life. You can lose the weight you've been wanting to lose. You can do better in school, and at work. You can learn to love yourself and have others love you as well. You can get the job, get the promotion, get the raise. You can put the nagging insecurities and anxieties, the guilt, fear, anger, and frustration behind you. You can do away with a long list of physical problems, from headaches, to ulcers, to fatigue, to pain. You can make the miracle of having your life be what you want it to be.

Boy, it sounds great, it sounds so easy. Well, Making Miracles is a time-tested, medically approved program based on over 30 years of experience as a medical doctor, and bolstered by the great works of the Reverend Norman Vincent Peale, whose *The Power of Positive Thinking* and many other books have helped millions overcome adversity and negativity; Maxwell Maltz, M.D., the plastic surgeon who found that making a person look beautiful doesn't bring happiness unless that person also feels beautiful inside; Professor René Dubos, whose philosophical reflections on medicine, science, and man have done much to humanize medicine; and other giants. Yes, you can make the miracles you want in your life. We all can, but it takes work. This is a lifetime program, not a quick-fix diet or three easy guidelines for success.

Along with many of my patients, my son Barry and I have used the Making Miracles program for some time now. Like everyone else, we have to be on guard against the dark sides of human nature. We must always remember to keep our spirits strong, and every day renew our commitment to the Ten Pillars, the ten aspects of a healthy spirit we describe in the book. We make our mistakes, like everyone else. We sometimes give in to the negative thinking that harms our immune systems and shrinks the boundaries of our worlds. But it's all right if you fall down occasionally. As Fred Astaire sang to Ginger Rogers in *Swing Time*, you "pick yourself up, brush yourself off, start all over again."

Making Miracles is about living to your fullest potential, physically, mentally, emotionally, and spiritually. You can make the miracle of being all that you possibly can. Making Miracles is the easiest program of its kind to follow *and is certainly the most important, for the health of your body is absolutely dependent upon the health of your spirit.* As you will learn, that is a scientific fact.

Read the entire book through first. Then go back and work your way through the program one day at a time. Reread the chapter for the day carefully, more than once if possible. Try to put yourself in the case histories as you read them. Tell yourself that you can do the good things these people did, that you can be as spirited, as brave, and as resolute as they. And you know what? You *are* as spirited, as brave, and as resolute as they. These are ordinary people, just like you and I. They met the challenge: So can we!

Learn the affirmation/visualizations and special medical R_X for each day by heart. Write them down on index cards and carry them with you, until you have them memorized. Make them a part of your everyday life: Soon, your life will take on the colors of your dreams as you achieve goal after goal.

If you have trouble with a particular Pillar of Spirit (suppose you simply cannot forgive someone right now), that's all right. Skip that day of the program and come back to it later. We're striving for lifetime goals with a lifetime program; instant perfection isn't necessary.

If you need more than one day to get through a part of the program, that's all right, too. Take two days, three days, five, or as many as you need. The key is to keep your momentum and spirit up. Sticking to a rigid schedule is not important.

Barry and I will talk a lot about spirit, the gospel of your mind, and the Ten Pillars. We'll present laws and principles, case histories, quotes and summaries. But it really comes down to one simple concept: *Positive Addiction to Yourself.* Millions of us are addicted to alcohol, legal and illegal drugs, eating, gambling, risk taking, love and so on. Millions more are addicted to negativity, anger, fear, frustration, feelings of failure, grudges and hatred. It's as though we were taught, from our earliest days, to plant the seeds of negativity in our minds, to water them daily so they might flourish. But you'll learn in this book that these seeds of negativity are infectious germs of the spirit, every bit as deadly as the viruses that cause physical diseases. As a medical doctor with over 30 years' experience in treating desperately ill patients, I can tell you that the unhealthy germs of the spirit and mind can destroy our immune systems, weaken our hearts, turn our body chemistry upside down, bring on depression and despair, and predispose us to failure in every aspect of life. For many of us, too many of us, this tendency to self-destroy has already set in.

If we can break our addiction to negativity–and we can–we can strengthen our immune systems, protect our health, lift our spirits, and encourage great things to happen to us. You can do this by becoming positively addicted to yourself, absolutely addicted to the great feelings that come from being filled with joy, conviction, courage, love, forgiveness, dreams, and the other Pillars of the Spirit. That's what Making Miracles is really about.

The two sure signs of good mental health are (1) knowing that nobody really has it made, for we are all human; and (2) being happy when someone else succeeds or receives something, and sharing in the joy of it. When we are positively addicted to ourselves, when our spirits are soaring, we are able to partake of all the joy and love in the world, ours and everybody else's. At the same time, we're firmly grounded in reality, we recognize our strengths and our weaknesses, and we understand our role in this world. This awareness puts us in the best of all possible worlds.

Like most people, you have probably been told more than once that you aren't good enough, that you can't do it, that you shouldn't even bother to try. The truth is that you *are* good enough, you *can* do it, and you *should* try to live life to its fullest, most joyful and loving potential every minute of every day. Make the miracle of unleashing your spirit that great tool you can use to build exactly the kind of life you want.

ARNOLD FOX, M.D.

Acknowledgments

Many people helped shape this book. Our agents, Jim and Rosalie Heacock, guided us through the early drafts. Bill Gottlieb, Editor in Chief of Rodale Books, recognized the potential. Charlie Gerras, superb editor that he is, helped us refine and polish the words and ideas.

In a larger sense, this book has been in the making for over 50 years. It began with my maternal grandfather, who always told me to be as great as I possibly could be. And you're never better, he would say, than when you're helping others help themselves.

For my grandfather, every day was filled with opportunities for helping others. He spent his life helping the poor, the homeless, and those without hope. The little bit of money he and my grandmother managed to save for their old age was never used. Helping others so devoutly kept them both young and vital to the very end.

My parents had plenty of problems; my father fought a long and terrible battle with "demon rum." When my father couldn't get a job during the dark days of the Depression, my mother worked as a maid at the Germantown Poorhouse in Philadelphia. For 90 long hours a week, she received $5. She always worked, but those difficult days stand out in my mind. Not because they were so hard, but because she never forgot to smile. Nor did she forget to tell me that the future would always be great for me. Both of my parents poured all the positivity they had into me, their only child. Don't worry about obstacles, they told me, just keep going forward! And always do good, they said, echoing my grandfather. Do good, not for gratitude or for reward, but for the sake of doing good!

I learned later that my parents were special, but not unique. Many of my young friends, my street buddies in South Philly, were also forged in the crucible of enthusiasm, positivity, and perseverance.

All along the way I was helped by people—people I often hardly knew. Many kindnesses were given to me without strings—a kind word, an introduction, a free meal, a few dollars until payday. Most of the givers received no reward, save my gratitude, and the great feeling that comes from doing good for the sake of doing good.

How lucky I was to meet Hannah, who married me, a penniless student, then went with me through ten more years of schooling. Lovingly, she devoted herself to our family. She was always there for all of us, carrying on the tradition of teaching children to believe in themselves.

Hannah and every one of my children contributed to this book, this lifetime accumulation of teaching and learning. Howard, Eric, Barry, Steven, Barbara, Bruce: As each new member of the Fox family entered onto life's stage, he or she presented a new thrill, a new challenge, and a new person with whom to share our love and enthusiasm. As I repeated to my children, the positive maxims I had heard from my predecessors, I could feel the magic in those great ideas and see their effect. As I helped transfer the ideas from generation to generation, I felt as if I were part of an endless chain of positivity and possibility, beginning far in the past, extending forever into the future.

I began by saying that this book began 50 years ago, with my grandfather. Perhaps it's more accurate to say that the book began ages ago, with my grandfather writing the first words in my little chapter. I wrote alone for a while, then with and for my family. Now I proudly write with my son Barry, watching with amazement as a little boy I once carried now shapes my ideas and philosophy with his own. Someday, the baton will be passed to the next generation.

We all "write" a little in the book of life, our thoughts influencing the thoughts of others. What went before helped determine what we are today. What we write into the book of life will help shape those who follow us.

ARNOLD FOX, M.D.

Day 1

SPIRIT!

Quench not the spirit.
1 Thess 5:19

There I was—a third-year medical student waiting for a baby to be born. A little over 30 years have passed, but I remember that day as though it were yesterday, for that very morning I had watched my son Barry enter the world. Then, just a few hours later, a classmate and I were in a ramshackle little house by the rail yards, where we'd been sent with a birthing table and all sorts of sterile equipment. Eight or nine little children ran around the yard, playing, chasing each other, as the father anxiously paced about.

We had been told that the baby was not due for another hour or so. It was obvious, however, that the baby had its own timetable. The obstetrics resident who was to handle the birth hadn't arrived yet. I may have appeared to be cool and confident as I joked around with my fellow student about what would happen if we had to deliver the baby, but inside I was shaking.

Suddenly the woman cried out, "It's coming!" And come it did, quickly pushing its way out of the womb and into the world.

I frantically grabbed the emerging head and held it as the baby seemed to fall right out of the mother. Everything was happening so quickly! My classmate hurriedly searched through the medical manual we had with us, trying to find out what to do next.

Time seemed to stop as I laid the tiny baby, covered with birthing fluid, on its mother's belly. We waited for the baby to breathe, to give us a sign of life. "Oh, God," I gasped. "How long does it take?"

Then we heard the cry we had been waiting for. The breath of life had entered the baby. A new spirit was among us. I knew that this new spirit, like my new son's spirit, and all new spirits, was a bundle of unlimited potential. This new spirit, like all spirits, could conquer the world if it remained strong.

> **We're all born with unlimited potential in the form of spirit!**

SPIRIT!

> *The Lord God formed man of the dust of the ground, and breathed into his nostrils the breath of life; and man became a living soul.*
>
> Gen 2:7

As dust we begin and as dust we end. What distinguishes us from the dust is that intangible something called spirit.

Our word *spirit* comes from the Latin for breath. Spirit is our spark of life, the animating principle that gives us energy, creativity, and the will to thrive. Spirit is the spark of the divine within us. Spirit is a marvelous tool with which you can make miracles–the miracles of health, happiness, and success–for yourself and for others.

This is a book about the spirit. This is also a medical book based on the latest scientific principles. I was trained as a medical doctor–as an internist and cardiologist. But I am a spiritual man as well, a physician who believes that the best medicine for most of our ills is not to be found in a syringe or a pill. Rather, it is in the strength and quality of our spirit.

More people than ever are physically ill. We suffer from terrible, often terminal afflictions such as heart disease, cancer, stroke, and diabetes. We've been hit by a virtual epidemic of headaches, backaches, neckaches, ulcers, bowel disorders, fatigue, sleep problems, inability to concentrate, and many other ailments. More than ever before, we are depressed, lonely, and unhappy. Millions are consumed by anger, rage, or frustration. We feel as though we've failed in life. We're unable to forgive ourselves our sins, or forgive others for theirs. Traditions seem to fall by the wayside. Family is no longer a strong support center. Opportunities seem to vanish as the boundaries of our lives shrink. Diseases we didn't even know about when I was going to medical school are scaring the daylights out of us—with good reason.

Patients come to me with laundry lists of complaints, and paper bags filled with medicines. A 42-year-old mother of three had been to 17 different doctors in search of a cure for her back pain. A man with a 20-year history of asthma had gone to physicians and clinics in seven different countries, but found no relief. A young woman wore a neck brace for 3 years after a car accident. Despite drugs and therapy, she could barely hold her head up straight. A very famous old-time actor brought three thick books into my office. "There are my sickness diaries," he said with a rueful grin. In the back of one of the diaries he had tallied up his sick and healthy days for the past 40 years. An incredible 60 percent of those days had been surrendered to sickness!

Other patients aren't able to tell me what's bothering them when I first see them. They're lying unconscious in the intensive care unit, needles and tubes sticking in their bodies, and surrounded by many high-tech monitoring devices. Standing next to their beds, amid all the machines, I feel as though I were inside the space shuttle, not a house of healing.

The medical community has responded to our epidemic of distress in the traditional way, calling for more drugs and more surgeries; stronger drugs and riskier surgeries; more specific drugs and more complex surgeries. As a member of the American medical community, I am proud of our accomplishments. It is increasingly obvious, however, that our traditional tools are failing us. *More Americans are taking more drugs, being plugged into more machines, and wearing more surgical scars than ever, but we are not nearly as healthy as we can be. As we* should *be.*

We stagger into our doctors' offices in record numbers. It seems that we are virtually buried under an avalanche of diseases. We look to pills as our saviors, and we unwittingly trade burial by disease for burial by pills and their side effects. *Most of the time, the pills cannot possibly work, because pills are for the body and most of our physical distress is of the spirit.*

The first billion-dollar-a-year drug was an ulcer medicine named Tagamet. It remained the world's best-selling prescription medicine until a new drug called Zantac claimed the crown. It is also for ulcers. In fact, Zantac takes out advertisements in the medical journals to boast about being listed in the *Guinness Book of World Records* as the most prescribed ulcer drug on earth.

We will spend about $3.6 billion on ulcer medicines alone next year, and more every year after that. Despite swallowing record numbers of pills, we will continue to suffer from ulcers. None of these medicines can really cure our ulcers, for most ulcers are symptoms of spiritual distress, not physical disease. *So long as we persist in treating ulcers in the stomach, not the spirit, we condemn ourselves to pain.* This is not a new idea. Back in medical school I was taught that the stomach is the sounding board of our emotions. *Still, we continue to treat the symptoms and overlook the root problem, unknowingly condemning ourselves to disease and distress.*

Most medicines do exactly what they promise to do. But their promises, unfortunately, have nothing to do with the real cause of our pain.

It doesn't have to be that way. God has given us the tool we need to flourish: He gave us spirit, the best medicine of all.

When the spirit is in pain, the body cries out. Modern medicine can sometimes help the body, but the best medicine for most of our ills is ages old: A strong spirit.

The Medicine Called Spirit

The best doctors recognize and use the spirit, although physicians as a group adamantly refuse to acknowledge it. That seems odd, for doctors see the spirit in action almost every day. I have treated many patients who refused to let their terrible illness beat them. You could see their spirit blazing defiantly in their eyes. You could hear it shouting "I will live!" in their every word, even when their voices were soft and weak. You could sense its electrifying power filling the room.

As a young doctor fresh from training at the Los Angeles County Hospital, I was asked to examine a man who was very ill.

He was only a few years younger than I, and like me, he had three young sons. My examination confirmed what the man's general practitioner suspected: This young father had a rare and virulent form of cancer.

During the examination he told me about the printing business he had founded several years ago, how he began it from scratch with a small shop and built it into three stores. He spoke of the fun he'd had at work–the challenges met, the obstacles overcome. I could feel the incredible enthusiasm and confidence, the joy of life leaping out of him. I wanted to wrap some of it up and take it home to show my boys.

"Something is wrong with my body," he said without fear. "But my spirit is strong." Then he grinned and said, "My spirit can lick your spirit any day!"

I knew he had spirit enough for 50 people. I also "knew" that he didn't have long to live.

A year later I had learned a lesson about the tremendous power of the human spirit. All traces of this man's cancer had vanished. The drugs we doctors gave him undoubtedly played a role, but the drugs we had back then were even less potent than those of today. I am convinced that his indomitable spirit was the medicine that beat the cancer.

In this man's hands, spirit was a powerful hammer which he used to build a monument to life: to health, happiness, and success.

Each of us is born with a very powerful "doctor within" called spirit.

WHAT MAKES US MIGHTY?

"Wait a minute, Dr. Fox," some patients say when I tell them that their spirit is a powerful medicine. "How can spirit do anything to me, make me healthy? Doesn't spirit have to do with God?"

Absolutely. Spirit is the touch of the divine within us. Spirit is the tool with which we build our lives. Spirit is the filter through which we touch, hear, see, smell, and otherwise sense the world. Spirit is the looking glass that reflects the world as we see it.

Your spirit is a special kind of magnet, one that draws like things to you. The strong spirit tends to bring good things into your life: vibrant health and energy, joyfully positive feeling, success in every aspect of life. A weak spirit is an even more powerful magnet, drawing negatives down upon you.

There is a spiritual "body" within the natural body of each of us. Or perhaps it is more accurate to say that our spirit is the motor that drives our body. When the motor is powerful, the body is full of health, energy, enthusiasm, curiosity, love, and delight. When our motor is running smoothly, we can easily grasp all the wonderful opportunities life always places before us. The body will almost always follow a willing spirit.

Even before I made the connection between strong spirit and good health, it was clear to me that there was a certain something within each of us. I'm reminded of an old man–he seemed very old to me–who used to take me with him in his old truck out to the farms in New Jersey. He would bring fresh bread to the farmers, and return to the city with their produce for the markets. At night he used the same truck to gather food and clothing, which he took to the poorest families in South Philadelphia. He was still at it years later, as he approached his eightieth birthday. This man was my grandfather. I used to wonder why he was so much healthier than his friends. After all, they were about the same age as him, had similar backgrounds, had eaten the same foods, and had even come from the same countries. Why was Grandfather so much healthier and so much happier? He had worked hard all his life, physical, back-breaking work, yet he was still at it in his seventies, his back still straight, his shoulders broad and strong, his spirit sharp and focused.

My grandfather smiled often. He never worried unduly. He was filled with belief in himself, with love for others, with courage, joy, forgiveness, and goodness. He always dreamed of what might be and worked toward his goals. And you'll learn throughout this book that belief, love, courage, joy, and other positive qualities are the ingredients of the strong spirit.

Grandmother and Grandfather saved very carefully for their old age. Often today, when a 20-year-old takes a job, he immediately wants to know what the retirement benefits are. Then he spends the next 40 years unhappily waiting to retire. I used to kid with my grandparents about their saving for old age. Not because they already seemed so very old to me, but because it didn't look as though Grandfather would ever stop working. Even in his seventies he was working, helping what he called the "old people," bringing them food, taking them to the doctor, and so on. Grandmother would say it was time to start using the money they had saved for old age, but he always replied, "Old age isn't here yet."

"I don't have very strong muscles," he would tell me. "That doesn't matter because the might of a man has nothing to do with his muscles. His strength is in his spirit. God gave me a strong spirit, and every day I say to myself that my spirit is growing stronger every minute. *That's* why I'm so healthy. And *that's* why I always smile." That's why his life, which lasted more than eight decades, was so healthy.

> **The might of man lies in his spirit! The health of his body, the clarity of his vision, the scope of his grasp, the length of his days: All depend upon his strong spirit!**

The Secret of Success

As a child, I wasn't sure I agreed with Grandfather's assessment of his life. He considered himself a success. To me, however, the successful people seemed to be the ones who had the most money, or were movie stars, captains of industry, or at least drove a big car.

Having gone from being an economically deprived South Philadelphia street kid to becoming a Beverly Hills physician, I can tell you that success has nothing to do with money. Success is happiness. That's all there is to it. The most successful people in the world aren't the richest or the most powerful. The successes in life are the people who enjoy living, who find happiness everywhere, who look forward to every day with enthusiastic anticipation, who love and are loved. These are the winners in life.

How can we become successes? It all begins with *spirit*!

A strong spirit ensures that all the channels in your heart are opened wide, allowing you to love and be loved. And love–love for yourself and for others–is a prime ingredient for success: The strong spirit has plenty of room for forgiveness. The ability to forgive freely–to forgive yourself and forgive others–guarantees you a large measure of happiness and contentment. A strong spirit is fired by optimism and enthusiasm, allowing for belief in yourself, courage, and joy.

Spirit may seem an elusive concept right now, but as you'll learn later, your spirit has direct and immediate effect upon your body. For example, the good thoughts engendered by a strong spirit spur the body's release of substances such as endorphins, the hormones that lift the mood, block certain kinds of pain, and strengthen the immune system. Your spirit can actually change the biochemistry of your body for the better.

A strong spirit can even make you healthier, more vital and energetic. Recent studies are proving what we've known for years: There are strong links between the mind and immune system. The strong spirit works through the mind to rev up the immune system, to give you energy, to make you feel great. The health of every single cell in your body depends on having a vibrant spirit. Even the seemingly independent macrophages, those powerful immune soldiers that engage germs in hand-to-hand combat, have receptors with which they receive messages from the spirit by way of the brain.

Success is having vibrant health. We all want to be full of energy and vitality, to feel young and healthy to a very old age. The young oldster who has lived many years in health and joy is a great success. When your spirit is strong, your odds of living to be vibrant and healthy to a very old age are increased.

Success is being the person you want to be, having the things you want to have, and doing the things you want to do. Being, having, and doing does not necessarily mean accumulating possessions and money. Many people are very happy, though they have only a modest amount of money. Others, including some of my very rich Beverly Hills patients, find no joy in their millions of dollars. Being, having, and doing means exploring life in hundreds of different ways, living life to its fullest.

Exuberant happiness, vibrant health, and being, having, and doing: These are the components of success. These are the miracles we want to have in our lives, and these are the miracles your spirit can make happen.

> **Strong spirit is the door through which you enter into the world of exuberant joy, boundless love, and unlimited potential. With strong spirit you have the potential to be the great person you want to be, do the good things you want to do, and have the fulfilling things you want to have.**

When Your Spirit Is Weak

Properly used, spirit can be the best medicine you can have. Unfortunately, many of us unknowingly turn our spirit into a weapon we use against ourselves.

A man came to my office some years ago complaining of back pains, headaches, nervousness, and insomnia. I took his medical and personal history, performed a careful physical examination, and called for the appropriate laboratory studies. After the examination, we sat down in my office to talk. "I don't know what's wrong with me, Dr. Fox. It's always been like this for me. My life is lousy. I don't know why I was ever born."

This wealthy man didn't realize it, but he was using his spirit against himself, using it to knock himself down instead of using it to build himself up. The words he spoke and the thoughts that filled his head were instructions to his spirit: Life is lousy. His spirit responded by altering the biochemistry of his body, thus encouraging disease and unhappiness.

A beautiful actress recently came to my office suffering from recurrent colds and flus, menstrual cramps, difficulty in concentrating, constipation, heart flutters, and what she called uptightness. She had a few easily treatable physical problems. But the problems were symptoms of deeper distress. It was her answers to some written questions, not the traditional physical examination, that revealed the underlying disorder. I asked her to complete a series of sentences. Here is a sample of her writing. The words following the dashes are hers.

I am–*fat.*
If I should die today–*no one would notice.*
I have achieved–*I'm still alive. Does that count for something?*
My life is–*painful. I want to cry all the time.*
The thought of suicide–*has occurred to me. But who would care?*
More than anything, I want–*I don't know. I don't think about lofty things, just about getting through each day.*

This woman was spiritually ill. Like the businessman, she had little spirit, little spark of life, little joy or happiness.

A strong spirit energizes the immune system. But when your spirit is weak, your immune system falters, and the biochemistry of your body tilts in favor of disease and depression. When your spirit is weak, you see life through half-closed eyes that miss all the wonderful possibilities and opportunities that are always out there. The weak spirit is a powerful magnet, drawing in all the bad things we work so hard to avoid.

When your spirit is weak, you are filled with pessimism and gloom; you feel small and helpless; you wonder if it's possible to find any joy in life. Without realizing it, you are closing the channels of your heart to love, stopping the flow of endorphins and other substances, stopping up the flow of thoughts and ideas in your brain.

When your spirit is weak, life is a chore, not the pleasure that it can be.

I've delivered many babies: boys and girls, black and white, small and large. I never delivered a success or a failure in life. I never delivered a lawyer, a doctor, or a truck driver. Only babies. At the moment of birth they were all successful because they were filled with unlimited potential. Some were physically stronger than others, some had more innate wisdom or inborn courage than others. But all had unlimited potential as far as their spirit was concerned. And spirit, as we know, is the real key to success in life.

The key to success is always in your hands. It's called spirit!

"THOUGHT DISEASE"

I am a physician with more than 30 years experience in the front lines of crisis medicine as an internist and cardiologist, responding to the needs of desperately ill people in intensive care units and coronary care units. I can tell you that very few of the people who come to doctors' offices need the highly technical skills we spend so much time perfecting.

As superbly trained as doctors are, we are not equipped to treat the loneliness, estrangement, disenchantment, frustration, guilt, and lack of spirit that are the cause of most of our physical and emotional ills. We are trained to treat the end result–the diseases that come from poor spirit–but the underlying cause remains to haunt us.

What is the underlying ill? For many of us it is a weak spirit, or, to put it another way, what I call "thought disease."

Thought disease is an illness of the spirit. We're familiar with diseases of the body, diseases caused by bacteria and viruses. We know that infectious germs can enter the body and harm us.

Likewise, there are very specific germs that cause thought disease. These germs are all around us every day; in us, of us. These germs are called anger, frustration, loneliness, animosity, resentment, fear, and guilt. We can neither put these germs under a microscope nor fully describe them, but it is increasingly obvious that these germs can be deadly.

For years we've felt that mind and body were separate entities. Mind and body happen to be attached to each other, but it was medical heresy to suggest that what happened in the mind actually influenced the body. Today we know that mind and body are tightly linked. That is why *there is never a thought without a thing*. Every thought we have acts through our brain to create the "things" of health or disease, happiness or depression, success or failure. These things are very real chemical and electrical messengers, such as cortisone, adrenaline, endorphins, and many more. It's these things that turn thoughts into physical reality.

The brain is the largest gland in the body, producing a constant stream of substances, messengers that are sent to every part of the body, every single cell. Our thoughts, or words and actions, are the stuff of our spirit. They are the spirit influencing the body.

Good thoughts spur the production of beneficial biochemicals such as endorphins which, in the right amounts, make us healthier and happier. Good thoughts are medicine to the spirit.

Bad thoughts, however, unleash waves of highly charged substances such as adrenaline, noradrenaline, 40-plus varieties of cortisone, and others that can pound our system just as a hammer can shatter glass, and literally make us sick. These things, born of bad thoughts, increase the chances that you'll get cancer, have a heart attack, or suffer from innumerable other diseases. Negative thinking also stops the flow of joy through your body, and even decreases your chances of success. Negative thoughts are infectious germs to the spirit. That's why the overwhelming majority of people flooding doctors' offices today are suffering from diseases caused initially by their thoughts, not bacteria or viruses.

Thought disease is a terrible scourge because it attacks our spirit, because it attacks through the spirit, and because it is of the spirit. Tens of millions of us are addicted to negativity, like the businessman and the actress. We have eyes that see only the bad in life, ears that hear only sorrow, arms that embrace sadness. With each jot of negativity we allow into our mind, each bit of unhappiness savored and chewed over, we weaken our spirit. And as the spirit goes, so goes the body.

I've been fortunate to meet many people with soaring spirits, like John, a 69-year-old plumber who had been a patient of mine for some years. He was married to a woman he loved deeply, was the father of two, and had six grandchildren. John loved life, and loved people. He made it a point to spend one full day a week doing plumbing work for poor people for half or a quarter of his usual rate–even for free if they couldn't afford to pay him. John never struck it big, and he was never important in the usual sense of the word. He struggled with the headaches many of us know: high taxes, a problem child, an auto accident that left him with a permanent limp, his wife's breast cancer, and so on. Through good or bad, his spirit was strong. Everywhere he looked he saw joy, he saw new possibilities, he saw love. It's no wonder he lived to be vibrant and healthy well into his seventies.

I've also known people with low spirits, like Martha, a 42-year-old housewife who saw misery everywhere. She developed breast cancer but it was detected early, and the prognosis was excellent. I had the feeling that she almost welcomed the cancer as proof of the fact that life was miserable. The surgeons removed all traces of the cancer, but Martha wasted away during the next several years, coming down with one disease after another until she finally died. Although the death certificate gave pneumonia as the cause of death, I believe her spirit died, and her body followed.

Thought disease is one of the most terrible diseases of our time, of every time past, and probably, of the future as well.

> **Thought disease is the weakened spirit's means of asking for help.**

Curing Thought Disease

We doctors have a panoply of powerful prescription pharmaceuticals, yet there are no drugs to heal the spirit, for the spirit is the touch of God, not a thing of the flesh to be manipulated by chemical substances. There are only words, yet, for the spirit, words are powerful medicine. Words of faith, enthusiasm, love, joy, forgiveness, courage, conviction: These are physicians to the spirit.

In a sense, our words are our spirit, for it is our words that are the concrete expression of our thoughts, beliefs, and attitudes. The actress, whose every word shouted out her depression, anxiety, fear, alienation, and her lack of self-esteem, unknowingly allowed her words to destroy her health.

We all know the words that harm us. We need to learn the words that heal. Some of the most powerful words of healing are those contained in the Bible. Because they are the words of God, and because we are all a part of God, they are our words as well; words to nourish and strengthen our spirit, mind, and body.

Good thoughts are the antidote to thought disease. More

than that, good thoughts are the key to success in every aspect of life; for words control your spirit, and your spirit directs your life.

Not long ago, I received a letter from an old friend and patient named Don. He was the only one of his large family who went to college and graduate school, and he later became a wealthy and powerful businessman. Only 47 years old, this native Californian had everything anyone could want, except for health and happiness. It was no wonder, for his every word seemed to be negative, his every thought one of anger, his every act designed to help himself at someone else's expense. In his letter, Don wrote:

> I'm not surprised I became as rich as I did, considering I was so dedicated to making money. What surprises me, however, is that I did not completely ruin my health, so dedicated was I to quashing every bit of joy, love, enthusiasm or forgiveness that dared enter my mind.
>
> Two years after I last saw you I hit bottom. Nothing in life gave me satisfaction, not even the money which was for so many years my sole reason for being. I would have committed suicide, but, to do so, I would have had to care passionately about something (killing myself). I couldn't even interest myself in ending my misery.
>
> Perhaps I would have continued in that state forever if not for my youngest. Last year, at the age of seven, she told me I was a miserable old man who hated the world. She was right. I didn't mind ruining my own life but I couldn't ruin hers as well (having done so poorly with my older children). I resolved to cure my spiritual ailments for her sake.
>
> Arn, thank you for giving me the tools with which to turn my life around. For the first time since I can remember, I am sincerely happy. I'm even enthusiastic about life. (But don't tell anyone. It'll ruin my reputation!)

Through this book I'll be urging you always to speak and think of things that are good. Whatsoever is enthusiastic, loving, joyful, forgiving, inspiring, honest, just, pure, or lovely—think constantly on these things, speak of them often. Fill your mind with these thoughts; for your thoughts, beliefs, and attitudes determine whether your spirit will be healthy or weak.

Yes, your spirit is the breath of God within you, the spark of the divine. But while it is given to you, it is also of you. Spirit is a dynamic process between you, the Creator, and all that He has created. Every thought you think, every word you utter, every act you perform becomes part of your spirit, for better or worse.

> **Your words are reflections of your spirit, and your spirit is made by your words. Your spirit makes you what you are, and you make your spirit what it is. The potential is unlimited; it is all within your grasp.**

When "Wishes" Come True

> *Whatsoever things are true . . . honest . . . just . . . pure . . . lovely . . . think on these things.*
>
> Phil. 4:8

"If the spirit is so wonderful," a patient asked me, "why are so many people unhealthy and unhappy? Why do they get thought disease so easily?"

The spirit's greatest power is also its undoing in so many of us. Your spirit absolutely "trusts" you; your word is unconditionally accepted. If you say the world is great, your spirit believes you, and it acts on that great belief. It opens wide the circuits in your brain, throws open the channels of your heart, sharpens your vision to make you quicker to spot opportunity, energizes the immune system, spurs the production of endorphins and other beneficial biochemicals, and does everything else it can to ensure that your world is indeed great. But if you say the world is not so good, your spirit immediately responds by prompting the overproduction of adrenaline, cortisonelike substances, and other biosubstances that, in excess, weaken your immune system, slow the flow of creativity and thought, dam the channels of your heart, and otherwise work to make your unhappy thoughts come true.

Your spirit makes your "wishes" your reality—even if you don't know you've made the wish.

You don't have to speak your wishes out loud, or even realize that they are wishes. You see, your spirit examines your every thought, word, or action. From these thoughts, words, and actions it derives your wishes. So think about things that are true, honest, just, pure, lovely, enthusiastic, joyous, forgiving, giving, and optimistic. Let these great thoughts be the wishes your spirit acts on, the wishes your spirit makes come true.

Wishes can come true, do come true every day. Always wish for the stuff of health and happiness for yourself and for others.

We Achieve by Spirit

Not by might, nor by power, but by my spirit. . .
Zech. 4:6

Our modern approach to health is seriously flawed. Our health philosophy celebrates disease, giving it the red carpet treatment. Instead, we should strive to create the conditions that encourage vibrant health, exuberant happiness, and success in life.

Drugs, surgeries, and the various medical procedures are all useful, each in their ways. Their ways are powerful, yet limited. The way of the spirit, however, is both pervasive and powerful. Your spirit is already a part of you: it *is* you. Your spirit is a magnificent "doctor within." You have a direct connection to your spirit. Your spirit responds to you, and you to your spirit. That's why working with the spirit is so effective.

You can make miracles in your life. You can strengthen your spirit, bolster your immune system, learn to see the world through eyes of joy, lose weight, get that better job, and be successful in every aspect of life. The key is to stretch your spirit to its fullest potential. There are ten aspects of spirit, the Ten Pillars that, if kept strong and tall, will lift your spirit high. They are:

1. Choosing
2. Writing
3. Giving
4. Doing
5. Praying
6. Being Determined
7. Being Joyful
8. Forgiving and Making Amends
9. Dreaming
10. Pleasing

These Ten Pillars of Spirit are the foundation upon which your success in life is built. When you believe in yourself; when your self-esteem is good and you love others; when you take responsibility for your success and look to God for guidance, not a handout; when you face life with courage, determination, *and* joy; when your heart is full of friendship, forgiveness, and goodness; and when you dream of the great things that can be: When you do all this, your spirit will soar. With a spirit that soars, you can make miracles in your life.

R_X for Spirit!

A time to be born. . .

Eccles. 3:2

Each chapter in this book represents one day of your two-week Making Miracles program. Today is Day 1 of Making Miracles, the Day of Spirit! Tomorrow, Day 2, looks at the Gospel of Your Mind. Each of the ten following chapters examines one of the Ten Pillars of Spirit. On Day 13 we teach you how to become Positively Addicted to Yourself, and finally we gather all that you've learned for Day 14, The Beginning.

Read through the entire book quickly. Then work through it again, one day at a time, studying the lessons for each day carefully, one per day. Make what you learn a part of your life. Pay special attention to the affirmations/visualizations and medical R_X for each day. Memorize the daily R_X; take it to heart, etch it into your mind. Carry the R_X's image with you, see it, in your mind's eye, all day long.

Today you will begin building a strong spirit by practicing the R_X for Spirit! I'm going to give. Your R_X for Spirit! consists of a specially designed affirmation and visualization.

Affirmations are short, positive instructions to your spirit. With affirmations, you tell yourself how to act, believe, behave, and be. With affirmations, you plant an idea in your mind, in your spirit, on purpose. Affirmations are a powerful medicine for healing. Acting through your spirit, affirmations actually change the biochemistry of your body, making the things which you desire much easier to obtain. Visualizations are affirmations you "see" with your mind's eye.

Enter into the world of your R_X for Spirit! several times a day, with energy and conviction. Here's how. Set aside some time today to sit in a quiet room, on a comfortable chair. Tell everyone that you do not want to be disturbed; take the phone off the hook. Close your eyes. With your mind's eye, see a key. It's a golden key, gleaming, solid, resting on air. This key is no place in particular, it's simply there, in your mind. This key represents your spirit. Your spirit is the key that will unlock all the doors in life.

Take a good look at your golden key, your spirit. It's solid, and it fits every door and every lock. Although giant in size, like your spirit, the key fits easily into your hand. See it resting in your hand, always there, waiting to be used.

As you see your key resting in your hand, say your affirmation for spirit out loud:

> Today marks the exciting beginning of my joyous journey toward health, happiness, and success. I now see myself, with the help of the Lord, as the vibrantly healthy, exuberantly happy, and very successful person I know I am.

With this R_X for Spirit! you are giving your spirit a shot in the arm. Visualize yourself holding your key to life several times a day, as often as possible. Repeat your special R_X for Spirit! over and over during the day. Each time you see the key to success with your mind's eye, take an extra moment to recite today's affirmation, loudly, with enthusiasm and belief. Feel the key in your hand. Squeeze your fingers shut and really feel that golden key. It's yours. You can use it as often as you like.

It's best to do your R_X in a quiet place the first time. After that, do it anytime, any place you can. I often take a moment when getting in my car, or after parking it, to do an R_X. You can also use a quiet moment at your desk, during lunch, or when you're at home.

Keep a picture of your key in your head all day long. Recite your affirmation for spirit over and over during the day, out loud and to yourself, as many times as possible.

With this R_X, you are beginning to create the conditions that lead to success in every aspect of life. Repeat your affirmation when you lie down and when you rise, as you drive to and fro, when you are at work and when you are home. See yourself, with your mind's eye, as the happy, healthy, successful person you want to be, you *deserve* to be. Feel yourself imbued with the spirit of success.

Today is the day the Lord hath made; now is the time to begin. The Lord will make us plenteous in every work of our hand, starting right now. Make this day, and every day, a new beginning, another opportunity to add a blossom to your garden of life.

GET STARTED

Boldness has genius, power and magic in it.

Goethe

There's a crippling syndrome I see over and over among patients and other people I've met through the years: "But-itis." But-itis is a terrible disorder that prevents people from getting started. If you don't get started, of course, you'll never finish, you won't make your dreams come true.

You can tell right away if someone is a victim of but-itis. They'll say, over and over, "I wanted to do (fill in the blank) and to be (fill in the blank) and to have (fill in the blank), but. . ." And the "buts" are unending: "but I couldn't afford to," "but I got married," "but we had kids," "but I didn't have the background," "but they didn't hire me," and on and on.

I was lucky to learn very early in life, from my parents and especially my grandfather, that the only way to do something is to do it. There's no other way. I also learned not to waste too much time worrying about how you're going to do it. Just get started. That's the key. Everybody else will tell you why you can't do it, why it's impossible. Everybody else will have plenty of "buts" for you. Your job is to get started.

Ever since I was 12, I had wanted to be a doctor. People told me to forget it, it was impossible. You're too poor, they told me. You can't afford to go to college, let alone medical school. People from our neighborhood don't go to college; they get a job to support themselves. Besides, only one other person in your whole family, including all your cousins, was graduated from high school, let alone went to college.

But I was going to be a doctor, and that's all there was to it. Not only that, I would go to college at the expensive Ivy League University of Pennsylvania. There was simply no doubt in my mind. I wasn't any smarter than my friends who also had dreams. The difference was that while they realistically "knew" they couldn't do it, I absolutely knew I could. I took the first step.

I got married during college, then went off to medical school. Again, I didn't have nearly enough money for the tuition, let alone rent and food. And this was in the days before student grants and loans were readily available. To make things tougher, my wife became pregnant.

We were very, very poor during those difficult years. I wangled a job as a pharmaceutical representative for what is now one of the largest pharmaceutical companies in the country. Calling upon hundreds of pharmacists and other allied medical professionals, I heard it over and over again: "Gee, kid you're in medical school! I wanted to be a doctor, but. . ." But, but, everybody had a "but." "But I got married," "but I didn't have the money," but, but, but.

And so it went. I ran into many people who told me they would have done this or that, if only they had had enough money. Or enough time. Or enough training. Or enough talent. I never had enough of anything, except desire. I guess that's the only cure for but-itis: tremendous desire. It's wanting something so much you'll allow nothing to stand in your way.

I can't tell you how many times I nearly fell flat on my face during the dozen years it took to work my way through college, medical school, internship, and residency. Were it not for my wife picking me up so many times and the helping hand I got from so many others, I may not have made it. I took it step by step, always making sure that one foot was going forward. Sometimes I wondered if I were headed for a dead end. Still, I knew the only way to do something was to do it.

Every "Failure" Is a Success

For years I've been telling people in my office to get started! For God's sake, for your sake, get started with your weight-loss diet, with exercise, with stopping smoking, with positive thinking, treating your family better, or whatever it is you want to do. For many people, the hardest thing in the world is to get started. I believe many people are afraid to get started because they feel they're going to fail. If they don't run the race, well, at least they haven't lost again. In the meantime, their goals become harder to attain, and dreams grow dim.

Get started now. Get started with the idea that you're going to succeed. Lack of success is not failure, it's simply some negative feedback. Negative feedback has been given a bad rap. Missiles, rockets, airplanes with autopilot and other devices all have something called a servo mechanism to keep them on track. If the missile is off the course, the servo mechanism says, "You're two feet off course to the right," or, "Tilt down two degrees." The machine joyfully accepts the negative feedback, because the feedback gets it back on course. There's no concept of failure involved. The missile is simply on course, or off course and correcting.

We humans have a similar mechanism inside of ourselves, a success mechanism. We're built for success. Just like the servo mechanism, our success mechanism keeps us on course by responding to negative feedback. Without negative feedback, we would never reach our goals! So when you get that negative feedback from your success mechanism, say, "Great! Now I know what I'm doing wrong, so I can correct it. I see I smoked that cigarette, took that drink, ate that cake. Now I've got to get back on course."

I tell my weight-reduction patients to weigh themselves regularly. The scale is your friend, I tell them, because it tells you when you're off course.

It's OK to go off course, we all do it many times in life. It's OK as long as we keep correcting ourselves. Every failure leads to success.

So get your "buts" out of the way and become a winner! Want something so much that you're willing to do whatever it takes to get it. Put the "buts" aside, and take that first step. Don't worry about the other steps. Take that first one. Let every step be your first step. With each step, firm and long or halting and small, you'll find yourself coming closer and closer to your goal.

There *is* something you want more than anything else, *something you absolutely deserve to have*. That something is success in life. That something includes vibrant health, boundless joy, and endless love. That something is within your grasp. You can be the success you want to be. All the potential is within you, for you have spirit! Unleash your potential, strengthen your spirit. Stand on your toes, reach for the stars! All the good in the world is yours for the taking.

Day 2

The Gospel of Your Mind

In the beginning was the Word, and the Word was with God, and the Word was God.

John 1:1

In the beginning was the Word, and from the Word came the world. Your words also create a world: your world, the world as you see it.

Your words, studied or casual, are as powerful within the confines of your world as those that created the universe. Your words and thoughts create worlds of difference in the biochemistry of your body. Your words, spoken or not, are instructions to your spirit *that must be carried out.*

No matter how much of a skeptic or critical analyst you may be, your spirit automatically accepts that you tell it. You may refuse to accept a billion words hurled at you by friends, teachers, books, and television, but every single word you utter or think is quickly written into the gospel of your mind.

The gospel of your mind is a record of every word you have ever uttered, every thought you've thought, every act you've performed. As you think, talk, or act, a mental pen records your every notion, good or bad. It's automatic and inescapable. Whatever you say, think, or do becomes *your* truth.

From your word comes your world, the world of your spirit. From your word comes the power of your spirit.

Psychoneuroimmunology: The Mind-Body Connection

. . .of whom shall I be afraid?

Ps. 27:1

A couple of years ago, I received a call from a frightened patient of mine named Steve. It was obvious that something was very wrong–his voice was weak, full of fear and pain. It seems he had recently applied for an insurance policy. As is customary, the insurance company required Steve to undergo a medical examination. Steve was healthy and young, only 32 years old, so he expected to breeze through the checkup. He was confidently awaiting the good news that he had passed when his world fell apart: The insurance company told him that he had the AIDS virus. Now he was on the phone with me, desperately looking for help. I told Steve to come to my office right away.

He looked terrible. His skin was pale, his eyes bloodshot, his hands trembling. When I shook his hand, I noticed how weak and sweaty he was. Steve collapsed into a chair, saying he couldn't understand how he had gotten the AIDS virus. "I've been faithfully married for five years. I mean it, I don't cheat, and neither does Robin. I don't do drugs, I've never had a transfusion. I played around a little before I got married, but. . .do I really have AIDS?"

Hoping to reassure the frightened man, I said: "Sometimes these test results are wrong. You haven't any of the risk factors, so let's do a recheck. And while we're at it, we'll run some tests on your immune system." He agreed to the recheck.

A few days later I received the results of his immune-system tests. Things looked bad. His total T-cell count, T_4 count, T_4/T_8 ratio, and other indices of immune strength were very low. It looked as though he did indeed have the AIDS virus and possibly the beginnings of the full-blown disease. But a few days later I got the result of his AIDS test: It was negative.

I called Steve to give him the good news–the AIDS test result was negative–and the bad news–his immune system was weak. He was somewhat reassured. Still, he was worried. "Can we do the test again," he asked, "just to be sure?"

"Sure. Come on down to my office tomorrow."

The tests were repeated, and soon the results were on my desk. Once again, the AIDS test result was negative. His immune-system test results were better than before, but still low. When I called Steve to tell him there was no trace of the AIDS virus in his body, he was overjoyed. However, I was still worried about his immune system. I asked him to come in for more extensive tests. He happily agreed. Two weeks later he was back in my office for the tests.

About a week after that, when I received the results of the third check on Steve's immune system, I was astonished to find that his immune system was in tip-top shape! What had happened, in just a few weeks, to turn everything around?

The answer is simple: The gospel of Steve's mind had been entirely rewritten–twice.

Initially, before the insurance company wrongly informed Steve that he had AIDS, this young man's mental gospel was in fairly good shape. His book of truth told him that he was a pretty healthy, happy individual. Then he got the false but very bad news. Immediately, his unhappy and terrified words and thoughts began writing new chapters in his mental book of truth, hundreds of pages filled with descriptions of the disasters that awaited him. He could see himself, with his mind's eye, becoming very sick, wasting away, suffering a cruel and painful death. Horrible scenes were written into his mental gospel, by his own hand, with his own thoughts and words.

And all the terrible things written there became his truth. It was written that he would become weak, and so he did. It was written that his immune system would fall apart, and so it did. When he got the good news, when results of the second test told him that he did not have the AIDS virus, fewer terrible things were written into the gospel of his mind. His immune system improved a bit. Then, when the third test confirmed that he did not have AIDS at all, he filled hundreds of pages anew with good thoughts describing how healthy he was, how great he felt, how strong his immune system was, how long he would live. The good words buried the bad, and his immune system returned to full strength.

All this, simply on the basis of words and thoughts. What incredible power we have within our spirit!

In scientific terms, what happened to Steve illustrates the relationship between mind and body. There's a whole new branch of medical science called psychoneuroimmunology (psycho-neuro-immunology) that examines the way mind and body interact. We're finally developing hard, scientific proof for what we've intuitively known all along, that there is never a thought in the head that does not affect the body. We've discovered, for example, that nerves from the nervous system run deep within the spleen and other "staging areas" of the immune system. There are special receptors on the tiny immune system cells, putting mind and body, mind and immune system, in direct communication.

Like many of us, Steve unknowingly turned the power of his mind against his body, especially against his immune system. His bad thoughts were converted by his brain into the harmful "messages," the hormones and other biochemicals, that ordered his immune system to drop into low gear. Now he was at grave risk for acquiring whatever diseases the germs around him happened to be peddling. Fortunately, his good thoughts, his exuberant joy and relief, were transformed by the mind into the endorphins and other substances that kicked his immune system back into high gear and made him feel great!

The pen of your mind is a careful secretary, writing your every word, thought, and action into your mental gospel. This gives you a powerful way to strengthen your spirit as you make your truth one of health, happiness, and success.

You Are the Sole Author of Your Gospel

A word spoken in due season, how good it is!

Prov. 15:23

Steve's story illustrates a very important point, perhaps the single most important point in this book: You are the sole author of your gospel. There is only one person who can write upon your mental book, and that is you. Yours is the only hand that can grasp the pen, that can hold it to the page, that can write, that can turn the pages. The AIDS virus itself wrote nothing in Steve's mental gospel. There was no AIDS virus anywhere near his mental book. But his thoughts took on the complexion of the terrible invader; the texture, the taste, the feel, look, and smell of the killer. Pictures of the virus and the deadly damage it could do were slapped into his book. That's all it took to send his immune system into a tailspin. And with his immune defenses so low, he was easy prey to any germ that happened along. Luckily, he recovered quickly.

"Take this situation, Dr. Fox," a 55-year-old fashion consultant proposed. "You finish a job for someone and they hate it. Or the man you love walks out on you. They're telling me I'm no good when they do that. *They* are writing 'you stink' into my mental gospel."

"They" don't write anything into your gospel. They can't. They simply provide information. You interpret the data. You decide what your truth is going to be, what your world is like, what thoughts will produce which things in your body. You are the sole author of your mental gospel. It's your perception that counts.

"But they tell me I'm not good," she insisted. "That's why I feel so bad."

"What makes you feel good?" I asked.

"My daughter. She just got married," she answered, with a smile.

"Look at the difference!" I said. "You've got a big smile on your face! Now what did your daughter do to make you smile? Nothing. She's not here, she doesn't even know we're talking about her. She didn't make you smile: You did it. Your good thoughts about your daughter are all it takes to make you smile, to fill your head with happy thoughts, trigger the release of endorphins and other good biochemicals within your body, and write happiness all over your mental gospel.

"You did it, not your daughter. You did it with your thoughts."

The pen of your mind is always ready to write every little thought, detail, or incident, trivial or consequential, into your mental gospel. You instantly respond to what is written.

Remember, I said that your spirit creates and controls you, yet you create and control your spirit? The same idea applies to your mental gospel. You act according to what is written in your mental book, yet you are the sole author of your gospel.

Your every thought, even an unintended misinterpretation based on other people's errors, is carefully recorded. If the pen writes the rainbows of good into our books, it also writes in the black colors of fear, anger, and pain. As Eleanor Roosevelt said, no one can make you feel inadequate without your permission. Neither can any person "make" you feel good. What we feel is up to us.

Some unhappy thoughts will be written into each of our gospels. That's inevitable; after all, we're only human. But we have a choice, and we have power. For every unhappy thought that is occasionally written, we can make sure to follow it with ten thousand good thoughts. No, we can't keep out all the bad. But we can surround and bury the bad with good. You'll learn how to do that as part of our Making Miracles program.

The pen is always poised, ready to write. Use this God-given gift to fill your mental gospel with the stuff of success, the thoughts, words, and deeds that bring health and happiness.

Is Your Truth Good News or Bad?

I bring you good tidings of great joy.

Luke 2:10

Are your words messengers bearing glad tidings, or harbingers of disaster? Many, perhaps most, of the ill patients I have treated over the years spoke words that were as daggers to their health and happiness. They didn't know, and neither did I then, that though we tend to write "disease and despair" into our mental books, it is just as easy to write "health and happiness."

Check the items in the "Good News" and "Bad News" columns that best reflect your attitudes.

Good News	**Bad News**
Toward Life in General:	
❑ Today's a great day!	❑ Today's another day to get through.
❑ I thank God for making me just as I am.	❑ I wish I were someone else.

Good News	Bad News
Toward Life in General: (cont.)	
❑ The world is great because I make it great.	❑ That's the way things are; there's nothing I can do about it.
❑ If I could do it all over again, I'd do everything pretty much the way I did.	❑ I made a mess of my life. I'd like to start all over again.
When Faced with a Difficult Task at Work:	
❑ Great! An interesting problem to solve.	❑ Another pain in the neck.
❑ I'll probably get a raise when I solve this.	❑ If I don't figure this out quick, I'll be in trouble.
❑ This is a chance to stretch myself.	❑ Why can't they give this to someone else? Are they trying to make me look bad?
About People:	
❑ People in general are good, honest, and kind.	❑ Most people would like nothing more than to cheat you.
❑ I enjoy helping others.	❑ I have to take care of myself.
❑ I'm happy when other people do well.	❑ I wonder whom they cheated to get what they have?
❑ I enjoy being with other people.	❑ Most people are boring.
About Relationships:	
❑ Everyone gains in a relationship.	❑ People use each other.
❑ When relationships start to fall apart, it's time to work on repairing them.	❑ It's not worth the effort to keep relationships. Just move on to the next.
❑ I enjoy my relationships and look forward to establishing many more just like the ones I have.	❑ Knowing people is good for business, but most people are a pain in the rear.

Good News	Bad News
Regarding Health, Happiness, and Success:	
❑ What I do determines my fate.	❑ Only a few people are "allowed" to be successful.
❑ I can take positive steps to keep myself healthy.	❑ When you get sick you just have to suffer it out.
❑ Happiness is a state of mind, and my mind is always set on happiness.	❑ I'd be happy if certain things happened, like I got more money. Lots more.
❑ I already consider myself successful because I'm happy.	❑ Success is having money and power.
❑ I can accomplish most anything I put my mind to.	❑ I'm not as talented as I'd like to be.

Are you writing good things or bad things into the gospel of your mind?

Say It And You'll Believe It

The inspiration of the Almighty giveth them understanding.
Job 32:8

Our words and thoughts about ourselves are self-fulfilling prophecies, for our every word and thought is written in our mental book. Keep telling yourself that you're sick, and that prophecy will come true. But tell yourself that you are healthy, and that thought becomes the thing that will strengthen your immune system. The same holds true for your spiritual and emotional health. If you stubbornly insist to yourself that you're unhappy, you will be miserable. But telling yourself that you are happy, predicting that you will always be happy, *and believing that prophecy* is a powerful medicine.

Here's one of my patient's experience with words. It began when she came to my office complaining of constant colds and infections, gastrointestinal disorders, fatigue, and irritability.

"It's my nature to be like I am," she said. "I was fated to be unhappy."

"I believe you can learn to be happy. And healthy," I replied.

"Sure, you're a rich Beverly Hills doctor. The world looks rosy to you. Look at the world through my eyes. I'm 33 and unmarried. I work eight hours a day in a job I don't like so I can pay for a crummy apartment and buy food that turns my stomach. The men I meet are jerks. Even if they weren't, I'd be afraid of getting AIDS or herpes in a relationship. I spent six years in college and grad school to earn worthless degrees, and I'm being laid off next week because the firm's cutting back. The way I see it, my world stinks."

"I agree," I said. "Objectively speaking, your world is not very nice. Not now. But that doesn't mean you have to add to your misery by being negative. Worry has never solved any problem."

"Oh, Dr. Enthusiasm here," she scoffed. "You think I should go around with a smile on my face and pretend life's peachy-keen." She looked me right in the eye, challenging me. "There is no way you'll get me to believe I can be happy."

It took some doing, but I finally got her to agree to try a little experiment. Every hour on the hour, all day long for the next two weeks, she was to tell herself that she was happy. No matter what happened, she was to do this.

"I'll say it but I won't believe it," she told me.

"You don't have to believe it," I answered. "Just say it."

When she left my office, she looked grim and haggard. When she returned two weeks later, she looked relaxed. Her speech was calm and soft, not the rapid-fire assault of her previous visit.

"I guess it works, Dr. Fox," she said. "Objectively speaking, my life is no better. I was laid off, I don't have any prospects or money. But I'm able to sleep nights, I don't blow my top all the time like I used to, and my stomach feels better. I met a guy yesterday and for the first time in years I didn't immediately become defensive and hostile. Saying 'I'm happy' made me feel all right. What can I say to make me feel great?"

This woman was still out of a job, she had neither money nor prospects. Yet her world was relatively good, for she was at peace with herself. She was not eating away at her health, her resolve, and stamina with angry, self-defeating thoughts. She was not filling her mental gospel with garbage.

Yes, there was much hard work ahead. But she had already taken great strides. She could sleep at night. Her stomach was better, she didn't blow her top like she used to. In other words, she was learning how to take control of her life. She was learning how to make the world–her world–a great place to be. She was turning her spirit into the kind of good magnet that would attract other good things to her. With her new, positive attitude, it did not take her long to find a new job. A better job, in fact.

You can't always change the world, but you can always change your attitude. And when you change your attitude, you change your world.

How to Write Your Own Gospel of Success

Write the vision. . .

Hab. 2:2

This woman used a simple affirmation to rewrite the gospel of her mind. For years she had been filling the pages of her mental book with negatives, resulting in physical disease and mental distress, plus failure in love and life in general. Simply affirming her happiness over and over was all it took to begin writing a new chapter in her gospel.

You can do the same thing this woman did; you can wipe thought disease right out of your life. You can write the gospel of good news into your mind and spirit, starting now, in both words and pictures.

Open a new, clean page in your mental book. What went before doesn't matter. You're going to start writing a new vision of the world. You're starting anew with prophecies of success, health, and happiness. I'm going to give you a special prescription "diet" of affirmations and visualizations, like the ones you learned earlier. This menu of food for thought is to be repeated every day, for the rest of your life. With this diet for the spirit you'll be filling page after page in your mental gospel with the positive thoughts that set the conditions for health and happiness.

Each time you repeat an affirmation, you make a positive entry in the gospel of your mind. The more positives written there, the better! You can't overdose, so repeat your affirmations–to yourself and out loud–as often as possible. Reinforce the words by making the pictures with the pen of your mind into your mental gospel. Write each of the affirmations on an index card and carry them with you until you've memorized them.

Here are your affirmations for health, happiness, and success in every aspect of life.

It Is Good to Give Thanks

Being successful in every aspect of life depends upon a strong spirit. Strengthen your spirit, energize it by affirming that you already have the things you want. Make this affirmation of thanks a part of your daily program.

> It is good to give thanks unto the Lord for making me the healthy, happy, and successful person I so richly deserve to be. I am open to receiving all the blessings of His abundant universe.

When you recite this affirmation, close your eyes for just a moment. With your mind's eye, see yourself surrounded by stacks of beautifully wrapped gift boxes. There are big boxes, little boxes, red wrapping, blue wrapping, shiny wrapping, glittery wrapping, bows and ribbons. See yourself with a big smile on your face, jumping for joy. And know in your heart that these presents represent all the blessings of our great world. All these blessings are yours for the taking.

Rejoice and Be Glad

Things occasionally go wrong, even in the best of worlds. The problem isn't so much that life sometimes upsets us, it's that we dwell upon the bad feelings. Steel your spirit against problems with this affirmation of joy:

> This is the day that the Lord hath made; I shall rejoice and be glad, be gladder than glad. I give myself permission to see all the happiness that is in my world, to think of the happiness, and to speak of the happiness. The Creator has filled the world with unlimited joy that is mine for the taking.

When you recite this affirmation, close your eyes for just a moment. With your mind's eye, see yourself standing on top of a hill. It's a beautiful, clear day; you can see forever. You're slowly turning around, looking at the world below. Everywhere you look you see something that makes you smile.

A Merry Heart
Continually remind yourself that good thoughts are medicine for the spirit.

> A merry heart is a good medicine. My heart and spirit and the gospel of my mind are filled with joy. I am full of the thoughts and things of health, happiness, and success.

When you recite this affirmation, close your eyes for just a moment. With your mind's eye, see yourself wearing a doctor's white coat. You're holding a stethoscope. The two earpieces are in place. You're holding the round disc to your chest, listening to your own laughter. It's loud, enthusiastic laughter; it's great and it's never-ending.

Spiritually Minded
Serenity is an important personality trait among those who live young and healthy to a very old age. This affirmation will help you develop inner peace:

> To be spiritually minded is life and peace. I give myself permission to be as calm and serene as the quiet waters of a beautiful, still lake.

When you recite this affirmation, close your eyes for just a moment. With your mind's eye, see yourself sitting at the edge of a mountaintop lake. In front of you is a beautiful, blue, quiet and calm expanse of water, absolutely still. Behind you are giant redwoods, born hundreds of years ago. There are no thoughts in your mind, only peace.

Endless Enthusiasm

I give my patients this "prescription" for enthusiasm because being enthusiastic unlocks the flow of endorphins and other beneficial biochemicals within your body. In addition to helping you feel good, endorphins block certain kinds of chronic pain and work with your immune system against disease.

> The Creator has filled me to the brim with enthusiasm. I gladly and generously pour my unlimited enthusiasm over my every thought and action. Armed with endless enthusiasm, I find excitement and adventure in every day.

When you recite this affirmation, close your eyes for just a moment. With your mind's eye, see yourself dressed for safari. Where are you going? Everywhere! How will you get there? That's easy. There's an endless line of porters behind you, each carrying a big box filled with enthusiasm.

Put on a New Me

There's a new you inside the old, just waiting to burst out. The new you is enthusiastic, joyful, loving, forgiving, and determined. The new you is on the fast track to health, happiness, and success. Use this affirmation to bring the new you to the fore:

> Today was another successful step toward the new me. With enthusiastic anticipation and absolute certainty that I'll make even more progress tomorrow, and every tomorrow, I'm putting on the new me.

When you recite this affirmation, close your eyes for just a moment. With your mind's eye, see yourself standing easily atop stilts. You're taking one giant step after another, without any fear of falling. There's a big smile on your face. All around you, down on the ground, your loved ones are urging you on, cheering your every step.

These are your affirmations for success! In just a few pages I'll give you a daily "diet" of these great affirmations, a diet that will trim away all the ugliness from your mental gospel, making you into the great person you deserve to be.

A New Beginning

You've opened a new page in your mental gospel; you've begun life anew. Inscribe these affirmations right there, on that new page. They are your new beginning. Write them in big, bold letters. These affirmations are the forward to your mental gospel, your new guide to life.

Recite these affirmations often, today and every day for the rest of your life. Say them firmly, with conviction and enthusiasm. Repeat them in your mind as you get ready for your day. Say them over and over as you drive to work. Run them through your mind as you work, exercise, eat, and relax. You can't write too much goodness into your mental gospel!

Do affirmations work? Can they really rewrite the gospel of your mind? Can they really revive a weak spirit and turn your life around? You bet they can!

Lisa was a waitress in a hotel restaurant. I met her a few years ago while traveling around the country lecturing on health and stress. Business in the restaurant was slow that night, so she had time to talk. She told me she wanted to be a computer programmer, but was "too dumb."

"Who says you're dumb?" I asked.

She looked surprised. "Why, everyone. It's common knowledge."

"You don't seem dumb to me."

"Well, everyone's always told me I was dumb."

"Who's everyone?"

"Well, my mother always said I took after her side of the family, the dumb side."

"And that thought was written into your mental gospel. It

became a prophecy that had to be fulfilled. Have you gone to computer school?"

"No."

"Have you taken any tests to see if you have an aptitude for computers?"

"No."

"Here's what I want you to do," I instructed, rapidly jotting a few sentences down on my napkin. "Say this affirmation every hour on the hour, from the time you wake up until you go to sleep. Stop whatever you're doing and say this affirmation. Say it loudly, enthusiastically, as if you really believed it. When the next semester begins, I want you to enroll in computer school and do whatever it takes to be what you want to be."

This is the affirmation I gave her:

> With the help of God, I'm on my way to success! I have the talent to accomplish my goals. I am becoming the person I want to be.

I heard from Lisa a year later. She was in computer school, and doing well. Not at the top of her class, but doing well enough to be confident of graduation and the career she really wanted.

> **"They" say this, "they" say that. It doesn't matter what "they" say. What *you* say is the only thing that counts.**

Prophesy the Good

In order to make the miracle of health, happiness, and success for yourself, you must become a prophet. You must continually prophesy unlimited health and unbridled happiness for yourself. In other words, you must always see yourself as being absolutely successful in every walk of life. Say it with your every word and thought, shout it out loud. In your mind's eye, see it as already accomplished.

We are all prophets, and our every prophecy is reverently written in our mental gospel. Be a prophet of only glad tidings.

You will be rewarded as you recast the world, your world, in the image of the good you so richly deserve.

The bad news will take care of itself. It should not be encouraged. Neither should it be ignored. Bad news should be examined, placed in perspective, and filed in the appropriate place. Our task is to focus on the good. The more good we see for ourselves, the more good we will bring upon ourselves. That is a basic law.

Make the prophecy now and forever. Develop a vision of joy and success. Hold that vision dear.

Rx: WRITING

How beautiful upon the mountain are the feet of him that bringeth good tidings...

Isa. 52:7

Today is Day 2 of your Making Miracles program, the Day of Writing Glad Tidings. Today, and every day for the rest of your life, think of yourself as always bringing glad tidings, to yourself and to others.

Your prescription of Writing is broken up into two parts. First is your daily series of affirmations. I've arranged the affirmations in this chapter into a complete daily "diet" for health, happiness, and success in every aspect of life. It's a special kind of diet, one that relies solely on the tremendous power of your mind. As you begin the gospel of your mind anew, indeed, as you begin your life anew, you will trim away the harmful negatives from your mind, replacing them with the good thoughts that you want–and deserve. With this special diet, you are setting up the conditions that make vibrant health, enthusiastic happiness, and unlimited success possible.

Recite these affirmations throughout the day, today and every day. Be sure to "see" each affirmation as you recite it. Write the affirmation/visualization on index cards and carry the cards with you. Pull them out during the day, look at them, read them, and see them with your mind's eye.

Upon awakening: "Rejoice and Be Glad"
This is the day that the Lord hath made; I shall rejoice and be glad, be gladder than glad. I give myself permission to see all the happiness that is in my world, to think of the happiness, and to speak of the happiness. The Creator has filled the world with unlimited joy that is mine for the taking.

Morning: "It is Good to Give Thanks"
It is good to give thanks unto the Lord for making me the healthy, happy, and successful person I so richly deserve to be. I am open to receiving all the blessings of His abundant universe.

Noon: "Endless Enthusiasm"
The Creator has filled me to the brim with enthusiasm. I gladly and generously pour my unlimited enthusiasm over my every thought and action. Armed with endless enthusiasm, I find excitement and adventure in every day.

Afternoon: "Spiritually Minded"
To be spiritually minded is life and peace. I give myself permission to be as calm and serene as the quiet waters of a beautiful, still lake.

Evening: "A Merry Heart"
A merry heart is a good medicine. My heart and spirit and the gospel of my mind are filled with joy. I am full of the thoughts and things of health, happiness, and success.

When going to bed: "Put on the New Me"
Today was another successful step toward the new me. With enthusiastic anticipation and absolute certainty that I'll make even more progress tomorrow, and every tomorrow, I'm putting on the new me.

Recite each affirmation out loud, with enthusiasm. This

daily menu sets up the daily minimum requirements of glad tidings. But I tell my patients to go beyond the minimum and recite their affirmations all day long: 5, 10, 20 times. You can't overdo it with affirmations!

Whether you believe in the affirmations or not is not important in the beginning. Just say them. Your words have a profound influence upon your beliefs. Say something long enough and you'll begin to believe it. Most of us do this all the time with negative thoughts. It's going to be a rotten day, we tell ourselves. And it *is* a rotten day, because we have set up the conditions that encourage misery. I'm going to fail the test, we tell ourselves. And we *do* fail, because the negativity we place in our mind impedes the flow of thought.

One little caution: Don't set a time limit. You may feel the changes in your thinking and health right away, or it may take a while. Keep repeating your affirmations over and over until your new positive outlook on life becomes firmly embedded in your mind.

Special R_X for Writing Glad Tidings

In addition to your daily diet of affirmations, put into your world this special R_X for Writing Glad Tidings. Say it several times today with energy and conviction.

Set aside some time today to sit in a quiet room, on a comfortable chair. Tell everyone that you do not want to be disturbed; take the phone off the hook. Close your eyes. With your mind's eye, picture a large book. It's a thick book, covered in gold leaf, sitting on a shiny black surface. On the cover of the book, written in beautiful calligraphy, is your name. This book is the gospel of your mind.

A hand, your hand, opens the book to the first page. The gleaming white page is blank, waiting to be written on.

See your hand holding a pen and writing in your mental gospel. The writing is bold, beautiful. With your mind's eye, watch as you write in your book of life, right in the center of the first page:

> In the beginning is the word. All my words, thoughts and deeds are of joy, love, and enthusiasm. My world is filled with joy, love, enthusiasm, and endless possibilities.

Now turn the pages. See on every page the same great message of glad tidings. Every page in your mental gospel, every thought you think and word you utter is filled with the knowledge that your world is filled with joy, love, and enthusiasm—and endless possibilities. There is no limit to your spirit, so there is no limit to your potential.

Visualize yourself writing in the gospel of your mind several times a day, as often as possible. Repeat your special affirmation for today—and all your affirmations—over and over during the day. Each time you see the gospel of your mind with your mind's eye, take an extra moment to recite today's affirmation, loudly, with enthusiasm and belief. Feel the pen in your hand. Squeeze your fingers shut and really feel the pen as it writes health, happiness, and success into your book of life.

Repeat your special R_X for Writing several times during the day. It's best to do it in a quiet place the first time. After that, do it anytime, anyplace you can. I often take a moment when getting in my car, or after parking it, to do a special R_X. You can also use a quiet moment at your desk, during lunch, or when you're at home.

Repeat this special R_X for Writing as many times as possible. It's very important that you get into the Glad Tidings habit. Keep that picture in your head all day long. Recite your special R_X affirmation over and over during the day, out loud and to yourself, as many times as possible.

Your mind believes what you tell it to believe; it does as you direct. So does your spirit. As your thoughts go, so goes your spirit. Begin directing yourself toward the happy and successful life you so richly deserve by filling your mind with Glad Tidings.

Day 3

Paint the Picture

Better is a handful with quietness, than both the hands full with travail and vexation of spirit.

Eccles. 4:6

The Reverend Paul Barrett of Palm Springs, California, uses the parable of fishermen sorting fish when he teaches people how they can separate the good from the bad in their lives. The brief episode from the Bible tells of how fishermen put their nets into the water, pull the nets up, and carefully divide the fish into piles.

We all cast our nets, our mental nets. As we rise from bed and get ready for work, our nets are gathering "fish." As we listen to the radio during the drive to work, go through the work day, speak with other people, study and play, take a quiet walk, our nets are catching fish. By the end of the day our nets are filled with fish–the sights, sounds, reactions, relived memories, and physical sensations of daily living.

Our mental nets capture everything that comes our way, good, bad, or indifferent. Like any fisherman, we don't want our nets clogged with bad "fish for thought," for the bad we catch in our mental nets can harm our heart and immune system, prompt cancer, worsen diabetes, and otherwise destroy our health.

Your spirit lives off the "fish" you catch in your mental net. Good fish or bad, your spirit takes it in. Controlling what's in your mental net, therefore, means you can make sure your spirit is properly nourished.

Good or Bad, the Choice Is Ours

What are these bad fish we catch in our mental nets? What is the difference between good thoughts and bad?

In one sense, there is absolutely no difference between good and bad thoughts. All our thoughts are bits of information, nothing more. They are data to be analyzed and stored. The thought itself has no inherent goodness or badness: It's how we interpret the thought that matters.

Let's say, for example, two workers are told that the boss is going to review their work in five minutes. The first worker panics, shoves papers into the desk, tries to get his files in order, and thinks of 20 excuses for being so far behind. The second worker, on the other hand, welcomes the review. He knows that his work is properly done and up-to-date. He can't wait for the boss to come; he's hoping for a raise.

Both workers received the same piece of information: The boss was going to review their work in five minutes. What made the information good for one and bad for the other was their interpretation, their response, their perception.

A thought is what you make of it.

Filters and Colors

The soul is colored the color of our thoughts.

Marcus Aurelius

How do our perceptions "create" good and bad thoughts? Every thought, sight, sound, smell, memory, and sensation entering our minds passes through our mental filter before coming to rest in our mental net. This filter is made up of all the memories, thoughts, sights, sounds, sensations, and perceptions that have ever entered our heads. It's a crazy-quilt filter alive with colors: flashing neon sign colors, soft pastels, inviting warm colors, cold and harsh colors, jagged and angry colors, slick magazine colors, faded old-picture colors, jarring colors, calming colors, laughing colors, crying colors.

All the colors, hues, and shades are there in our filters. One person's filter has more laughing colors; another's has more angry and jagged colors. The filters are dynamic, ever-changing as more colors are added every day. And different colors already on the filter move forward and back, up and down as different thoughts come into our heads.

Yes, there are constant changes, but the basic color scheme remains fairly constant for most people. The friendly, relaxed person's brightly colored filter may occasionally darken, but only briefly, before regaining its happy coloration. The angry, stressed person's jagged and dark filter may occasionally brighten, but it's rare. Some people's filters are constantly changing kaleidoscopes, shifting rapidly from rainbow brights to midnight blacks and everything in between. Most of us, however, tend to find a color scheme and stick with it.

As our newly formed thoughts are processed through our filters–and all thoughts are–they take on the colors of the filter. And so the filter made up of purple anger, blood-red hurt, and green envy thoughts paints the new thought with the colors of anger, hurt, and envy. This new notion is written in our mental gospel in one of those colors. It becomes part of the filter, and its dark pain adds to the blackness already present.

But when a thought comes to the rainbow-soft filter painted the colors of joy, the lively colors of energy and enthusiasm, it takes on these same warm and lively colors, writes the good news into the gospel, and joins the joyful filter.

When the first worker got the news of the coming inspection, he panicked, and his filter quickly turned dark (if it wasn't already). The colors of fear were pushed to the front of his filter, and these were the colors that painted his notions. The bad news, arrayed in the colors of fear, was written into his mental gospel, and then became a part of his mental filter, ready to paint any future news with the blackness of fear. If the worker is like most of us, that bit of darkness will remain there forever as a stain on his mind.

The filters of our minds color all the sights, sounds, thoughts, impressions, emotions, and memories. It's this coloration, this perception, that determines whether our thoughts are good or bad. This is not to say that every thought entering our heads is absolutely neutral. Some thoughts–a loved one's death, for example–contain much more explosive emotional potential than others–say a drop in the price of bananas. Still, our thoughts and our filters are what we make of them. We can't often change the outside world, but we can, to a surprisingly large degree, determine how to respond to events.

What are the colors of your mental filter? These are the colors of your future.

Stress: The Result of Negative Thoughts

What happens once good or bad thoughts come into our mind that are already colored by our filters? Let's look at the negative thoughts first. Each negative thought represents stress. Rather, each is a stressor, a cause of stress. Stress itself is the response of the body to demands made upon it. Stress is the reaction of the body to the stressors.

When the first worker heard that the boss was going to review his work, he became frightened. The colors of his mind were fearful. He was afraid of being embarrassed or reprimanded, demoted or fired. He was horrified by the prospect of facing his family and friends after having been fired. He was thinking how difficult it would be to find a new job.

Immediately: Panic! Fear! Embarrassment! Fired! No income! Hard job search! Tremendous danger! These were written into his mental gospel.

The man's brain picked up these unhappy thoughts. The human brain is the largest gland in the body and it has a tremendous impact upon our organs, systems, tissues, and cells. The negative thoughts were quickly sent to the part of the brain where the intellect meets the emotions. Here the bit of information was pushed through his filter and colored with fear.

This fear was instantly read by a part of the brain called the hypothalamus, the great "pilot" of the brain which controls so many functions. The hypothalamus immediately instructed the pituitary gland to inject adrenocorticotropic hormones (ACTH) into the bloodstream. The ACTH shot down to the adrenal glands (two half-thumbs-sized glands, one of which sits atop each kidney). Instructed by the ACTH, the adrenals pumped noradrenalin (nor-epinephrine, or NE) into the nervous system, and more ACTH into the bloodstream.

In less than a second the piece of information, colored by this worker's filter, written into his mental gospel, turned his body chemistry upside-down. Powerful, high-voltage chemicals flooded his system. His bronchial tubes were jacked open for deeper breathing. His heart beat faster and contracted more strongly. His blood pressure rose. Sugar poured into the blood stream for extra energy. The digestive system shut down. Blood vessels of the skin contracted, slowing the flow of blood (this is why our skin turns pale when we're frightened or angry). His eyes dilated so he could see better. The blood vessels in his muscles opened wider, allowing more blood to flow through the muscles. The muscles themselves contracted.

This is stress. Not the information or thing which frightened him, but this incredibly complex and rapid reaction. This biochemical cascade which turned a relaxed man into a whirlwind of energy is stress. The process is a lot more complicated than this, but the basic idea is that the stress reaction prepares us to fight for our lives, or run away (the "fight or flight" response). As you can imagine, stress is a real shock to the body.

Sometimes stress is a good thing: It gets us going–fast–when we have to. It revs us up, prepares us to take on challenges. In this case, it got the lazy employee working faster than he had worked in a long time. Stress can give you instant energy to jump out of the way of a car, to run from a mugger, or to lift the heavy tree that fell on your friend. In cases like these, the shock to the body is worthwhile, and only temporary. We're frightened, we undergo the stress reaction, we respond, and then we relax.

Sometimes stress is a good thing. Most of the time, however, stress is harmful. We turn on the stress reaction way too often without good reason. Shocking the body to save our life, or someone else's life, is fine. Shocking it for other reasons can be dangerous in the long run. And shock it we do. Every time a negative thought invades our mind, the trip wire is jangled.

Sometimes gently, sometimes loud and long.

Forced to undergo the stress reaction too often, the body starts to give way. The blood pressure which goes up during stress stays up. The immune system, which kicks into high gear during stress, weakens. The high-voltage bio-substances released during stress begin to ravage our heart and other organs. The adrenal glands and other parts of the body involved with the stress reaction begin to wither and rot.

> **The full-blown stress reaction is great–once in a great while, in an extreme emergency. When it is turned on too often, however, this savior can become our worst nightmare.**

"Thought Medicine"

What of our good thoughts? What happens when notions wearing the colors of joy and love come into our minds?

What happens is similar to the stress reaction, but the results are very different. When the good worker heard that the boss was coming to review his work, he immediately began thinking things like "my work is good," "my files are in order," "all my customers are pleased," "my output was up 20 percent last month," and so on. These thoughts are written into his mental gospel: Pleasure. Satisfaction. Enthusiastic anticipation of a raise. Proud family. These great thoughts were quickly sent to the part of the brain where the intellect meets the emotions. Here, they triggered the release of a gentle sunshower of bio-substances such as endorphins, hormones that block pain, lift the mood, strengthen the immune system, and make us feel great!

Rather than ring the alarm bells, good thoughts gently massage and relax the heart and immune system–the entire body. Good thoughts are a combination vacation, pep talk, and tune-up for the body–every part of the body. Every good thought that comes through our filter into our mental net is a golden nugget of health and happiness.

Whether your mind is filled with good thoughts or bad can

mean the difference between health and disease, happiness and depression, success or failure in life. That's why it is vital that we learn to sort things out, learn to banish the negatives as much as possible. It's also vital that we learn how to keep the filter of our mind radiant with the colors of joy and love. I'll get to that later. Right now, let's see what happened to a man who clung to negative thoughts.

Thoughts and Your Heart

Let not your heart be troubled. . .

John 14:27

Smitty, a 53-year-old executive, lives in what used to be the relatively quiet seaside city of Santa Monica. The drive to his firm's downtown headquarters was always a little slow, but never too bad. Over the years, however, the traffic has become increasingly worse. Now he has to leave 30 minutes earlier than he used to, and he curses every minute of the drive.

Smitty used to enjoy his job and looked forward to climbing the corporate ladder. Now that he's near the top, however, he's disillusioned and burnt out. This morning he oversleeps. He blames his wife. "You know today is a big day!" he shouts. Today, of all days to oversleep: Today he's presenting his plan for reorganizing the company. If they like it, Smitty's future is assured. If they don't, well, another one of the executives has a different plan, one that will eliminate Smitty's job.

Relax, he tells himself as the traffic on the Santa Monica Freeway grinds to a halt. Think about the presentation. Gotta look good. But how can I look good when I've been up every night for a month worrying about my job? he asks himself. Gotta get them to take my plan over that so-and-so's, or I'm out on my butt.

The traffic's moving again. A car cuts in, barely missing him! "Jerk," Smitty mutters. He's about to hit the horn when he remembers that people shoot each other on the freeway now. He doesn't honk his horn, but everyone else does; loud, blaring noises banging back and forth in his brain.

Smitty can feel his heart slamming up against his chest wall. He can almost feel his blood pressure rising as he checks the clock for the tenth time in two minutes.

He arrives at the office on time but feeling lousy. His secretary greets him; he snaps out some instructions. His reports aren't ready yet; he calls the copying department and chews out a clerk. When the reports arrive, they're not covered in exactly the shade of blue he ordered. This time he shouts at the young summer employee who was unlucky enough to be sent to his office with the box of reports.

Nine o'clock, time for the meeting. Smitty strides into the meeting room. There's Bill, his old buddy. Bill will vote with me, Smitty tells himself. But how come he didn't come over to shake my hand? How come he's sitting so close to that so-and-so Tom? Are they planning to do me in? What's going on?

The meeting goes poorly for Smitty. Although the final decision won't come for a week, he's sure the other plan will be adopted. He's also sure that all his old buddies were bought off by the other side. He can feel the tightening in his chest and neck as he shuffles back to his office. For the rest of the day Smitty sits at his desk unable to work, trying to convince himself that his chest pain is due to stomach acid. And he reviews the meeting over and over in his head, thinking about the things he could have done. If only I had said this instead of that, put this section there, gotten more statistics, been more aggressive in cutting. If only. . .if only.

Smitty never did find out whose plan the company decided to adopt. He had a heart attack and died early the next morning.

Stressing the Heart

How did Smitty's thoughts trigger his heart attack? What physical mechanisms translate thoughts into disaster?

Make a fist with your left hand, thumb on top. Put this fist up to your breastbone, slightly to the left of center. Squeeze your fist, strongly, rhythmically. Your heart beats like this some 100,000 times a day, pushing four or so quarts of blood through your body every minute. When you're stressed or are exercising, even more blood is pumped.

It all seems so very mechanical. Dark-colored "used" blood from all over the body comes by way of the superior vena cava and inferior vena cava into the right atrium, the small chamber on the upper right side of the heart. But it hardly has time to realize where it is before dropping through the tricuspid valve, on the bottom side of the right atrium, into the right ventricle.

The right ventricle, directly below the right atrium, is a larger chamber. This ventricle pumps the used blood into the lungs. Inside the lungs, the blood is oxygenated, exchanging its carbon dioxide, which we exhale, for fresh oxygen. Now the blood has the red color we expect it to have.

From the lungs, the now bright-red blood returns to the heart. This time it goes to the "left heart," first visiting the left atrium, the smaller, upper chamber on the left side of the heart. Like the right atrium, the left atrium is essentially a thin-walled collecting room. In no time at all, however, the oxygen-rich blood passes through the mitral valve down into the mighty left ventricle.

Strongest of the four heart chambers, the left ventricle has the thickest muscular walls. This part of the heart keeps the blood flowing through the entire body, head to toe. Put your fist to your breastbone again, thumb up. Squeeze it hard, as hard as you can. Again and again, hard enough to keep fluid running through endless miles of arteries and veins. Imagine doing this all day long, year after year, for a lifetime.

Blood does not flow randomly through the body, of course. It is carefully directed through a seemingly limitless series of arteries and veins. When blood leaves the heart, it moves through large arteries, then smaller arteries, then the very small arteries. Finally the arterioles give way to the very tiny capillaries. Only when the blood has reached the capillaries does it exchange its oxygen for carbon dioxide. Having done so, the blood begins its journey back to the heart. From capillaries to venules then to the veins, blood flows through ever-wider pipes back to the heart.

The arterial vessels–carrying freshly oxygenated blood from the heart–can be looked upon as the life-giving side of the vital exchange, bringing oxygen, nutrients, hormones, and other substances to the body tissue. The venous (veins) side–guiding the used blood back to the heart–is sometimes called the refuse disposal half of the system.

It all seems so well-programmed. How can the health of our hearts be so dependent upon the color of our thoughts? How can our thoughts raise our blood pressure and cholesterol, and even cause the heart to beat abnormally?

From Thoughts to High Blood Pressure to Disaster

Back in medical school we learned a simple formula: *Blood Pressure=Cardiac Output x Arterial Resistance.* This means that your blood pressure depends on how much blood your heart pumps per unit of time (cardiac output), and how difficult it is for the blood to move through the pipes (arterial resistance). In other words:

Factors That Increase Blood Pressure	*Factors That Decrease Blood Pressure*
Heart pumping harder	Heart pumping gentler
Narrower pipes (arteries)	Wider pipes
More fluid pumping through the system	Less fluid pumping through the system

(There are, of course, other factors involved with the regulation of blood pressure.)

Stress can make your heart beat harder and faster. In fact, I believe that stress is a major cause of elevated blood pressure. Under stress we may feel as though everything were going wrong–we're going to blow the big job; we're always rushing to get somewhere; we're always behind; people are standing in our way; we're upset about being caught in traffic. When we're stressed, the brain stimulates the sympathetic nervous system. In turn, the sympathetic nervous system prompts the adrenal medulla (the inside part of the adrenal glands) to pump out adrenaline-like substances. This in turn increases the heart rate, and the strength with which the heart beats. So, essentially, stressful thoughts equal higher blood pressure.

That's not all. When the hypothalamus, the pilot of the brain, "reads" all your negative thoughts and other signs of stress, it tells the pituitary to release ACTH. This ACTH goes down to the adrenal glands on top of the kidneys. There the ACTH directs the outer part of the adrenal glands to put out a number of hormones, including aldosterone and some 42 varieties of cortisone. Among other things, these hormones cause your body to retain salt and water. Extra fluid and sodium in the body means that there's more fluid in the blood stream, more fluid that has to be pumped through the body. This elevates blood pressure.

And there's more. With chronic stress, the blood vessels constrict, they tighten up and narrow. When that happens, it's harder for the blood to flow through, which means blood pressure goes up.

Furthermore, with chronic stress, the chemistry of the blood changes, making it more likely to clot. This means there's a greater chance that a clot will form and trigger a heart attack by getting stuck in a partially narrowed artery in the heart, or prompt a stroke by getting stuck in a narrowed artery in the brain.

With chronic stress—that is, stress after stress after stress—the heart begins to suffer. For many, it is a never-ending cycle of stress, increased blood pressure, more stress, another increase in blood pressure, more stress, and on and on until the mechanisms break down.

It's a simple formula: Negative thoughts equal stress, and stress equals elevated blood pressure.

Our Thoughts and Cholesterol

Put your fist back up to your chest. Let it stand in for your heart again. Look down at that fist, at the back of it. See the veins just a little under the skin? Imagine that those are some of your coronary arteries, the arteries that supply fresh, oxygen-rich blood to the heart muscle itself. I remember, from the days when I used to do autopsies, that some of these vital arteries had become as narrow as the tip of a pencil.

Let's suppose you've been eating the high-fat, cholesterol-rich Standard American Diet, and some of your coronary arteries have narrowed. Not fatally so; a 50 percent blockage in this artery, a 60 or 75 percent narrowing in that. You can do reasonably well in spite of these kinds of blockages, unless stress causes cholesterol levels in the body to rise. Many studies have shown the relationship between stress and elevated cholesterol. If you stress people by throwing them into ice cold water, for example, their cholesterol level will rise. If you threaten them, say they're going to be fired, or they're going to have to take difficult tests, their cholesterol level will go up.

Years ago, studies of doctors, lawyers, and accountants showed that all three of the groups had elevated cholesterol levels because of bad diets. However, even though they did not change their diets, the accountants' cholesterol levels rose during tax season though the levels of the doctors and attorneys did not. The accountants were eating the same food as before but they were under increased stress, and that is the reason their cholesterol levels went up. So even if you're on a healthy diet, stress can keep your cholesterol level high. And that puts you at increased risk of heart disease and stroke.

Again, notice how important perception is. It was the accountants' feeling of being rushed and under the gun that led to the rise in cholesterol. *It was their thoughts that caused the problem.*

One researcher reported on 43 studies that showed changes in cholesterol levels under a variety of stressful conditions. The cholesterol levels rose anywhere from 8 to 36 percent above those of the controls.

Stress and elevated cholesterol levels are intimately related. Anger, fear, "hurry-itis," feelings that you are a failure, that life is out to get you: These thoughts increase blood pressure *and* cholesterol. These thoughts are killers.

Every year 1.5 million Americans suffer a heart attack. More than a third of those people will die. If you are under stress, if you have high blood pressure or high cholesterol level, if you smoke, if you don't exercise regularly, if you have diabetes or certain genetic tendencies, your risk of having a heart attack is above average. We can't change our genes, but we can reduce our stress by deciding how to interpret what happens to us. This along with good diet and exercise, will help us keep our blood pressure and cholesterol levels down–and will also help control diabetes among those who have it.

Sorting the good from the bad is excellent preventive medicine for the heart. And not only for the heart.

Our Thoughts and the Immune System

Many studies have shown the relationship between stress and the immune system. For example, men whose wives developed breast cancer and died were depressed and anxious, which is natural. Tests showed that the number of their immune system cells had fallen, and that their immune systems were weak in general.

It's been well established that the brain oversees the immune system. The hypothalamus controls the autonomic (automatic) nervous system and the body's hormonal system. This powerful part of the brain is in direct contact with the lymphocytes, the most important of the immune system white blood cells that battle invading germs. (There are receptors on these lymphocytes that allow the hypothalamus to "talk" directly with the immune system.)

When a person is under stress, the cerebral cortex (the thinking brain) signals the hypothalamus. The hypothalamus in turn activates certain neurotransmitters and hormones, and the Stress Reaction is underway. As part of the Stress Reaction, the adrenal glands pump out cortisone. This is temporarily beneficial, but in the long run, all that cortisone suppresses the immune system.

A strong immune system is absolutely vital. When our immune systems are flying high we can resist all kinds of diseases. When I was a young resident in internal medicine, people would cough all over me when I examined them. Weeks later we might find out that they had pulmonary tuberculosis. I kept expecting to come down with TB but never did. Neither did any of the other young doctors, because we had strong immune systems. Yet there were enough TB germs and other threatening organisms in the wards to infect the entire city of Los Angeles. The mere presence of infectious organisms is not enough to cause illness–not when the immune system is strong.

Our Thoughts and Cancer

As far back as 3,000 years ago, during the time of the great Greek physician Hippocrates, we've known that depressed women are more likely to develop cancer of the breast or uterus than women who are not depressed. Much depression, like stress is born of the negative thoughts we take into our heads and hearts. Factors such as diet, the environment, genetic disposition, and smoking can all contribute to stress. But we know that our moods, our thoughts, our outlook on life, are major factors in preventing or inviting cancer. That's why it is so very important to banish the bad from our mind.

Our Thoughts and Diabetes

I have seen many people who are healthy and have no family history of disease but suddenly come down with symptoms of fatigue, weight loss, and, often excessive urination during a period of severe stress. This is often interpreted as depression and anxiety associated with stress. Upon checking a little further, I sometimes find that their blood sugar is very high, that they have sugar in their urine, and that they show other signs and symptoms of diabetes mellitus.

We treat these people for diabetes. If we get their diabetes under control, and if we can teach them how to handle their stress, the diabetes will go away and never be a problem again.

It's likely that these people had a genetic tendency toward diabetes, but the disease did not manifest itself until stress struck. How does stress encourage diabetes? It's believed that the immune system turns on itself in many of these cases, that the body itself damages the beta cells of the pancreas. (The beta cells secrete insulin, which regulates sugar metabolism.) It's well-known that certain types of work stress, such as role conflict, work overload, and severe harassment, can cause people who never had diabetes suddenly to come down with it. And those who do have diabetes, but keep it under control, found that their disease had worsened.

In some people who have never had diabetes before, or who have mild diabetes controlled by diet, severe stress will create the need for large amounts of insulin in them. They may never get back to a nondrug treatment of their diabetes again.

How serious is diabetes? Its complications can include blindness, heart disease, stroke, gangrene, and kidney failure. All these side effects are hastened by severe stress. That's why we've got to keep our minds filled with loving, joyful, sharing, caring, positive thoughts.

Our Thoughts and Sudden Death

Can stress kill suddenly, right on the spot? I believe it can, and does. Suddenly flooding the body with high-voltage chemicals such as adrenaline, noradrenalin, and ACTH can cause the coronary arteries to constrict, thus impeding the flow of blood to the heart muscle. It can also overwork the muscles of the heart, raise blood pressure by constricting the peripheral arteries, and make the heart beat abnormally. A 60-year-old man accompanied his wife to the emergency room in an ambulance. She was pronounced dead on arrival. He immediately collapsed. The doctors quickly took an electrocardiogram and found that he was suffering from ventricular fibrillation, which interferes with the heart's pumping blood through the body. This man who had no symptoms of a heart problem before suddenly had a heart attack and died. Such cases are surprisingly common.

I Am Upset by—By What?

It's too bad God didn't give us a release valve, didn't fix it so that we could release excess and inappropriate stress by twisting an ear, or something like that.

We don't have a safety valve, but we often have warnings that trouble is brewing, that we're overloaded or in conflict. The warnings may be seemingly minor problems such as headaches, neckaches, backaches. Or the warning may be in the form of heaviness in the chest, heart palpitations, or high blood pressure. These are more serious warnings and must be looked into right away. Unfortunately, our warnings sometimes come too late. For many, the first warning is a fatal heart attack, or the news that they have advanced cancer.

No, we don't have a safety valve. That's why we must learn a lesson from Epictetus, the famous first century philosopher who said, "I am upset not by events, but rather by the way I view them."

Like him, we are upset less by events, or by the information coming into our nets, than by the way we view them. In other words, it's our perception that counts, not the actual thing, or stressor. It's the color our thoughts are painted by the filters of our minds that counts. It's how we view the world and what happens to us that makes the difference.

We can't always get rid of the unpleasant things in our lives, *but we can always change our attitudes toward them.* Ours is the only pen writing in our mental gospels. That means we have tremendous power–and equally tremendous responsibility: Our errors are written large in our mental books. But it also means that we have tremendous power. If we can change the tenor of our thoughts–and we can–then we can ensure that only the good is written into our mental gospels.

You have tremendous control over your thoughts, and every thought in your head influences your body, your immune system, and your health.

By the way, it's interesting to note that people who are legally insane have a lower incidence of stress-related diseases (heart attacks, stroke, cancer, diabetes, and so on.) They don't "know" when they're being stressed.

Choose a New Palette

You cannot drink the cup of the Lord and the cup of devils.
1 Cor. 10:21

The human mind is a marvelously complex instrument, capable of holding an incredible variety of facts, attitudes, and emotions, some of them absolutely contradictory. According to the manual, the computer I'm using to write this can make 16,000 different colors. That 16,000 is nothing compared to the colors in our mind and filter.

We all have access to an endless spectrum of colors in our mental filters, but we tend to use the same few over and over. Thus, everywhere you look on an unhappy person's filter, you see the dark colors of despair and depression, the colors of hopelessness and helplessness. Bright spots are few and far between.

Imagine that you have a big box full of colored poker chips. There are thousands of brown chips, black chips, and gray chips, with just a few reds, whites, and blues. Reach into the box and pull out a chip at random. What color is it? Odds are it's brown, black, or gray. Grab another chip, and another, and another: They're probably all dark. Now let's suppose that you want to find a bright-colored chip, a red, white, or blue one. It'll take forever to find one by reaching randomly into the box, so you have to search through it. It's hard to find the bright chips. Even when you shake the box, the brights don't come to the top. They're buried down on the bottom of the box, trapped beneath piles of dark chips.

When your filter is mostly painted with darks, it's unlikely that a new thought will find a joyful color and be painted with the joy. Odds are the new thought will be dark. And if you wanted the new thought to be colored with joy, *really* wanted it to, that would be difficult, for all the bright colors on your filter are buried by the dark.

Yes, your mind can hold onto an amazing variety of thoughts, your filter can be painted with thousands of colors. But it is rare to find the colors equally represented, exactly X percent of each. We generally put just a few colors on our palette, and use them over and over, day after day. That's why it's tricky to suddenly change your thoughts, to simply decide to repaint your mental filter. If the good colors are not on your palette or are only there in small amounts, you don't have much color choice.

Rx: Choice

Old things are passed away; behold, all things are become new.

2 Cor. 5:17

Today is Day Three of Making Miracles, the Day of Choice. This day is dedicated to choosing the life you will lead; to writing the vision of happiness into your mental gospel; to painting your life with the colors of love and joy.

Recite these affirmations throughout the day. Be sure to "see" each affirmation as you recite it.

Upon awakening: "Rejoice and Be Glad"
This is the day that the Lord hath made; I shall rejoice and be glad, be gladder than glad. I give myself permission to see all the happiness that is in my world, to think of the happiness, and to speak of the happiness. The Creator has filled the world with unlimited joy that is mine for the taking.

Morning: "It Is Good to Give Thanks"
It is good to give thanks unto the Lord for making me the healthy, happy, and successful person I so richly deserve to be. I am receiving all the blessings of His abundant universe.

Noon: "Endless Enthusiasm"
The Creator has filled me to the brim with enthusiasm. I gladly and generously pour my unlimited enthusiasm over my every thought and action. Armed with endless enthusiasm, I find excitement and adventure in every day.

Afternoon: "Spiritually Minded"
To be spiritually minded is life and peace. I give myself permission to be as calm and serene as the quiet waters of a beautiful, still lake.

Evening: "A Merry Heart"
A merry heart is a good medicine. My heart and spirit and the gospel of my mind are filled with joy. I am full of the thoughts and things of health, happiness, and success.

When going to bed: "Put on the New Me"
Today was another successful step toward the new me. With enthusiastic anticipation and absolute certainty that I'll make even more progress tomorrow, and every tomorrow, I'm putting on the new me.

Recite each affirmation out loud, with enthusiasm. This daily menu sets up the daily minimum requirements for spiritual nourishment. But I tell my patients to go beyond the minimum and recite their affirmations all day long: 5, 10, 20 times. You can't overdo it with affirmations!

In addition to your daily diet of affirmations, enter into the world of your special R_X for Choice several times today, with energy and conviction.

Set aside some time today to sit in a quiet room, on a comfortable chair. Tell everyone that you do not want to be disturbed; take the phone off the hook. Close your eyes. With your mind's eye, picture yourself standing in front of an artist's easel. There's a canvas on the easel, and you've penciled in a picture of your mental filter. It's a giant filter that fills the canvas. It's all sketched out, and you're ready to color it in.

You pick up your painter's palette, that flat, roundish board that has all the paints on it. With your mind's eye, look at your palette. There are a lot of colors on your palette. Some are bright, glowing colors. Others are soft and warm. Each is a color of joy, of love, of peace, of courage. They're beautiful, inviting, energizing, exciting colors, each and every one of them. There are more bottles and tubes of paint on your workbench.

Like the colors on your palette, the others are colors of happiness and success.

See all the colors. With your mind's eye, see yourself dipping your brush into the great colors on your palette and painting your filter the colors of health, happiness, and success. Sure, there may be a few dark spots, tiny and in the background, for life has its downs as well as its ups. But the overall look of your filter is one of joy.

As you see yourself coloring in your filter with the colors of joy, say:

> The colors of my palette, of my filter and life, are the bright, soft, warm, inviting, exciting, electric neon colors of success. Filled with joy, I choose to make each thought joyful, and my life a joyful life.

With this R_X for Choice, you are scraping away the dark colors encrusting your mental filter and replacing them with the colors of health, happiness, and success. Relive your special R_X for Choice several times today–as many as possible. See it. Feel it. Make those mental colors so real, that painting of your filter so real you can touch it. Believe it. Believe it with all your heart, and your spirit will repaint your mental filter.

Write Your Own Vision of Health and Joy

Can the Ethiopian change his skin, or the leopard his spots?
Jer. 13:23

As a commissioner for the California State Board of Medical Quality Assurance, it is my pleasure to help give oral examinations to the mostly young physicians applying for licenses to practice medicine in California. These doctors have already been graduated from medical school, completed residencies in their various specialties, and passed the written examinations. Some already have licenses to practice and have been practicing in other states. As a group, they are highly educated, motivated, and intelligent.

I've been curious to see how much they know about stress. At the last examination, I asked the doctors to pretend that they were examining a 50-year-old man complaining of fatigue. One of the most common complaints of stress is fatigue.

"What are some of the causes of fatigue?" I asked. "Give me five or ten possibilities."

All these bright physicians quickly suggested heart disorders, lung problems, and all kinds of exotic diseases that the average doctor sees once in a lifetime. None of them seemed to know that depression is one of the main causes of fatigue.

I then instructed them to question me as if I were this 50-year-old, fatigued man. They all asked me "straight" medical questions: "Do you have heart disease?" "Do you have trouble breathing?" "Is there a history of fatigue in your family?" "Do you have diabetes, lupus, or polyarteritis?"

They were very concerned with the organs of the body, with the systems, tissues, and molecules. Not one even peeked into my spirit. No one asked me what I thought of life, if I loved my wife, if I felt harassed or unappreciated at work, or if I had good relationships with my children.

Unfortunately, it's taking a long time for my fellow doctors to understand and appreciate the tremendous impact of the mind on the body. The medical system is making progress, but slowly. Doctors are still being taught the disease/drug equation: For every disease there is a drug, or will be soon.

You already have something more powerful than any drug ever devised, and it's exactly tailored to your needs: Your spirit. Unleashed, your spirit can be a whirlwind of health, happiness, and success in life.

"Write the vision, and make it plain." Make your choice. Color your filter with the colors of loving, daring joy, and write the vision of Spirit! into your mental gospel.

Day 4

YOUR CUP RUNNETH OVER

My cup runneth over. . .

Ps. 23:5

Many years ago I was privileged to learn an invaluable lesson from Deborah, a beautiful 38-year-old woman who was dying of cancer. Formerly a model, now a wife and mother of two teenagers, Deborah had developed breast cancer some years before. The surgeons had removed one of her breasts, but some of the cancer had evaded the scalpel, or perhaps had grown anew. The scourge now held that area where chest, neck, and arm meet.

I was called in to determine whether Deborah was well enough to withstand yet another surgery, one which the surgeons sadly admitted was a long shot. A very long shot, at best.

It was well into the night before I arrived at her hospital. As I sat at the nurse's station reviewing her chart, I was struck by a wave of sorrow for the so-far faceless patient described in clinical terms on these pages. Female. . .38 years old. . .mother of two. . .three previous surgeries. . .laboratory studies, surgical reports, progress reports, and on and on; correct, factual pages filling her thick chart, saying, without saying, that this woman was going to die.

Slowly I walked through the dimly lit corridors, in no hurry to confront the specter of death I could imagine hovering above this cancer victim. I was signing three, four, five death certificates a week back then. It was easy to believe that this woman's name would soon appear on one of those terrible papers.

Standing by the sleeping woman's bed, looking at the pale face swathed in shadows, I saw, with my mind's eye, the exact pattern of scars from her surgeries, the precise spot where the first surgeon touched scalpel to her skin, and where the second did, and third, and where the fourth would soon. Was the room as cold as it seemed, or was it me?

Suddenly her eyes opened. She was instantly awake, a beautiful, warm smile struggling to break through her weakness and illness. "You look tired," she said to me.

"*I* look tired?" The words shot out of my mouth before I could think.

"Yes, you do. Have you been working all day?"

"Since seven this morning. Oh, I'm Dr. Fox. Your surgeon asked me to examine you."

"How do you do? He told me about you. You're the specialist who gets all the hard cases."

"Well. . ." I didn't know what to say.

"It must be difficult," she said, sympathetically, "to deal with death every day. The psychological strain must be enormous. How do you do it?"

How do *I* do it? How do *you* do it, I wondered. The conversation was making me uncomfortable, so I put on my professional "mask" and began the examination. Head to toe, I carefully evaluated Deborah, trying to determine whether she was strong enough to survive the rigorous, risky surgery described in her chart. As I realized that she was too weak to undergo the surgery, I grew even more uncomfortable, even more "professional" and detached. Deborah undoubtedly sensed this, for she asked: "What's your diagnosis, Dr. Fox?"

"Well," I said evasively, "I'll be talking to your doctor."

"Good. What's your diagnosis?"

"Uh, your doctor will discuss it with you."

"I'd like to hear it from you," she said, friendly but firm.

It was difficult to look her in the eye as I said, "I'm going to recommend against the surgery." I could feel the room turning cold again, and it seemed as if the lights were dimming. But Deborah didn't seem to notice.

"You don't think I'm strong enough to survive it?"

"In my professional opinion, weighing your condition against the risk of the surgery, and the potential benefits. . ." I was unable to finish telling this woman that I could see no hope for her.

"I want you to change your recommendation, Dr. Fox. With

all due respect, you don't know me well enough to say I won't survive the surgery."

The look in her eyes was mesmerizing. I could almost feel little lightning bolts of determination flash out at me, yet, at the same time, sense her complete confidence and peace.

"My father gave me this cup when I was a little girl," she said, pointing to a beautiful silver goblet standing on the night table next to her bed. "Read the inscription."

I bent over to read it. " 'My cup runneth over.' That's from the Bible."

"Yes, but the source is not as important as the message. My father told me that the cup of life is never half-empty or half-full; it's always overflowing with possibility. He said that it didn't matter what terrible things were happening, if I had conviction, if I believed in myself, my cup would never run dry. My cup would always be a source of life, inspiration, strength, love, and everything else I could possibly need."

Then she took hold of the water pitcher on the night stand and poured water into her cup, more water than it could hold. As the water flowed over the brim and splashed on the table top she said, her voice so weak yet stronger than any I had ever heard, "My cup runneth over with conviction, Dr. Fox. It will never run dry. I will have the surgery and somehow I will survive, and I will live to see my two boys become men. You doctors take care of my body. God and I will take care of the rest."

Deborah had the surgery, and she did survive, and she lived to see her two boys become men.

Was her survival a statistical quirk? Spontaneous remission? A tribute to the genius of her surgeon? Perhaps. I've seen enough patients to know, however, that the ones who are convinced that their cups run over do better than those who see their cups running dry.

Your cup of life is a never-ending fountain of spirit, and spirit is the stuff of life.

There Is No Sin in Sorrow

By the sorrow of the heart the spirit is broken.

Prov. 15:13

"That's an inspiring story, Arn," a friend said. "But she's obviously an extraordinary lady with a Herculean spirit. How can a normal person like me believe that my cup is running over, given the downside of life which we all face daily? Let's be realistic. No one can have that kind of conviction all the time."

My friend was right. It is impossible to find dazzling silver linings in every storm cloud, to contentedly count our blessings even as the world falls apart about us. In fact, the person who never feels even the smallest bit of unhappiness or disappointment, who never acknowledges experiencing a negative feeling, is probably psychologically ill. Psychologists would suggest that such a person is manic.

There is no sin in sorrow. It is perfectly all right to be unhappy occasionally, to cry, to feel sorry for yourself, even to think negative thoughts. In one 18-month period I lost my mother, a daughter, and a good friend. Yes, I cried. I was depressed. I felt sorry for myself. That was ten years ago. I still think of them with sadness. Time dulls the sting of sorrow but it cannot erase the pain entirely.

There is no sin in sorrow. The key to facing sorrow, to surviving sorrow intact, is to have firm convictions. Especially, believe that you are a good person deserving the best of health and happiness. Be convinced that your cup always runneth over.

There is no sin in sorrow; rather, the sin is in loving sorrow, clinging to the feeling, making it the stuff of your life.

"Tragedy Is Not Static"

A time to weep, and a time to laugh; a time to mourn, and a time to dance.

Eccles. 3:4

While traveling around the country talking about our earlier book, *Wake Up! You're Alive,* Barry and I appeared on many radio and television shows. During one of the radio shows, a woman called in and taught us an important lesson. We don't remember that great woman's name, and we never saw or met her, but her message is one we will never forget.

She told us that her two young children had been killed in a fire, and her husband horribly burned over his entire body. A tragedy like this is enough to make most of us believe that our cup of life is very dry, but this woman had an inspiring lesson we can all take to heart.

"Tragedy is not static," she said. "It does not have to put a stop to your life."

Wow! What a powerful thought, one that will keep her cup overflowing forever. What an incredible thought she had stamped into her mind. A powerful thought like that can paint over the sorrow or despair.

During our conversation, it became clear that what kept this woman going, what gave her the courage to continue, was her conviction that her cup of life was still overflowing. From deep within her heart, she knew that life was good and worth living. She absolutely believed that her life was a gift from God. She knew that she would find a way through–a happy way.

As we spoke with this anonymous woman by telephone, I could picture her sitting at a table, with a beautiful silver goblet in front of her. I could see her cup was filled to the brim. Then, from somewhere, an ugly hand knocked her cup over, spilling out all the precious spirit, the stuff of her life. Only a few drops remained. The woman cried, yes, and wondered why she should go on living. But even as she said she'd rather be dead, she righted her cup. Tears were still running out of her eyes, yet she immediately began refilling her cup of life.

There will always be a tear in her eye for her children and husband. But there will always be plenty of spirit in her cup of life.

Tragedy need never be static, not if you keep moving ahead in life. Right your cup. Even as you grieve, begin refilling your cup of life with spirit. Fill it all the way to the top.

The Law of Conviction

When I see a patient for the first time, after I take the personal and medical history, I ask many additional questions: "Are you happy?" "Do you love your spouse?" "How is your relationship with your children? Your parents?" "Do you enjoy your work?" "What do you look forward to?"

I never fail to ask this question, which often startles my patients: "Do you have any strong convictions?"

At first I hear a lot of "ums" and "ahs." "What do you mean?" my patients often ask.

"Do you have any strong convictions or beliefs about anything, family, politics, religion?"

When I asked one man, a very famous retired politician, what he truly believed in, he said, after a very long silence: "Golf? No, not golf. Um, I like drawing. Family. I believe in family. My children are very important to me."

Why does a doctor like me, an internist and cardiologist, want to know about his patient's convictions? *Because conviction produces spirit, and spirit fortifies our convictions. That is the Law of Conviction.*

The woman with cancer had a very strong conviction. She believed that she was deserving of health and life. And her family was very important to her: She wanted to live to guide her sons into manhood. She had all the conviction she needed.

How about you? What are your convictions? Without taking time to think, jot down your convictions, the things you believe in most strongly.

I have found that strong convictions go hand in hand with a strong spirit, and vice versa. The important thing is not *what* your convictions are; the important thing is having some strong convictions—*whatever* they are.

The First Conviction

The First Conviction is the most important. It's a three-part conviction that says:

1. Spirit is the stuff of life.
2. I am filled with spirit!
3. I deserve all the good things that happen to me–and more!

The woman with cancer had this conviction, but it was never spoken. And she would never have written this onto her list of convictions. But it was there, written in-between the lines.

When we are filled with strong convictions, this First Conviction is usually there as well, in-between the lines. It's a given. When we're lacking in conviction, we must write this three-part First Conviction onto our list in big, bold letters. As other convictions join our list, this First Conviction will fade into the background. But it's always there. It's the foundation upon which our convictions, and our spirit, are built.

The Wounded Spirit

. . .a wounded spirit who can bear?

Prov. 18:14

Let me tell you about a man who almost lost his life because he became convinced that his cup had run dry.

Now in his thirties, this man had served in Vietnam during the 1960s, at the height of the conflict. Like most of our soldiers there, he was young and frightened. For many months he lived in or near the jungle. When they patrolled through the jungle, he was the lead man, the one up front who had to look for land mines, booby traps, ambushes. With every step he risked death; he and his entire patrol would be endangered if he should make a mistake.

Death never knocked on this man's door, but it seemed to know all of his friends' addresses. One by one his buddies died. Some were walking by his side when they were hit by a mortar shell. They simply disappeared. Some quietly crumpled to the ground, shot dead instantly. Others cried in anguish as they awaited death.

Though this man escaped physically untouched, he was

riddled with spiritual shrapnel. He couldn't believe he had come out alive. He believed that he *should* have died; the odds said he should have. And he felt he would have been better off if he had died, rather than live to die ten thousand times as he relived the death of his friends over and over and over in his dreams through the year. He often wished he could die now, to make up for Death's earlier omission. He lost the First Conviction. He no longer believed that he was filled with spirit, and that he deserved all the good things that could happen to him.

We doctors can usually tell quickly how much damage a physical wound has caused. Spiritual wounds, however, are difficult to assess. That was the case with this man. Slowly, over the course of twenty years, his spirit was robbed of life. Drop by drop, his cup ran dry. Shrapnel is bits and pieces of jagged metal which the enemy hurls at you. If it enters your body, it cuts and tears, rips into tissue, slashes arteries. There is spiritual shrapnel that does the same, in a way we cannot explain.

By the time I saw him, this veteran was in serious trouble. His chart was a thick book filled with descriptions of his diseases, syndromes, symptoms; it had many records of doctors' findings and recommendations, plus the results of innumerable laboratory studies. He had tried to kill himself twice. Neither the internists nor the cardiologists nor the neurologists nor the psychiatrists nor the gastroenterologists nor any of the other specialists had come up with a cure for his myriad ills, most of which got worse as time passed. We doctors know how to find problems in the body, how to pluck them out or fight them with medicines. But no surgeon can cut open the spirit to remove the shrapnel, repair the damaged tissue, sew together the broken arteries of the spirit. There is no cast, no sling, for the broken spirit.

Luckily, this man came upon his own medicine. During a period of relative health, he went to the Vietnam Memorial in Washington, D.C., to honor the memories of his friends. Picture the scene: A gaunt man, not well, walking slowly along the wall, touching the names of his buddies chiseled into the hard black stone, as if by touching their names he could somehow touch them again. Tears flowed freely as he remembered each one, remembered how each died. And as he remembered, he realized how easily it could have been him. And he wished it had been him.

He found every name, but still he looked for one more. Back and forth he walked, fingers on the wall, looking for one last name. His own. He believed that he *did* die back in the jungle, that he *did* die alongside his friends.

Finally he went to the book that listed all the names of the dead in alphabetical order and described where to find each name on the wall. He asked the attendant to find one more name. The attendant carefully looked through the book, but couldn't find the name.

"Are you sure that's the right name?" the attendant asked.

"Yes," the man replied. "It's my name."

The attendant looked at him, not with surprise, nor with sorrow, and said softly: "Your name isn't here. You must be alive. Go home and get on with your life."

This man did go on with his life. He sought the appropriate counseling, and rewrote the First Conviction into his mental gospel. He has become a much better man, father, and husband than he had been before.

I've heard this story, or something close to it, from other patients. It's as if their cup of life had been shot through by bullets, and all their spirit had flowed out of the cup. They no longer believed they had any reason or any right to live. They no longer had a desire to live. The vision of death they held in their minds was written into the mental gospel, time and time again. Their spirit responded to the sad words by drying up more each day. Luckily, our spirits have a tremendous will to live. It's hard to pour all the spirit out of your cup. The last drops of spirit cling stubbornly. That gives us the extra time we need to find the healing medicine for our spirit, or to find someone who can give it to us.

Strong convictions are a shield protecting us from blows to the spirit. Strong convictions are a sword with which to shatter life's obstacles. Strong convictions are the stuff of spirit, and spirit is the stuff of life.

The Enemy Is You

One day, a colleague I knew only casually—a dour-looking, listless, paunchy, 40-some—sat at my table in a coffee shop. I heard that this doctor, call him Dr. Hoffman, sometimes sarcastically referred to me as "Dr. Good Talk." I hadn't seen Dr. Hoffman for some time. To be honest, I hadn't missed him. Surprised as I was that he suddenly joined me, I was even more surprised to see him smiling so easily and naturally in greeting.

He wanted to thank me, he said, for helping him restore his immune system to health. (I hadn't known anything was wrong.) He had been ill for some time and upon checking his immune system, his total T-cell count, his T_4/T_8 ratio, and other indicators of immune strength had registered alarmingly low.

"When I read the results," he explained, "all of a sudden it hit me that you were right. I was making myself sick because the only thing I believed in was that I should be miserable. I was convinced that the world was full of doom and gloom, so my immune system got doomed and gloomed. I didn't think much of myself. I just didn't believe that I deserved the nice things I had. So I took a lesson from 'Dr. Good Talk' and gave myself a prescription of conviction. I decided that every day I would thank God for making me such a happy and healthy guy. That's the only change I made. I had my immune system checked last week. It's back to norm. I feel great!"

Write the First Conviction into your mental gospel; write it big and bold, write it over and over again. Your spirit will be replenished, and will respond to your great belief by drawing to you the good things that you desire.

Conviction Is the Key

Let every man be fully persuaded in his own mind.
Rom. 14:5

We can all learn a lesson from the marvelous woman and her

cup of life, from the woman who knew tragedy was not static, from the Vietnam veteran who found a way to go on living, and from the doctor who gave himself a prescription for conviction.

From the bottom of our hearts, we must believe that our cups always run over. No matter who we are, what our station in life or our present situation, we must believe that our cups run over.

Our cup of life is a gift from our Father, and it is our Father's good wish to grant us all the joy that can be yours. Our cup is always overflowing with all the things we need to thrive. It is filled with spirit!

Our spirit makes our wishes come true. When we believe that our cup runneth over, our spirit converts the wish into reality. Therefore, be fully persuaded in your own mind that you are a worthwhile person who deserves the best life has to offer.

When you're down, as we all are occasionally, know in your heart that your cup continues to overflow. All that strength, energy, and inspiration are always there, waiting for you to take advantage of them. Tragedy need not be static.

Conviction puts us into a positive feedback loop. The more we believe, the stronger our spirit. The stronger our spirit, the easier it is to believe in ourselves.

When we lack conviction we break the circle, we stop the flow. Now we're thrown into a negative feedback loop: Less conviction means a weaker spirit, and with a weaker spirit it is more difficult to believe. Luckily, negative feedback is positive guidance.

Step into the circle of conviction. Take the first step forward by writing the First Conviction into your mental gospel. The woman with cancer believed that life was joyful, and worth living. She believed that she was full of spirit–and so she was!

Your conviction is the faucet through which spirit flows into your cup of life. Throw the faucet wide open and prepare to drink of all the good stuff of life.

Rooted in Spirit!

Because they had no root, they withered away.

Matt. 13:6

"What do you mean I deserve the best life has to offer?" a patient asked me. "In all honesty, I'm not so hot. Why do I deserve the best?"

I believe that every single one of us deserves to live to the fullest extent of our potential. God gave us all that great physical, mental, and emotional potential for one reason: to be used.

We're told that he who does not believe will not be established. This means that belief in yourself is the prerequisite for health and happiness. Health and happiness, of course, are what makes us successful in life.

It doesn't matter who we are, who our parents are, where we came from, or where we are now. I've cut into many bodies in anatomy class and the surgery rooms. White bodies, black bodies; men and women; rich and poor; young and old; educated and ignorant; powerful and powerless. We're all the same. We were all given life and potential by the Creator. Our job is to take root in the rich soil of spirit. In this great soil are all the nutrients we need to flourish, to reach our fullest potential.

"OK," this same patient said. "You said we should believe and live to our potential. What if we haven't got much potential? What if we're deformed?"

I answered: "If your spirit is strong, physical deformities are irrelevant. You can still fulfill your potential."

The whole world saw an excellent illustration of this principle at the 1988 Summer Olympic Games in Seoul, Korea. The American baseball team was led by a young man named Jim Abbot. Jim was a star college pitcher, had won the Sullivan Award as the best amateur sportsman in the entire United States, and had been drafted by the California Angels, a major league baseball team. There he was on the mound, pitching at the Olympic games.

What made this baseball player so special? His belief in himself. His determination. The fact that he had only one hand was utterly secondary, especially to him. His body was a little flawed, but his spirit was absolutely perfect.

Inspiring examples like this are all around us. Last summer I read about a computer specialist who works for the F.B.I. This man, who has a top-secret security clearance, uses his computer to track down white-collar criminals. He types with his toes because he hasn't any arms or hands.

Barry and I recently went to radio station KMPC in Hollywood to be interviewed about our book, *Wake Up! You're Alive*. We arrived a bit early, so we sat down in the greenroom (the waiting room). Over the speaker we could hear the host of the show we were going to be on as he interviewed another guest. This guest was talking about a book he had written on George Washington. It sounded interesting, so Barry and I listened. The guest had a nice voice, he was obviously well educated, intelligent, and articulate. Soon it was our turn to go on, so Barry and I walked into the studio.

We were surprised to find that this guest had a hole in his throat. Every night he had to plug a respirator into his throat to do his breathing for him, or else he would die. He was small in stature and twisted; one arm hung at his side, apparently useless. A few days later we saw a picture of him in the *Los Angeles Times*. He was taking on the entire government over the issue of medical treatment for the handicapped. Physical deformities couldn't stop this man, whose body had been crippled by polio. He was living to his fullest potential. He earned a Ph.D. He wrote a great book, and he was still young.

Oh, yes. We also discovered that the host of the radio show was blind.

When that great First Conviction is written into your mental gospel, when you have things you can't wait to do, you can live to your fullest potential. Physical or mental handicaps become irrelevant.

Spread your roots in spirit. Everything else will fall into place.

Rx: Conviction

A land flowing with milk and honey.

Exod. 3:8

Today is the Day 4 of Making Miracles, the Day of Conviction.

We're told that the Promised Land is a land flowing with milk and honey and all the good things of life. If we keep our spirits strong, we can enjoy a never-ending flow of all the good things in life.

Recite these affirmations from your index cards throughout the day. Be sure to "see" each affirmation as you recite it.

Upon awakening: "Rejoice and Be Glad"
This is the day that the Lord hath made; I shall rejoice and be glad, be gladder than glad. I give myself permission to see all the happiness that is in my world, to think of the happiness, and to speak of the happiness. The Creator has filled the world with unlimited joy that is mine for the taking.

Morning: "It Is Good to Give Thanks"
It is good to give thanks unto the Lord for making me the healthy, happy, and successful person I so richly deserve to be. I am open to receiving all the blessings of His abundant universe.

Noon: "Endless Enthusiasm"
The Creator has filled me to the brim with enthusiasm. I gladly and generously pour my unlimited enthusiasm over my every thought and action. Armed with endless enthusiasm, I find excitement and adventure in every day.

Afternoon: "Spiritually Minded"
To be spiritually minded is life and peace. I give myself permission to be as calm and serene as the quiet waters of a beautiful, still lake.

Evening: "A Merry Heart"
A merry heart is a good medicine. My heart and spirit and the gospel of my mind are filled with joy. I am full of the thoughts and things of health, happiness, and success.

When going to bed: "Put on the New Me"
Today was another successful step toward the new me. With enthusiastic anticipation and absolute certainty that I'll make even more progress tomorrow, I'm putting on the new me.

As I told you before: Recite each affirmation out loud, with enthusiasm. Go beyond the minimum and recite your affirmations all day long. You can't overdo it with affirmations!

Many people find it difficult to believe that they deserve the best life has to offer them. Others can hold that First Conviction only when things are going well for them. How can we believe our cup always runneth over, even in the face of tragedy or adversity? Here's how you'll use these affirmations for conviction–your prescription for conviction.

Sit down, in a quiet room, on a comfortable chair. Tell everyone that you do not want to be disturbed; take the phone off the hook. Close your eyes. With your mind's eye, picture a beautiful silver goblet standing on a shining black table. It's dazzlingly bright. Take a closer look. Engraved on the goblet in bold letters is "My cup runneth over." Below that, your name.

Now look at the goblet's rim. Liquid is running over the top, like a waterfall. The color and texture of the liquid are whatever is most beautiful, exciting, or meaningful to you. The liquid isn't coming from anywhere, it's just there, in the goblet, continually overflowing.

Now look into the goblet from above. It's enormously wide and deep, filled with an ocean of possibilities for you: unlimited strength, endless energy, vibrant health, exuberant happiness, and energizing inspiration. In the middle of this giant ocean of potential floats a shining golden key. This key is your spirit, your power to unlock all the doors in your life.

With your mind's eye, see yourself holding your cup in one hand, pouring the liquid over your other hand. The flow is never-ending, a cascade of liquid energizing your entire body with health and happiness. You keep pouring, and out of the cup comes the golden key. It falls into your hand and you grasp it tight, knowing that all the keys to success are now in your hand.

See your cup running over. *Feel* it. *Believe* it. *Feel* that key in your hand. It's there. It's real. It's yours.

Now *say* it. After you've seen the key falling into your hand with your mind's eye, after you've held it tightly for several seconds, say out loud:

> My cup of life runneth over with endless possibility, with strength and inspiration, with never-ending enthusiasm, energy, and belief. I hold the golden key to success, life, and health in my hand. All the good things I want and deserve are within my reach.

See, say, feel, and believe that your cup runneth over. And it will! The woman with cancer proved that you can do it, if you believe you can!

Visualize your silver goblet of life running over several times a day; do it as often as possible. Enter into the world of your R_X for Conviction over and over, all during the day, at least 20 times. Every time you see the goblet overflowing with your mind's eye, say your affirmation loudly, with enthusiasm and conviction. Feel the key in your hand. Squeeze your fingers shut and really feel that key. It's there. It's yours. Use it!

> **All things are possible, if you believe. You can *be* the person you want to be. You can *have* the things you want to have, and *do* the things you want to do.**

YOUR CUP OF LIFE

You've seen it, said it, felt it, and believed it. Now make it an absolute reality. Go out and buy a silver goblet; beautiful and shiny, simple and tall. Have an engraver write "My Cup Runneth Over" on the goblet in big, bold letters. Below that, your name.

Every morning hold your goblet in one hand, over the sink. With the other hand, pick up a large pitcher filled with water or any other liquid. Feel the goblet in your hand: This is the cup of *your* life. Read the inscription: "My Cup Runneth Over."

Now pour the liquid into the cup, slowly. Fill the cup of your life, then let it overflow. Keep pouring. As you pour, and as the liquid overflows, say your affirmation:

> My cup of life runneth over with endless possibility, with strength and inspiration, with never-ending enthusiasm, energy, and belief. I hold the golden key to success, life, and health in my hand. All the good things I want and deserve are within my reach.

Let your cup of life overflow as long as possible. Let it be a symbol, a physical representation of the great belief you have in yourself.

> **God promised that there would never again be a flood to destroy the earth. What He gave us instead was the power to flood our cups with the spirit of life.**

Day 5

MAKING MIRACLES

No man can do these miracles that thou doest, except God be with him.

John 3:2

God created the heavens and the earth. Moses struck a desert rock with his staff, and from the rock poured forth water. Daniel emerged unscathed from the lion's den. Jesus made the blind beggar see, roused the child from the sleep of the dead, and rose from the tomb himself.

The wonders of God are many indeed, but we are created only a little lower than the angels, and we are not without powers of our own. God's greatest miracle, perhaps, is that He made us miracle makers, too. When the spirit of God is within you, you can create a universe; you can turn one substance into another; and you can perform what has hitherto been impossible to do. With nothing more than the power of your mind, you can perform the miracle of giving life, to yourself and to others.

God gave us the incredible power to perform miracles when he taught us how to love–instructing us to give that love freely. He who loves is full of the spirit of God. And when we are filled with the spirit of God, we can perform the miracle of life.

By love do we serve one another, giving to others what we prize most.

THE LAW OF LOVE

Give and it shall be given unto you.

Luke 6:38

Throughout this section I'll be talking about giving. Giving of yourself, your attention, your time, your concern, your help, giving charity. Most of all, however, I'll be talking about giving your love to others; giving freely, unconditionally, and gladly.

Love is the most precious gift we can give, for love is the perfect expression of all good things on earth. In order for us to give our love to others, we must be loving people. We must see that the world is filled with love. And if we are loving people, we will automatically be givers. Loving and giving are one and the same. That is the Law of Love.

He who loves, gives. He who gives love, gives life.

The Medicine Called Love

Perfect love casteth out fear.

John 4:18

Giving begins with being. How loving can we be? Can we even love in the face of tragedy? A 77-year-old woman named Rose Nelson taught me that we can never be too loving, and we can always find a way to love.

I first met Mrs. Nelson at a senior citizen's home where my family and I used to entertain. We would sing old-time songs, dance a little, tell jokes, and do some magic. Mrs. Nelson was always there in the front row, a big smile on her face, singing right along. Although confined to a wheelchair, she always seemed to be dancing. One of the other senior citizens told me that Mrs. Nelson had been brutally beaten by two drunk teenagers who didn't even remember what they had done. That was ten years ago; she had been confined to a wheelchair ever since. Medical bills had eaten up her modest savings, so she had been forced to sell her family home and move into the seniors' home. I also learned that although Mrs. Nelson and witnesses identified the assailants, they got off on a technicality.

Mrs. Nelson had every reason to be angry, fearful, and depressed. "I wouldn't even think of it," she said with a big smile. "It doesn't matter where I am, how I am. As long as my brain is working and I can think of love, I'm doing great!"

"How can you be so loving after what happened to you?" I asked. "The world was not very loving to you."

Again she smiled. "The world is what I decide it is. Oh my, I could have dried up after the boys beat me. I was afraid I would. And I was afraid that they would do it again because they were never put in jail. That's why I decided to be full of love, and to give my love to everyone. The more I love everyone else, the better I feel. And the better I feel, the more I love the world. Love cured my fear."

She continued. "Why do you think all the old people around here like listening to your family sing? Half the time you're off-key, but you sing with love. Your love is a medicine for these old people with their problems. And I'm not old; they are," she said, indicating the other seniors.

Love is a medicine for the spirit, ours and others. Love is the antidote to fear, anger, guilt, frustration, and more.

The Law of Projection

Mine eye affecteth mine heart.

Lam. 3:51

Mrs. Nelson is a beautiful illustration of the Law of Projection, which states that we see the world as we are, and as we see the world, so do we become.

Normally we think of our eyes as taking in light from all directions and sending it to the brain, where it is put together into the pictures of the world we see. But our eyes are also projectors, projecting images from our minds onto other people, things, and events. These images coat everything we see, painting them the colors of our thoughts.

If our minds are filled with loving and joyous thoughts, we project love and joy. Thus, the world seems to us to be filled with loving, joyful people and things. But if our minds are full of unhappiness and pain, we project negative visions. We see all the negatives, and we believe the world is a bad place.

In other words, all the world is a mirror—our mirror. As we look at the mirror of the world, we see deep within ourselves.

We see the world as we are. Our eyes *do* affect our hearts, our health, our happiness, our lives. Despite the terrible thing that happened to her, Mrs. Nelson projected love.

The Law of Projection also states that as we see the world, so do we become. Looking into the shiny mirrors of her world, Mrs. Nelson saw only love. Not fear, not anger, but love. And she became what she saw, always adding to her store of love.

Love is the antidote to fear, to anger, to guilt, and to all the other negative emotions that are as infectious germs to our spirit.

Whom Do You Love?

None of us liveth to himself.

Rom. 14:7

He who loves, gives. He who gives love, gives life. But what of people who have little love in their lives?

A 52-year-old man stopped me in the parking lot after I had given a talk in Century City, right next door to Beverly Hills. At first I wondered why he had sought me out, for his conversation seemed pointless, and he wasn't asking me questions about health, nutrition, or the spirit, as people often do. He was obviously distressed, however. Finally he said, "My whole life is a blah. Nothing interests me. I'm scared. What's wrong with me?"

"Whom do you love?" I asked him.

He was startled. "Love?"

"Whom do you love?"

"Uh, I, uh . . . no one. I don't love anyone. I can't think of anyone."

"Who loves you?" I asked.

"No one," he answered immediately, sadly.

Whom do you love? Who loves you? I ask my patients these questions, and find that a lot of people have little love in their lives. But love of life is vital, for loving and being loved go hand in hand with having a strong spirit.

A doctor can't diagnose a patient as having "lack of love": That would lead to trouble with the medical licensing board. And insurance companies would refuse to pay for claims based on "lack of love." So when a person comes to a doctor with, say, headaches, related to too many lonely nights in his or her apartment or to a profound feeling of being alone, doctors often write *cephalgia* on the insurance form. ("Ceph" refers to the head, and "algia" to pain.) Giving it a fancy name like cephalgia and prescribing a painkiller satisfies the requirements but helps no one.

The unloved Mr. Morrison later came to my office. He feared he was having or had already had a heart attack. "I get pains in my neck, chest, shoulders, and arms. Sometimes I can't breathe."

Tightness or pain in the chest, neck, or arm are common symptoms of heart disease, so I immediately did a very thorough physical examination of Mr. Morrison, and called for the appropriate laboratory work-ups and other studies. I paid special attention to his heart and his risk factors for heart disease, but found no evidence of an impending heart attack. In fact, his heart and coronary arteries were in better-than-average shape for a man his age. The other specialists I sent him to agreed.

I usually spend an hour talking with new patients, getting to know them. As Hippocrates wisely noted thousands of years ago, you can learn much about a man's disease by learning about the man's life. During our conversation, Mr. Morrison described himself as a heartless man.

"I don't mean I'm mean," he hastened to add. "I've just never loved anybody. Look, I was raised in foster homes. Everyone was nice to me, but I never felt any real love involved. I had girlfriends. They were nice, but I never loved them. One of them said I was born without a heart.

"It just seems like there's never been any love in my life. I don't love, and no one loves me."

Mr. Morrison saw little love in his world–little heart. And so he became even more "heartless" and unable to love. He carried it a big step further, as his psychic pain mimicked the well-known symptoms of a heart attack.

Mr. Morrison was caught in a loveless loop. He felt little love, so he projected little love. He saw no love in the world, so he became less loving.

Mrs. Nelson, on the other hand, was skipping through life in a loving loop. Nothing could knock her off her golden pathway. Nothing.

Can we step out of a loveless loop and into a loving one? Mr. Morrison worked diligently through the Making Miracles program. It took some time, for his mirrors were clouded over with lovelessness. But love became the cleanser that cleared the mirrors of his life. After a while he found that his eyes were affecting his heart—but only for the better, for his eyes were able to project and see plenty of love.

We see what we are, and we are what we see. See love to be love, and be love to see love.

THE LAWS OF EXPANSION AND CONTRACTION

He that watereth shall be watered also himself.

Prov. 11:25

In a sense, the world—your world—is alive. Like any living being, your world needs nourishment. Instead of vitamins and fiber, your world feeds on all the good feelings you project, like a plant feeding upon the sun's energy. You are the sun around which your world revolves. The brighter and warmer your light, the more alive your world will be.

The Law of Contraction states that when you pull into yourself, when you stop giving the light of your love to your world, your world contracts. Your world shrinks in on you like a fist. As your world shrinks, it squeezes the life out of you.

A 60-year-old man named Dan came to my office complaining of "a squeezing feeling in my upper body, like a giant hand is squeezing me." I took a careful personal and family medical history, performed a thorough physical examination, called for the appropriate laboratory studies, and reviewed the reports from his other doctors. As I suspected, Dan's problem was spiritual, not the result of some exotic bacteria or unusual genetic problem. He was a clear example of the Law of

Contraction.

Dan told me that he never gave his love to anyone, because "love is nonsense." Neither did he spend much time with his family, or give to charity, or help employees suffering from personal or financial difficulties. "Everyone gets paid, and that's plenty," he told me.

And so Dan gave nothing to the world. He thought of himself as being walled off. He projected that feeling out to the world. When he looked into the mirror of his world he was not connected, and he burrowed deeper into his cocoon. And so Dan became a victim of the Law of Contraction.

The Law of Expansion is the opposite of the Law of Contraction. Mrs. Nelson's world was constantly expanding, for she fed it endlessly with love. Giving is the cure for a diminishing world. The more light you "feed" to the world, the larger your world. The more you give love, the more alive is your world, the brighter are your mirrors.

Expand your world with love. Let all mirrors of your world shine brightly with the light of your love.

Ordering Cocaine Like Pizza

One of my patients was a very wealthy man who never gave anything to anyone: not a helping hand, not a thought, not a moment's concern.

Everyone thought this multimillionaire was leading the good life, and outwardly he was. He had a giant estate in Malibu, a mountaintop home up North, a Palm Springs getaway home, pools, servants, cars, and the other trappings of wealth. Inwardly, however, this man was a pauper. He had no joy, no love for anyone, not even himself. He picked up the cocaine habit. Soon he did nothing but stay in his room taking cocaine. "I was ordering it to be delivered like pizza," he said.

His family tried to get him off the cocaine, but had little success. Every so often the man would check into a rehabilitation hospital or go to a psychologist, but he never stayed long. He knew what the cocaine could do to him and he knew he should break the habit. He wanted to, but he didn't want to.

One day, one of his low-level employees came to his estate to deliver some papers. Like most everyone else, this employee, named Brian, knew the man was destroying his life. But Brian was a little different from most people. He stuck his neck out. He knew he could be fired on the spot, but Brian was a helping kind of guy. Brian told the man to go to Cocaine Anonymous—now.

This man, who often yelled at his employees and anyone else who annoyed him, argued a bit but Brian was convincing. He agreed to go. That evening Brian came back to the estate to pick his boss up and take him to the Cocaine Anonymous meeting. This really surprised the boss, who never went out of his way to help anyone. Then, at the meeting, the boss was dumbfounded to discover a roomful of people he had never met before who were willing to stand by him. They accepted him 100 percent, flaws and all, without judgment. Yes, everyone else in the room was an addict, and they were there because they needed help. But they were all willing to help one another. They were all ready to give.

This man got off cocaine in no time. He was off the drug for three years when he told me the story. Today, when anyone asks him for help, he jumps into action. Not just with his checkbook, because that's too easy for this wealthy man. He goes out in person to lend a hand.

"I realize that the only thing that keeps me from going back is the unconditional love, and the person-to-person help, I give to others. I've got millions of dollars, but I'll get my hands dirty if I have to. I enjoy helping people. And I know that helping them helps me."

For years I've gone with my patients to various self-help groups: Alcoholics Anonymous, Cocaine Anonymous, Al-Anon, Alateen, Overeaters Anonymous, and others dedicated to helping people get over their addictions. I even insisted that some of my non-addicted patients go. They would say, "Doc, I don't drink, why should I go to AA?"

I would answer: "You're not addicted to alcohol or drugs, but you are addicted to selfishness. I want you to see that there are people in this world who are totally nonjudgmental, who don't care what you've done in the past, and are willing to help you."

Many of my patients were amazed, for they had never

helped anyone themselves. They had never known that people would help them for nothing more than love. And they never knew how healing helping can be.

What Is Love?

Let us not love in word neither in tongue, but in deed and in truth.

1 John 3:18

Love is an essential ingredient in the recipe for health, happiness, and success; it's the leaven that makes the batter rise. Joy and courage tell your spirit how to be; love tells you why. It's said that if you have faith to move mountains but lack love, you are nothing. When you love, you know where to put the mountains, and why.

"I have lots of love," one of my patients, a famous singer, told me. "There are millions of women who love me. They mob me when I walk down the street. I can't go anywhere any more."

This man received endless adoration, and perhaps even some genuine love, but treated it no differently than he did money or the sales figures on his records. Love was just another commodity to stockpile, another boost to his ego. His life was an endless succession of drinking and drug binges, coupled with maniacal reckless driving sprees up and down the Pacific Coast Highway. After a three-day binge that nearly ended his life, he came to my office for help.

"If this keeps up I'm going to kill myself," he said. "Help me."

Fortunately I was able to convince him to join Alcoholics Anonymous and seek counseling. Actually, I had to take him there myself the first couple of times, sitting with him through the meetings. After much soul searching, he was able to open his heart to love. Drugs, alcohol, and reckless driving were traded in for love of his family and love of life.

Love has nothing to do with numbers, dollars, status, or power, and is never given with any expectations of reward. True love is always outer-directed, and is often given to people who have no idea you love them.

Many people confuse the love or admiration they receive from others with their own love, with the love they give *to* others. The love you receive from others is very important. But taking love without giving equal amounts or more back to the world breaks the circuit.

Love has a branching effect. Each person you touch with your love touches other people. Now, in a tree, the branches get thinner as they move away from the trunk. The highest, farthest branches are pretty small. But with love, each branch is thicker than the one before it, for your love is joined with the love of the person you touch. Your love does not diminish theirs, nor theirs yours. Together, your combined love is mightier than ever.

It's the love you have inside of you, the love you project to others, that brings the gift of life.

Fulfill the Obligation of Love

Owe no man anything, but to love another.

Rom. 13:8

How does love make the miracle of life? What is it about a simple emotion that makes miracles?

Love tells our spirit that there is meaning to life, that there is a reason to look forward to each new day. When you love yourself, love God, and love life, you write great thoughts of joy into your mental gospel. When you love others, you give them reason to write goodness into their mental gospels. And the more love there is in our gospels, the stronger our spirit.

Acting through the spirit and mind, love and other good thoughts boost our health. We can all learn a lesson from Frank, who was in his nineties when I used to see him as a patient. I asked him for the secret to his remarkable health and longevity. He told me it was "love for the world, and a good cigar every day." I don't know about the cigar, but I can tell you that goodly amounts of love will strengthen your immune system, helping to make sure that you have plenty of killer T-cells, macrophages, and other immune soldiers to defeat invading germs and nip cancerous growths in the bud. We know that there are strong links between the mind and immune system: What happens in the mind always affects what happens in the immune system.

Love is also a marvelous antidote to stress, a major cause of disease in our country. Stress (*dis*-stress) has a high probability of causing coronary artery spasm, which can lead to angina pectoris (chest pain) or heart attacks. And the victim may not even know what's happening. Irrefutable medical proof reported recently has shown that silent ischemia (lack of oxygen to the heart muscle, in this case) often occurs in stressed individuals, quietly producing irreversible damage to the heart. A great deal of the time, the person has no symptoms. Then suddenly, he or she has a heart attack. For a large number of people, the first chest pain is their last.

Fulfill the obligation of love by giving freely, without expectations, to everyone. Don't just give money; that's fine, but it's too easy, and it's not nearly enough. Give someone the most precious treasure you have: Yourself.

Teach a kid how to read, how to play ball, bake a cake, or ride a bicycle. If you can sing, dance, play an instrument, juggle, tell jokes, do magic tricks, or anything like that, entertain the people in a retirement home. It doesn't matter if you're not very good. What you're really giving is your concern and love, and that's much more important than your talent. Go back to your old neighborhood and tell the people they can do it. Give them the tools to do it, give them your time and attention. Give them love, and give them the desire to excel.

Love reduces stress, strengthens the immune system, puts smiles on our faces and joy in our hearts. Love is preventive medicine, holding off disease, despair, and even many of the ravages of old age. Love is truly a blessing in all seasons, for the one who is loved and for the one who loves. Everyone benefits from love.

Make the miracle of life by loving yourself, loving others, loving God, and loving life. Make the miracle for yourself and for others.

THE LAW OF GIVING

Every gift you give is given twice: Once to the person you give it to, and, simultaneously, to yourself. I find that taking my patients to Alcoholics Anonymous or any of the support groups is not a chore. It's a pleasure, for every time I give to someone else, I feel as I've been given a large measure of love and support.

How does the Law of Giving work? How can giving to someone else bring something to you? The act of giving with love is written into your mental gospel: Today I lovingly gave to so-and-so. Immediately, this new piece of information is cross-referenced, and a new entry is made in your chapter of love. Your brain notes that your chapter on love has grown and reacts accordingly. Now your eyes, which project out onto the world the pictures of the world you have inside your head, project even more love. Everywhere you look, everything you see, seems to have a bit more love. The "love quotient" in your world has increased. Living in a more loving world prompts the steady release of endorphins and other beneficial biosubstances in your body, making you feel better, happier, and strengthening your immune system.

Every gift you give to someone else is a gift to yourself.

WHEN SHOULD WE GIVE?

As we therefore have opportunity, let us do good unto all men.

Gal. 6:10

When is the best time to give to others? Anytime is a great time, of course, but is there a time when we especially need to give?

Barry and I recently drove out to Palm Springs, California, to tape a segment for a television show called "There Is a Way." We arrived quite early, so we sat down to watch the Reverend Leo Fishbeck of Glendale, California, taping his segment of the same show.

Dr. Fishbeck spoke about giving, saying, "You especially

need to give when you are lacking."

Give when you are lacking? How can we give when we're lacking? Shouldn't we hang on to what little we have, and try to increase it? If we give it away we won't have any left, right?

My cousin, may he rest in peace, was a poor boy who wanted to be an entrepreneur. He dreamed of setting up companies, buying and selling stock, putting multimillion-dollar deals together, and making a big name for himself. He had some good ideas, but he had no business education and no money. I remember being so horrified when he would spend what little money he had. He always said, "It takes some to get some." He referred to the money he spent as seed money, saying the money he was "planting" would grow and be harvested soon.

It worked for him. Since then I've seen it work countless times for people who are giving, as well. When you get to feeling that you have no love or no one loves you, give away more of your love than ever. As you give more love, you fill your head with loving thoughts. These thoughts will be projected into your world. Everywhere you look you'll see love. All that great love will be reflected by the mirrors of your world right back to you. And as there is more love within you, you will become a more loving person. That first bit of love you give away is the seed. Plant a thousand seeds. You'll be rewarded with a bountiful harvest.

The Reverend G. Arthur Hammons, host of "There Is A Way," summed up Dr. Fishbeck's presentation by saying: "As I give of myself, I develop the courage to succeed."

> **Give what you lack most, and give freely. What you give most and most freely, you shall receive back soonest and most joyfully.**

Teach the Gift of Giving

It's never too late to begin giving. Neither is it ever too soon to begin teaching people to give. Last year my little granddaughter Melanie and her friends proudly participated in a Girl Scout ceremony in which they graduated from the Daisies to the

Brownies. It was a happy, musical ceremony; all the parents were there with video recorders and cameras. At the end of the ceremony the girls took off their Daisy aprons and put on Brownie sashes. One of the mothers announced that she was collecting Daisy aprons for girls who could not afford them, and most of the little girls, without waiting for prompting from their parents, donated their aprons.

It's a great start for these girls. Sure, a skeptic could criticize this, saying it was easy for them to give; after all, they had all just moved up to the Brownies and didn't need their Daisy aprons any more. Yes, it was easy for them to give. The point is, however, that they were getting into the giving habit.

(Watching the little Scouts took me back to the days, so many years ago, when I was saving my pennies to buy my Boy Scout uniform. The last piece I got—and I finally had a full uniform—was the slide that held the neckerchief in place. It cost fifty cents. That was a lot of money back then in South Philadelphia.)

You don't have to be well-off to get into the giving habit. I grew up during the Depression. Most of the families in my neighborhood were just a step or two ahead of the bill collector. Everybody I knew was poor in money, but most every family kept a little can or bottle in the kitchen. It was a charity can, the can where we put our spare pennies for the "poor people." I knew we didn't have any money, but I also knew, because my parents explained this to me, that charity is a double gift: Once to the receiver and once to the giver.

We hadn't formulated fancy concepts, we didn't know about the Law of Love or the Law of Giving. We just knew that it felt good to help someone out.

Loving to Live with God

God is love; and he that dwelleth in love dwelleth in God and God in him.

1 John 4:16

I was lucky to have very loving parents. With their love, my parents performed miracles. Their great loves were the first words written in the gospel of my mind. The wonderful words they wrote there gave me a strong spirit, determined that the biochemistry of my body would favor health, and created in me a vast potential for success. Their love gave me my life, as it is today. We were extremely poor in money and things, but rich in love.

Many of us suffer like the 32-year-old woman who came to my office complaining of sexual problems, recurrent colds, stomach upset, anxiety, and nightmares. She had been to several doctors during the last six months, who gave her prescriptions for various drugs. One recommended surgery. During our discussion she told me that she had given up on love years ago. "It's practical relationships that run life, not phony-baloney love," she said disgustedly. "Love is a fairy tale advertisers use to sell us junk."

Love is absolutely real. Love absolutely affects your spirit, the chemical makeup of your body, your immune system and more. Love–the love you have for yourself, the love you have for others, the love you receive from others–is a decisive factor in your life. Love is the touch of God within you. When you love, you spread God's goodness.

When you love others, freely and unconditionally, you cannot hate. You can recognize the errors and bad things others may do, yes, but you cannot hate them, for you are too full of love. Thus you are spared the hellfires of hatred, of the angry thoughts that become destructive things within your body.

When you love others, freely and unconditionally, you are not consumed by envy, for you share in everyone else's joy. Their success reminds you that the world *is* full of unlimited goodness, and that you can succeed, too.

When you love others, freely and unconditionally, you cannot be prejudiced, for you look at others and see the goodness that is within them. Though they may be different in some very minor way, they, like you, are God's children.

When you love others, freely and unconditionally, you give them life, as my parents gave it to me. You also give life to yourself as you banish destructive thoughts and things from your body.

Love is the fountain from which so much good flows, yet

love is not dependent on anything else. Love is a never-ending, self-renewing resource. The more love you give the more you will receive. Love encapsulates all that is good in life. Many waters cannot quench love, neither can the floods drown it.

God gave you life and love. Now you can share love; now you can give life. You can write "love" over and over again, in big bold letters, in thousands of mental gospels. You can strengthen spirits, you can realign body chemistries, you can strengthen immune systems. You can pour love into many cups of life, and make sure that those cups overflow endlessly. You can make miracles.

Love is God, and he that lives in love lives with God.

What's Written in Your Gospel?

Is your mental gospel filled with love? Are you telling your spirit that your world is a lovely place to be? Quickly, without thinking about it, make a list of all the people, things, and ideas you love and why you love them.

The larger your list the better. If your list is small or nonexistent, there may be a lot of hate, anger, and unforgiveness in you. Let loose! Get rid of your hatreds and "hurtreds." Let loose of your negative feelings and make this list grow. (When you work through this program the second time, you'll be surprised at how much larger your list has grown.)

Love Too Much to Hate

Many waters cannot quench love, neither can the floods drown it.

Song of Sol. 8:7

One of my patients was an elderly woman who knew that love is medicine for the spirit. She had lived in Russia during a time when Jews there had a precarious existence, never knowing when the government or groups of haters would cause trouble.

She and her husband and their three children had been living in a little town where they had a small bakery.

One night some local troublemakers beat up several of the Jewish men and set fire to several of their houses. My patient's husband was one of the men. He died a few days later. And her house was one of those burnt to the ground. When she went to the authorities she was told there was nothing they could do, even though she knew who some of the murderers were.

"I had every reason to hate them," she told me in halting English. "I would see the murderers on the street every day but there was nothing a Jew in the old country could do to have justice. Rather than hating them and making myself sick, I put it in God's hands and went on with my life. I love God and the world too much to ever become a hater."

The Five Aspects of Love

A new commandment I give unto you, that you love one another.

John 13:34

We're told to love God, to love our neighbors, to love our enemies. We're told to walk in love. We're told to love not only in word but also in deed. Let's do all this, and in so doing, perform the miracle of giving life, health, happiness, and success.

Let us do this by embracing the five aspects of love:

First is love of God, for we are told to love the Lord our God with all our heart, soul, and might. When we love God we acknowledge that our world is a good place, for He created it and everything in it.

Next is love of yourself, or self-esteem, acknowledging that you are God's special creation, deserving of the best life has to offer: vibrant health, unbridled happiness, and limitless success. When you love yourself, modestly, honestly but enthusiastically, you write love into your mental gospel.

Love of others follows naturally from the first two loves, for when you love God and all that He has created, and when you love yourself, you have enough confidence and self-esteem to recognize the goodness that lies in others.

Love from others comes if you do this. If you adopt the commandment of love, your reward will be the fourth kind of love.

Love from God is the fifth love. That is always present and needs no explanation.

When you adopt wholeheartedly the commandment of love, you write volumes of good news in your mental gospel, and set up the conditions that promote health, happiness, and success. When you embrace the commandment of love, you become one with God, for the one who dwells in love dwells in God, and God in him.

Are you poor in money? Embrace the commandment of love. A young patient of mine named Harry embraced the commandment of love, after much persuading. All the time he had spent plotting revenge on his superiors and the people who were promoted ahead of him was now available to use for getting ahead. Instead of hating, his mind was free to work on designs to submit to his bosses. Within six months he was promoted from secretary/runner to assistant designer. Harry now had more money, better health, and was on his way to the top.

Has illness overcome you? Write love into your mental gospel. Anger is a terrible enemy of the immune system. So are rage, frustration, envy, and all the other negative feelings. When a 52-year-old actress and patient of mine tore the negative pages from her mental gospel and wrote in new pages of love, her five-year bout with mononucleosis faded into memory.

Do opportunities seem to pass you by? Look at life through the eyes of love. A salesman and friend of mine made a mighty effort to see his clients as good people in need of his fine products, not as "jerks who loved to keep me dangling." His income shot off the charts and within the year he was made regional manager.

"What made the difference?" I asked him.

"I wasn't willing to work hard to sell junk to jerks, but I'll bust my buns to make sure my friends have the opportunity to buy the stuff they need to succeed."

Is your spirit broken? Fill your cup with love, and it will overflow forever.

Rx: GIVING

. . .love covereth all sins.

Prov. 10:12

Today is Day Five of Making Miracles, the Day of Giving. This day is dedicated to keeping the cycle of love going, and strengthening it with our every thought and action.

Recite these affirmations you have written on your index cards throughout the day. Be sure to "see" each affirmation as you recite it.

Upon awakening: "Rejoice and Be Glad"
This is the day that the Lord hath made; I shall rejoice and be glad, be gladder than glad. I give myself permission to see all the happiness that is in my world, to think of the happiness, and to speak of the happiness. The Creator has filled the world with unlimited joy that is mine for the taking.

Morning: "It Is Good to Give Thanks"
It is good to give thanks unto the Lord for making me the healthy, happy, and successful person I so richly deserve to be. I am open to receiving all the blessings of His abundant universe.

Noon: "Endless Enthusiasm"
The Creator has filled me to the brim with enthusiasm. I gladly and generously pour my unlimited enthusiasm over my every thought and action. Armed with endless enthusiasm, I find excitement and adventure in every day.

Afternoon: "Spiritually Minded"
To be spiritually minded is life and peace. I give myself permission to be as calm and serene as the quiet waters of a beautiful, still lake.

Evening: "A Merry Heart"
A merry heart is a good medicine. My heart and spirit and the gospel of my mind are filled with joy. I am full of the thoughts and things of health, happiness, and success.

When going to bed: "Put on the New Me"
Today was another successful step toward the new me. With enthusiastic anticipation and absolute certainty that I'll make even more progress tomorrow, I'm putting on the new me.

Again, recite each affirmation out loud, with enthusiasm. Recite them all day long. You can't overdo it with affirmations!

In addition to your daily diet of affirmations, enter into your world of this special R_X for Giving several times today, with energy and conviction.

Set aside some time today to sit in a quiet room, on a comfortable chair. Tell everyone that you do not want to be disturbed; take the phone off the hook. Close your eyes. With your mind's eye, see yourself standing with a big smile on your face. There's an endless line of people in front of you, stretching farther than the eye can see to the right and to the left. You're walking down the line, one person at a time. As you stop in front of each person you touch your hand to your heart, then holding onto a big chunk of your love, you give it to that person. When you do, that person grows suddenly bigger and much brighter. And so you go down the line, giving your love freely to everyone you meet. As you do, say:

> This is always the time to give, this is always the place to give. Love is the greatest of God's many gifts. I am full of love, and I am sharing my great gift with the world.

We are commanded to love. Love God, love yourself, love others and receive their love in return. Love life with all your heart, with all your soul, and with all your might. Write volumes of love in your mental gospel. Fill your cup to overflowing with love.

No one can perform miracles unless God is with him. When you love, you are with God. Perform the life-giving miracle of love, for yourself and for everyone, starting here, starting right now, and never stop.

Bring Joy to the Living

As we have therefore opportunity, let us do good unto all men.

Gal. 5:13

One day not too long ago I drove out to the cemetery to visit the graves of my parents, my daughter, and two dear friends. As is my custom, I parked my car at the bottom of the hill and walked to the top, visiting each grave in turn, remembering the deceased and the joy they had brought in the world–and to me.

Usually I leave the cemetery feeling up, not down, because the realization that these people who meant so much to me have passed on is more than balanced by the memories of the love and good times we shared. That day, however, I walked to my car feeling lousy.

I didn't want to drive away feeling bad, so I sat in my car and thought about all the good times I had shared with each of the deceased, one at a time. Thinking of the good is an excellent way to drive the bad out of your mind, but that day it didn't do the trick. For some reason, I couldn't shake the blues.

I refused to leave the cemetery feeling unhappy, so I purchased a brass polishing kit from the mortuary shop and trudged back up the hill. One by one I polished the grave markers, and thought of the good times I had had with the deceased.

Now I felt that I had done something positive for my loved ones. I felt good, and now I could go on with my day.

Why was I feeling so low that day? Because I was afraid of facing the future without these people by my side. Because I was frightened of experiencing the death of another loved one. More than that, however, much more, it was because I was feeling guilty. What more could I have done for them when they were alive? What could I have done to enrich their lives? What things had I said to them in anger, or out of frustration? How often had I been so self-involved that I had overlooked their feelings, their needs?

Afraid to face the future, too guilty to look back at the past, I was caught in a sad and uncomfortable present, feeling fearful, and, especially guilty. Guilt is a harmful emotion that preys on our peace of mind, and, acting through the mind, on our body as well. What can we do to protect ourselves? How can we make amends and alleviate our guilt?

We can't make amends to the deceased, of course, but we can do good for others. All the good you wanted to do for those loved ones who have passed away, do for the living. All the joy you wish you had given, give to the living. All the good things you wanted to say, say to the living. All the love you have for the deceased, give to the living. Give it all, and more.

Tell your loved ones–your spouse or significant other, your children, parents, friends–that you love them. Tell them today, tomorrow, and every day–in word and deed–that you love them.

If you have trouble expressing love, a good way to start is to give compliments. Don't be phony; people will see through that. Look for things you sincerely like, and be generous with your praise. When you sincerely compliment someone, you're sharing a bit of your love.

Once you're comfortable giving compliments, reach out and touch someone. Pick a person you love–your lover, mother, father, brother, sister, child, friend, whomever you prefer–and tell them that you love them. If you can't use the word love, say, "I appreciate all the good things you've done for me," or, "I really enjoy your company."

Be sure to look them in the eye when you tell them you love them. Touch them. Hold their hand, put your hand on their shoulder, put your arm around their shoulder. Let them feel the warmth of your love.

Don't be afraid to give your love. Love isn't limited, like the money in a bank account. Love is infinite. The more you give, the more you'll have. You see, you're happy when you've loving. That happiness works in the brain to stimulate the release of endorphins and other biochemicals, that, in the right amounts, lift your mood. The happiness, the good feeling that results, helps reduce your fear, guilt, or other negative feelings. When you love, and when you give your love, you put yourself into a positive feedback loop that benefits everyone.

Make miracles. Give away plenty of love, and keep reminding yourself that you are a loving person. For if guilt is the antithesis of love, love is the antidote for much of our guilt. Love is a fountain of joy. The more we share our fountain with others, the more we drink of it ourselves.

It seems as if I've gotten far afield, away from my guilt that day at the cemetery. But I really haven't. I was feeling guilty because I wasn't sure I had done everything possible to express my love for these people when they were alive. Had I given them all I could? I was wondering who else might die before I had a chance to demonstrate my love for them. For whom else would I feel guilty?

I resolved that day never to feel this guilt again, for I would show the people I loved that I loved them, today, tomorrow, and every tomorrow until the end of my life.

Day 6

WHO IS YOUR SHEPHERD?

The Lord is my shepherd; I shall not want. . .

Ps. 23:1

"Code blue! Code blue!" The public address system spat out the words, galvanizing doctors, nurses, and technicians all over the hospital into action. The designated emergency teams and many others ran to the intensive care unit hoping to save the life of whomever was undergoing the emergency signaled by code blue.

I happened to be the first doctor to the patient's bed, there to find a man with a face full of agony, hands clutching his chest as if trying to yank the terrible pain out of his heart. Suddenly his features relaxed as the frantic beating of the monitor mounted on the wall gave way to a single sustained tone, signaling death.

I raised my right hand high in the air and brought its closed fist crashing down on the man's chest. Twice more I did this before his battered heart beat once again. But his soul hovered half in and half outside his body, awaiting the outcome of this struggle between life and death. It took a shot of adrenaline injected directly into the heart to settle the battle in favor of life.

The next day I spoke with the man, a 52-year-old salesman. "I was in church when the first heart attack happened," he told me. "We were reading 'The Lord is my shepherd' and I was thinking, some shepherd. My whole life I've asked the Lord for things but He never gave me anything. I didn't make it in business, two marriages fell apart, my kids don't like me, I had a heart attack, a bypass operation. When I felt this second heart attack, I thought I must be a sheep the shepherd didn't like." Then he smiled wryly, "I guess I was wrong again. I'm still here. Maybe he's giving me another chance to win the life I always wanted. I won't waste the opportunity this time."

I believe that our Shepherd loves us all, for God is love, and we are all granted equal measures of His love. We err, however, when we confuse His love with a handout.

DARE TO SUCCEED

Let not your hands be weak; for your work shall be rewarded.

2 Chron. 15:7

The loving Shepherd does not want us to be helpless sheep, waiting without wit or effort for our bellies to be filled. Our Shepherd has brought us to beautiful green pastures where we can find good soil to grow in, grasses to feed our animals, materials with which to build. And he has given us spirit, the best tool of all. The Lord our Shepherd brings us to the places of plenty. It is up to us to use what he gives us.

King David, who wrote the great Psalm, showed us exactly how to act. He knew the Lord was his shepherd. He also knew that while God is always with us, it is up to us to grasp rod in hand and make an effort. God was certainly with young David when he slew Goliath, for it was God's hand that guided David's. Yet before David was made great by God's hand, David took the initiative, took slingshot in hand. He showed courage in daring to face the giant.

David could not have succeeded without the help of the Lord. But neither would he have succeeded without daring to succeed.

Do the odds seem great? Many people have overcome tremendous odds. Abraham Lincoln failed many times in many ways before becoming one of the best presidents this country has ever had. Thomas Edison, the prolific American inventor, failed hundreds of times before finally developing the light bulb. The great English statesman, Sir Winston Churchhill, was removed from his position of power and banished to the polished wilderness for more than 20 years before being called back to lead his country through World War II. Dale Carnegie, an unsuccessful salesman who was afraid to speak in public, founded the greatest organization of its type in the world, teaching millions of people how to overcome their fears, how to speak in public and be good salesmen. Despite being rejected by every studio in Hollywood, Sylvester Stallone refused to give up on his idea for a movie. His *Rocky* became one of the most successful movies ever made.

These people were not helpless sheep waiting for someone to drop achievement into their laps. They went after what they wanted. They took responsibility for their lives, they said they were willing to do what it takes to succeed. That's most of the formula for success, right there.

One of my young patients overcame the odds by losing 100 pounds and lowering her cholesterol 75 points. How did she do it? "I prayed for guidance, and I kept a picture of what I wanted to be in my head at all times. Then I went on the diet and stuck to it. That's all there is to my secret to success."

A young man named Aaron, whom I know very well, had no money and only so-so grades in college. But he wanted to be an attorney. Not only that, he wanted to go to a top-notch law school. "Nothing but the best for me," he always said. He was turned down by every top-notch law school in the country, and most of the lesser schools as well. But he persisted. First, he targeted the one law school he wanted to get into. Then he went to the campus for an interview, despite being told not to bother. He met personally with some of the professors. He told them that he was going to get into their school, if not this year then the next. Or the next. He wrote reports on various topics of law and sent them to the professors. Meanwhile, he retook some of the college courses in which he had done poorly and earned higher grades the second time around. That kind of determination was rewarded, of course. The next year he was accepted. Why? Not for his grades, which were still low. For his spirit! That's what impressed the admissions committee.

Yes, this young man had help. He asked his friends to tutor him, and he signed up for a special study course to prepare him for the law school admission test. Get all the help you need. That's fine. But dare to succeed–that's the first step.

Don't worry about the odds. The odds will always be there; they'll take care of themselves. Don't let anything come between you and that picture of success in your mind. A fellow named Stratton played some years with the old Washington Senators baseball team, despite having only one leg. Last year I saw a high school play starring a boy who lisped. How can someone with such a glaring handicap become a great actor? Only by daring to succeed.

Trying does not guarantee success. Not trying, however, absolutely guarantees failure.

The Sowers Shall Reap

Sow ye and reap.

Isa. 37:30

When you sow, you reap. When you dream of what might be, you can change the world. When you screw your courage to the sticking point, you can overcome giant obstacles. Only when you are willing to face failure can you succeed. When you try, when you just try, success is almost in your grasp.

God gave you the courage, the willingness, the strength, the determination, and the dream. All that is yours. You have to do but one thing: You must try!

Yes, pray to God; pray regularly, enthusiastically. By all means, pray to God for spiritual guidance, wisdom, and peace of mind. But remember that you are not a helpless sheep. God gave you a good brain and a strong back because He wanted you to use them. *Pray to God but don't give up on yourself!* Thank Him for giving you the tools you need, praise Him for His great works, then do what must be done!

Prayer is one of the seeds to be sown. From prayer comes the confidence and serenity of knowing that God is on your side. But pray for guidance, not a handout. Meanwhile, sow all the seeds, knock on every door, take all the tests, learn what must be learned, do what must be done, try what must be tried.

God wants you to succeed. He wants to help you succeed. Tell Him you are ready. Give Him a sign by starting down the road to success all by yourself. Pretty soon you'll see that you have company.

TOGETHER

With God all things are possible.

Matt. 19:26

Martha was a 42-year-old homemaker and mother of two who came to see me, hoping I could "make" her lose weight. Bernice was a 35-year-old career woman who wanted me to give her a "magic pill," as she jokingly called it, that would "knock 15 pounds off my rear." Henry was a recently divorced 47-year-old who wanted a "shot or something to unload this spare tire" hanging around his belly.

And then there was Linda. Linda came to me for medical and nutritional advice. No, not advice, she wanted information. She wanted me to examine her to make sure she was fit. "I also want you to recommend some books on nutrition," she said. "Simple ones, because I have no scientific background."

Linda was 50 pounds overweight, and had been so for 20 years–since the birth of her first child. She had been on all the diets. She had searched frantically for the "magic pill." She had ridden the diet roller coaster up and down for two decades.

"That's all going to end now," she told me. "I'm not looking for someone or something to make me thin anymore. I'm looking to myself. I'm taking control of my life, with God's help. With God on my side, I'm in the majority. I don't know where I heard that, but it's true."

You know who lost the most weight, and kept it off? Linda. The others lost some, then quickly regained it all plus a few extra pounds. Linda took her problems in hand and began walking down the road to success. Pretty soon she found that she wasn't walking alone.

There are "two" in together. You are always one of the two, the one without whom there is no progress.

DEPENDENCE, DESPAIR, DISEASE

Our society encourages dependence. Our government, our

medical system, our institutions and experts all encourage us to surrender responsibility. We'll take care of you, they tell us. It's too complex. You can't handle it. You need us. Everywhere we turn, we're told in word and deed that we can't hack it.

It's no wonder we feel like helpless sheep. All our lives we've been told that we're not good enough, not smart enough, not talented enough, not brave enough, not far-sighted enough to handle our lives. Brainwashed into believing that we don't measure up, many of us have forgotten the incredible talents we all have.

I remember many patients who had been convinced that they were helpless sheep. They were victims of the false promise that others can give us what we need. No one can give us what we need: That only comes from within.

These patients invariably felt hopeless as well as helpless. They didn't think they could do anything to improve themselves, and they saw that the "others" were equally helpless. Hopeless and helpless, they often fell victim to despair and depression.

I don't know how many patients I've seen at my office or at the hospital with physical symptoms, with what we call "real" diseases, who were really suffering from hopelessness and helplessness, depression and despair. One of these was a very beautiful woman called Cindy, who was a snake dancer.

I first met Cindy when I was called to the hospital by a fellow doctor. He told me that a woman had been bitten by a snake and come down with tetanus. "I've never seen tetanus," he said. "I know you saw some cases at the county hospital, so I'd like you to handle this."

When I arrived at the hospital I saw what looked like a textbook case of tetanus. Cindy's face had the "lockjaw" look, a smile frozen on her face by muscles that were locked into place. Neck, shoulder, and back muscles were also rigid, forcing her head back, face up, unmovable.

We spoke for some time, although it was difficult for Cindy to speak through clenched teeth. Cindy told me she was a go-go dancer and in her late twenties. She was supporting an eight-year-old daughter and an ailing mother. To try to stand out among the other dancers, she danced with a snake. It was this snake that had bitten her.

It was obvious to me that Cindy was very bright but was

convinced that she could do no better than work as a topless dancer. She had saved some money for a down payment on a three-unit apartment complex, but couldn't keep up the payments.

This was "obviously" a case of tetanus, but something didn't ring true. I added some Valium to Cindy's intravenous. As the drug took effect, her muscles relaxed and she dropped her guard. Now, half-awake, half-asleep, she spoke to me of her fears, of her feeling that she was overwhelmed, that she couldn't possibly continue. She had been feeling helpless and hopeless for some time. When her snake bit her, she suffered a conversion reaction: Her mental distress was converted into the symptoms of a physical disease. Thus she abdicated all her responsibilities, putting her life, her daughter's life, and her mother's life in the hands of the government and the experts.

In some respects Cindy was a "success" story. She regained control of her life, secure in the knowledge that she had tremendous inner resources just waiting to be tapped.

We're told every day in many ways that life is too much of a burden for us poor humans to handle. Life can sometimes be difficult; we may require guidance and assistance. But we, with God, are the stalwart shepherds guiding our lives. And we have tremendous inner resources that only we can tap into. Others can give us money, and things, and information, and medicine, and shelter, and so on. But only we can give ourselves the will to thrive. Only we can give ourselves the burning determination to reach our fullest potential. Only we can fill the mirrors of our lives with joy and courage and love. Only we can give ourselves the things beside which all else pales.

Step out of the flock, grasp the rod, and become the shepherd of your life. You, with God, are the best shepherd you can have.

TAKING CONTROL: FIVE BASIC STEPS

Seest thou a man diligent in his business? He shall stand before kings.

Prov. 22:29

How do we regain control of our lives so we can tap into our great inner resources?

First, realize that you have that power. That's what Making Miracles is all about.

Second, remember that you are never alone. There is a Shepherd over all of us. But this Shepherd, unlike our worldly institutions and experts, does not want us to become helpless dependents. Our heavenly Shepherd wants us to grow strong and tall, to develop our minds and bodies, to reach for all that life has to offer. That's why He gave us spirit!

We are all partners with our Shepherd. God is the silent partner, we are the active. God put the potential into the partnership. It's up to each of us, working with God, to develop it.

Third, keep your helpers in perspective. This is a complex world. No one can know all there is to know. Neither can we master every skill, profession, and art. We do need experts, advisors, and teachers. Experts, advisors, and teachers are fine, as long as they remain experts, advisors, and teachers we call upon as needed. Keep them in perspective. They are there to help us, not rule us.

Fourth, be diligent in everything you do. Like any good shepherd, we must watch carefully over our flock. The fact that ours is a flock of one makes no difference. In fact, your flock is very precious; it is you.

Fifth, take someone else by the hand and guide them along. The best way to help yourself is to help others. When you help others, you are telling yourself that you are strong and wise and giving enough to go the extra mile for them. Writing these good thoughts into your mental gospel is a powerful antidote to feelings of failure. Don't take control of their life; help them find their inner strength, as you have found yours.

Your hand is the only hand that can light the fire of your spirit. With that fire lit, you're on your way to success.

The Law of Multiples

Am I my brother's keeper?

Gen. 4:9

Helping others is one of the best ways to help ourselves. The Law of Multiples, also known as the Law of Helping, states that for every one person you help, you are helping two. Who is that second person? Yourself. If you are helping 100 people, you are also helping yourself 100 times over.

You are your brother's keeper. In helping your brothers and sisters, you help yourself as well.

The Law of Blame

Thou shalt eat the labour of thine hands.

Ps. 128:2

Some people seem to be shepherding their lives, but have really given control over to others: They have fallen victim to the habit of blaming.

An angry Linda sat in my office one day, pointing verbal fingers in every direction. For seven years she had been trying to start up her own publishing company; seven years of repeated failure. Although she had raised quite a bit of money, her publishing company never got off the ground. She recited from her long list of blame: Mr. X didn't do this, Mr. Y failed at that, Ms. Z made a crucial error. Things fell apart because the attorneys drew up the company charter incorrectly; because the accounts didn't cross all the *t*'s and dot all the *i*'s on the stock-offering papers; because the authors who were to write the books didn't come through; because of government red tape; because. . .because. . .

Linda had someone or something to blame for every single thing that went wrong. She didn't realize, however, that every time she pointed a finger, she became a victim of the Law of Blame.

Simply put, the Law of Blame states that constantly blaming

others ensures continued failure.

Blaming others plants in your mind the negative notion that something is wrong with you. You must be inferior in some way. If not, why is it so easy for everyone to stand in your way?

Blaming gives control of your life to others. When you blame, you make people into the "bad" shepherds who don't take care of you.

Blaming others fixes your eyes on the negatives. This went wrong, that when wrong–wrong, wrong, wrong, wrong, wrong. Everywhere you look you see wrong. The wrong that fills your mind is projected out onto your world. Your mirrors are filled with wrong. Your whole life becomes wrong.

Blaming others turns your eyes away from the positives. Wrongs are harmful germs to the spirit, but positives are nourishment. When you blame, you starve your spirit.

Blaming others fills you with anger. Pages of anger are written into your mental gospel. This prompts the release of biosubstances that increase your cholesterol, weaken your heart, damage your immune system, and increase your risk for disease. Linda was sick. Her blood pressure was high, she had a bleeding ulcer, she was constipated and suffered from hemorrhoids. She had difficulty sleeping and concentrating, and was nervous and irritable. Linda had filled her mind with blame, and projected the blame out onto the world. Everywhere she looked she saw blame.

And do you know what? As we went over the history of her company, it was clear that she was right: A lot of her partners, consultants, and employees made crucial errors. In that respect, she was entitled to blame them. But even if you are right, even if "they" are to blame, pointing a finger at them harms you.

Blaming is a poison for spirit and body.

Grabbing the Buck

The buck stops here.

Harry Truman

I explained to Linda how blame poisons the spirit and body. She said that although she intellectually agreed with the idea, it was hard not to blame. In addition to treating her physical ills, I asked her to consider what all the blaming was doing to her.

Well over a year passed before I saw her again, this time for a regular checkup. I had hoped she had gotten over her disappointments and blaming, but was surprised to see how well she had done.

"You told me about the Law of Blame," she said. "I've got another law for you. The Law of Buck Grabbing.

"The Law of Buck Grabbing says that when you take responsibility you feel great. Don't wait for the buck to stop on your desk. Reach out and grab it! You know why it works? Because when you willingly take responsibility for your life you're telling yourself that you're brave enough to do it, which is good. You're telling yourself that you're strong enough to accept responsibility, which is good. You're telling yourself that it doesn't matter how many failures are piled on your desk, you're not going to let it get you down. That's good.

"Every time I feel like blaming someone I reach out and grab the buck. It makes me feel good. Strong. Brave. Like I'm in control. I am in control, because I'm not letting other people's shortcomings hurt me. I take their shortcomings and fix them."

She continued: "My stomach pain is gone. So are the constipation and hemorrhoids. I sleep easily now. I'm not nervous anymore. We're opening new offices next week. I think we're going to make it this time."

Grabbing the buck is a challenge–it's also the best thing you can do for yourself. Put yourself in charge of your life, feel that you're in control. That very feeling is a strong medicine.

"Like Heck He Won't"

My wife, Hannah, is a courageous example of what can happen when you insist upon guiding your own life. We were both crushed to discover that our infant son, Steven, had a severe birth defect that made him nearly blind. We consulted many eye specialists, but none could offer him any hope, despite three surgeries. According to the best doctors, Steve would eventually lose all his sight. I admit that I had just about given up, but Hannah was only beginning. For years she took him to doctor after doctor, spending countless hours driving him up and down southern California, waiting in doctor's offices and hospitals, going through procedure after procedure. She heard "No" and "I'm sorry" time and time again, but those words were not in her vocabulary, they didn't mean anything to her. Every time they said, "He won't see," she muttered under her breath, "Like heck he won't see!" She kept knocking on doors until one finally opened. It didn't occur to her to give up: Her son would have good vision and that's all there was to it. God answered her prayers by rewarding her effort.

I remember how she used to drive Steve out to UCLA every day. It was a long drive in those days before the freeway system was in place, with three other little kids in the car. But Hannah didn't care: She took on the responsibility for making her son's life the best it could possibly be. The UCLA doctors put Steve through the therapy routine once, with no results, and a second time, also with no results. They said there was nothing else they could do. Hannah replied: "Teach me how to do it."

Every day Hannah worked with Steve. Howard, our oldest, was then five, helped out. At the end of three weeks, Hannah piled Steve and the others back in the car, drove out to UCLA and asked them to run the tests again. This time the results were amazing: It looked like Steve was going to be able to see after all!

I asked Hannah what would have happened if none of the doctors in California could have helped Steve. She said there were plenty more doctors in the other 49 states. In fact, she was all set to fly Steve back East when the breakthrough came.

Do you know what gave Hannah the strength to go on, from doctor to doctor, disappointment to disappointment? One day, when Steve was just six months old, she was at the post office. Steve had no control over his eyes then, and they rolled around aimlessly. It was obvious to anyone who looked that something was terribly wrong. The woman standing behind Hannah in line tapped her on the shoulder and said, "Mother, don't ever lose faith. God will help you make your child right." We never knew who that great woman was, or why she spoke up, but we're glad she did. Her words were Hannah's inspiration.

Taking Stock

Are you willing to start down the road alone? Circle the number that describes how you feel about the following statements:

1. I have the power to improve my life
   Always — *Not at all*
   10 9 8 7 6 5 4 3 2 1

2. There is a greatness in me that has not yet been explored, has not yet surfaced.
   There is! — *I'm not so hot*
   10 9 8 7 6 5 4 3 2 1

3. If need be I could rise to the occasion, whatever it may be.
   Always — *No, I couldn't*
   10 9 8 7 6 5 4 3 2 1

4. I may be lacking some in education or other aspects of life, but overall I'm a pretty good person.
   Yes, I'm pretty good — *No, I'm not much*
   10 9 8 7 6 5 4 3 2 1

5. I look forward to solving challenges that come my way.
   I love a challenge — *I can't face difficulty*
   10 9 8 7 6 5 4 3 2 1

6. When I tackle a task, it's done right.
   Always — *Never*
   10 9 8 7 6 5 4 3 2 1

7. My life is what I make of it, and I'm making it great!
   Absolutely! — *Not at all*
   10 9 8 7 6 5 4 3 2 1

8. I've made positive contributions to other people's lives.
   Many contributions *No, I haven't*
   10 9 8 7 6 5 4 3 2 1

9. Every day is a great day!
   Always *Never*
   10 9 8 7 6 5 4 3 2 1

10. With God by my side, I'm on the way to the top!
    Yes! *I disagree*
    10 9 8 7 6 5 4 3 2 1

Tally your score. When you've finished working through the program, take this test again. You'll be surprised at how much higher you'll score–your confidence and determination will have improved.

Rx: Doing!

There is nothing better, than that a man should rejoice in his own works.

Eccles. 3:22

The menu for Day Six, the Day of Doing, includes a special affirmation thanking God for making you able to do for yourself. From this day forth consider yourself one who acts, not one who only listens.

People who only listen deceive themselves, for listening alone is not enough. Listen, yes, and absorb the lesson. Then do whatever it is that must be done to succeed!

Sit down, in a quiet room, on a comfortable chair. Tell everyone that you do not want to be disturbed; take the phone off the hook. Close your eyes. With your mind's eye, picture yourself standing in front of a big wooden door. The door is closed. See yourself standing in front of that door, holding your book of life, the gospel of your mind, under your left arm.

See yourself knocking on the door with your right hand. You're knocking on that door firmly, with great confidence. You know that the door will be opened to you.

No one answers. The door remains closed.

See yourself knocking again. Again no one answers, but your confidence and determination are unshaken. One more time you knock, knowing in your heart that the door will open, knowing that you will keep knocking until the door opens, no matter how long it takes.

This time the door opens wide! As it does, say:

> I am a doer! I thank God for giving me the courage, strength, wisdom, determination, and spirit to brush aside obstacles as I open the door to success in every aspect of my life. I can open the doors to success!

Visualize this prescription over and over again throughout this Day of Doing! Each time you see it, believe that you are unbeatable, be determined to succeed, no matter what the odds. Believe that you have the strength to keep knocking until the doors of life open to you. Believe that you will knock on a million doors if necessary, and know in your heart that the doors will finally open to you.

Each time you visualize yourself knocking on the door, feel the book, the gospel of your mind, that you are carrying under your arm. Remember that your book of life is filled with confidence, determination, enthusiasm, and belief. What's written in your book gives you the strength to keep knocking.

In addition to your special R_X for today, recite your daily affirmations at the indicated times:

> **Upon awakening: "Rejoice and Be Glad"**
> This is the day that the Lord hath made; I shall rejoice and be glad, be gladder than glad. I give myself permission to see all the happiness that is in my world, to think of the happiness, and to speak of the happiness. The Creator has filled the world with unlimited joy that is mine for the taking.

> **Morning: "It is Good to Give Thanks"**
> It is good to give thanks unto the Lord for making me the

healthy, happy, and successful person I so richly deserve to be. I am open to receiving all the blessings of His abundant universe.

Noon: "Endless Enthusiasm"
The Creator has filled me to the brim with enthusiasm. I gladly and generously pour my unlimited enthusiasm over my every thought and action. Armed with endless enthusiasm, I find excitement and adventure in every day.

Afternoon: "Spiritually Minded"
To be spiritually minded is life and peace. I give myself permission to be as calm and serene as the quiet waters of a beautiful, still lake.

Evening: "A Merry Heart"
A merry heart is a good medicine. My heart and spirit and the gospel of my mind are filled with joy. I am full of the thoughts and things of health, happiness, and success.

When going to bed: "Put on the New Me"
Today was another successful step toward the new me. With enthusiastic anticipation and absolute certainty that I'll make even more progress tomorrow, and every tomorrow, I'm putting on the new me.

How long will you keep knocking? As long as it takes.

How many doors will you knock on? As many as it takes.

Your spirit and the spirit of the Lord, combined together, can bring to you the best life has to offer. You take the first step—raise your hand and make the effort.

Who is your shepherd? You and God are your shepherds, in partnership.

Day 7

THE MEDICINE CALLED PRAYER

I have heard thy prayer, I have seen thy tears: behold, I will heal thee.

2 Kings 20:5

Late one night, many years ago, I sat at the nurses' station inside an intensive care unit, dispiritedly flipping through a patient's chart. I knew very well that reading the chart yet again would make no difference: Death was imminent. Still, I went through every page–pages I knew almost by heart–looking for the miracle I knew was not written there.

"Pray one for another, that ye my be healed." The quote ran through my head. Pray for a patient? Sitting at the nurses' station cluttered with lab reports, charts, medications, stethoscopes, and coffee cups–pray? Standing by the patient's bed, surrounded by other critically ill patients, amidst the uncaring machines with their beeps, hisses, and clanks–pray?

The usually sterile and unnoticeable air in this oh-so-clean room felt heavy, full of death. Where was the clue? On what page of the patient's chart, in which lab report, buried in which doctor's report?

"Dr. Fox." The patient called weakly to me. If the room hadn't been so deadly quiet, I wouldn't have heard his small voice. "Dr. Fox?" I went over to the patient's bed. He had been a strong, active, and decisive man, his wife told me. By the time I met him he was near death, shriveled, looking at me through eyes filled with pain and fear. "I don't want to die," he had cried over and over. "I don't want to die."

"When will I die?" he asked, tears slowly sliding down his gray, lifeless skin. I couldn't answer. He tried to raise his hand, but didn't have the strength. I sensed that he wanted me to take his hand in mine, so I did. "Dr. Fox, pray for me."

"Pray for you?"

"I don't know how. . ."

Embarrassed, I glanced over at the nurse. She was busy at her desk; she wasn't looking at us.

And so I prayed for my patient; prayed with him, for as I softly recited the Twenty-third Psalm, his lips began moving with mine. Three times we said the psalm, each time louder, with more conviction, with more certainty, with more belief. And the light was dim, but the change was easy to see: His eyes were calm, his grip was stronger, his voice steady. A look of contentment had replaced the tears.

I wish I could say the prayer saved his life, but the Lord had already made His decision. We spoke for a while, the man and I, then he asked me to bring in his wife. He spoke with her briefly, telling her of his love for her, asking her to say good-bye to their children and grandchildren, to some friends. This was the first time he had spoken to anyone since I had been called in as a consultant some weeks before. Calmly, he thanked his wife for giving him her love, closed his eyes, and died.

The man died, yes, but he died at peace, finally at peace with himself and with the world. He had been consumed by fear, self-pity, and tears. He had refused to speak to his wife, his children, his friends who came to visit. He had been so frightened that he could not accept what was happening. But he found his peace, through prayer, before he died. He was finally able to speak with his loving wife, and to have her pass on his wishes of love and a happy life to their loved ones.

A little later, after the formalities had been completed, after the wife had left, after his bed had been remade and the machines moved away, it was as if the man had never lain there. Almost as if he had never existed. All that was left of him in the room was his chart. I went through the chart again, not really paying attention to the words and the numbers filling the pages.

Passages from the Scriptures ran through my head: "He heareth the cry of the afflicted." "I will call upon God; and the Lord shall save me." "The prayer of faith shall save the sick."

Had the Lord heard our prayer? At first I thought not, for the man had died. Then I realized that our prayer had been heard, and granted, for the man died calmly, at peace with himself, speaking with his beloved wife. His cry *had* been heard.

And my cry had been heard, too, for I had been given a powerful new "medicine" to share with my patients: Prayer.

Not long after, when a woman heard that I prayed with my patients, she asked, somewhat amazed, "Why would a medical doctor trained in the latest scientific methods resort to prayer?"

I answered, not at all flippantly, that I believe in going right to the top, to the highest power. "We doctors are not the final answer on life and death. We're only instruments of God. Asking for His help is a good idea."

"That may be OK for religious people who believe in God," she said. "But what about the rest of us?"

That stopped me dead in my tracks. I believe God does hear our prayers, does love us and looks after us in this world and the next. To me, and to other believers, the value of prayer is obvious. But how about those who do not believe? Can prayer benefit them, as well?

I believe that prayer is for everyone, believers and nonbelievers alike. What are we saying when we pray? We're saying that someone loves us. We're saying that someone wants us to be healthy, happy, and successful. We're saying that there is rhythm and rhyme to the world; that there is a time to be born and a time to die. We're saying that there is reason to be good, to treat others as we would have them treat us. We're saying that there is someone who smiles with us in our success, and who gladly lends an ear in our distress.

As a physician, an internist and cardiologist, who has treated uncounted patients suffering from every kind of disease, I can tell you that knowing you are loved is a powerful medicine. To love and to be loved, to know that someone smiles with you and always wishes you well, these are powerful medicines indeed.

I can also tell you that to know there is rhythm and rhyme to the world, and to know you belong, provides the sense of security we all need to remain healthy and happy. We've known for a long time that our thoughts have a profound effect on our body. Only recently, however, have we been able to prove it to the satisfaction of laboratory scientists.

On one level, our thoughts are very different from the biochemical messengers they become. Thoughts are intangible; we can't touch them, analyze, describe, categorize them as we can the messengers. At a deeper level, however, our thoughts and the things they spawn are the same thing, the same idea, expressed in different "languages."

Whatever the language, be it the language of the mind or the language of the body, the message is the same. What is the message? That depends on your thoughts. When the thought is positive, the message is positive, and the result is increased energy and health, greater happiness, and a propensity toward success. When the thought is negative, the opposite is true.

Prayer is by nature positive. When you pray, you affirm the existence of someone who loves you, who will guide you, who shares your joys and tears. Properly done, prayer creates the thoughts that, when translated into the language of the body, strengthen your immune system, tip the biochemical balance of your body in favor of happiness, and carry you closer to success. Properly applied, then, prayer is a very strong medicine for mind and body.

In Psalm Twenty-five we read: "Unto Thee, O Lord, do I lift up my soul." When you pray, you lift up your entire being, body and soul. You lift yourself with the good thoughts that are your prayer, that carry you closer to being the person you want to be, having the things you want to have, and doing the things you want to do.

As a physician, I prescribe prayer for many of my patients. "Pray without ceasing," I tell them, for when you pray, you create conditions within you that promote the good things you want.

It's interesting that many people who never considered prayer find it quite to their liking. They often later tell me that they had felt a void in their lives, an emptiness that prayer and belief in God filled.

That's not surprising, for believing in God gives you quite a bit. Believing in God gives you reason to believe in yourself, something we can all use in these troubling times. When your soul is filled with trouble, remember that God loves you. And if God loves you and wants you to succeed, as He has stated He does, then you must truly be deserving of the best in life. When you believe in God, therefore, you can believe in yourself, and live life enthusiastically.

Believing in God also gives you reason to love, and love is a powerful medicine. "Let us love one another; for love is of God," it says in the Scriptures. God is love. To love is to be with God.

Believing in God gives you reason to persevere, to fight the good fight with Him by your side.

When you believe in God, you have reason to believe in yourself, reason to be enthusiastic about life, reason to love, reason to forgive and to persevere, and so much more. When you have all these good feelings, you carry yourself closer to success in every aspect of life.

Pray without ceasing, for prayer is a good medicine. And as you pray, believe you'll have the thing you pray for, and you shall. Feel yourself enjoying the thing you desire. See it, with your mind's eye, as being within your grasp. See yourself as already having that which you pray for; see yourself enjoying it. Tell yourself that you are already healthy, happy, and successful.

See your prayer as coming true. *Feel* that it has been accomplished. *Tell* yourself that you are what you want to be; that you have what you want to have; and that you are doing what you want to be doing.

Pray with feeling, with belief, with conviction. Pray without ceasing, and may all your prayers come true.

Ask, Seek, Knock

Ask, and it shall be given you;
seek, and ye shall find;
knock, and it shall be opened unto you.

Matt. 7:7

When you ask, whether you are asking of God or of your fellow man, be sure to ask completely:

A—ask
S—seek
K—knock

Ask: Ask for guidance, for an idea, for assistance, for reassurance, for confidence. Know what you want. Identify your goal. Want it enough to work for it. Want it enough to keep working for it, no matter how many times someone says you can't have it.

Seek: Search out the thing you want. Find out where it is and what it takes to obtain it. Must you pay for it? Change your diet or lifestyle? Go back to school, open a business, raise money, pass a law, persuade people–what?

Knock: Strive for the thing you want. Knock on every door that must be knocked on, open all the doors that must be opened. Knock with conviction and determination, knowing that for every door that shuts in your face you are one door closer to obtaining the thing which you want.

We are told that he who seeks, finds; and he who knocks gets the doors opened. The seekers and knockers may face a lot of obstacles, but the seekers and knockers are the ones who eventually find.

And the ones who have not asked, sought, or knocked? They're waiting for their ship to come in–but they never sent it out.

Ask, Seek, and Knock.

Rx: Prayer

Ask in faith, nothing wavering.

James 1:6

Today is Day Seven of your Making Miracles program, the Day of Prayer. It's said that the prayer of faith will save the sick, and that men and women ought always to pray. Let us pray without ceasing, always remembering to thank God for giving us all the tools we need to succeed. Prayer for what you *don't* have, for in doing so, you're telling yourself that you believe you will have it. In doing so, you act from strength, not neediness or emptiness.

Recite these affirmations throughout the day, today and every day. Be sure to "see" each affirmation as you recite it.

Upon awakening: "Rejoice and Be Glad"

This is the day that the Lord hath made; I shall rejoice and be glad, be gladder than glad. I give myself permission to see all the happiness that is in my world, to think of the happiness, and to speak of the happiness. The Creator has filled the world with unlimited joy that is mine for the taking.

Morning: "It is Good to Give Thanks"
It is good to give thanks unto the Lord for making me the healthy, happy, and successful person I so richly deserve to be. I am open to receiving all the blessings of His abundant universe.

Noon: "Endless Enthusiasm"
The Creator has filled me to the brim with enthusiasm. I gladly and generously pour my unlimited enthusiasm over my every thought and action. Armed with endless enthusiasm, I find excitement and adventure in every day.

Afternoon: "Spiritually Minded"
To be spiritually minded is life and peace. I give myself permission to be as calm and serene as the quiet waters of a beautiful, still lake.

Evening: "A Merry Heart"
A merry heart is a good medicine. My heart and spirit and the gospel of my mind are filled with joy. I am full of the thoughts and things of health, happiness, and success.

When going to bed: "Put on the New Me"
Today was another successful step toward the new me. With enthusiastic anticipation and absolute certainty that I'll make even more progress tomorrow, and every tomorrow, I'm putting on the new me.

Recite each affirmation out loud, with enthusiasm. Go beyond the minimum and recite the affirmations all day long. You can't overdo it with affirmations!

In addition to your daily diet of affirmations, enter into the world of this special R_X for Prayer several times today, with energy and conviction.

Set aside some time today to sit in a quiet room, on a comfortable chair. Tell everyone that you do not want to be disturbed; take the phone off the hook. Close your eyes. With your mind's eye, picture yourself praying. As you see this, you know that you are thanking God for making you such a talented, capable person. You don't need a handout, for you've got what it takes to succeed: You've got spirit!

With your mind's eye, see yourself as having finished your prayer. Suddenly, in front of you, a box appears. It's a shiny white box, wrapped in a wide red ribbon. You open the ribbon, take the top off the box. Inside of the box you see a beautiful golden goblet, a large one that fills the box. This goblet, a gift from God, is filled with spirit! You know that God has answered your prayer by giving you even more of His great spirit to pour into your cup of life, and you say:

> My cup of life is filled with the spirit of God, and the spirit He gave to me. Armed with nothing but this great spirit, I can conquer the world!

Enter into the world of the R_X for Prayer several times today, as many times as possible. Pray without ceasing, for prayer properly done produces a never-ending flow of spirit to add to your cup of life.

Day 8

FIGHT THE GOOD FIGHT

Be strong and be not afraid, for the Lord thy God is with thee wheresoever thou goest.

Josh. 1:9

Our word "determination" comes from the Latin word for boundary or limit. I like to think of determination as meaning boundless and limitless; that is, I will draw the boundaries of my life where *I* want them to be, not where others say they should be. To be determined is to be resolute, to persevere, to have the courage to stand steadfast in the face of adversity.

DETERMINATION VERSUS CANCER

Fear ye not, stand still, and see the salvation of the Lord, which he will show to you today.

Ex. 14:13

Jill came to my office for her regular checkup. Ten years before, she had lost her left breast to cancer. Two years after that, cancer was discovered in her right breast and her doctors wanted to remove it as well. She refused, though the doctors believed that the cancer would spread, and might kill her. Her concerned family pressured her to have the surgery. Still she said no.

Jill devised her own anticancer program based on healthy eating, exercise, guided imagery, and affirmations. Aware that she could wind up in serious trouble, Jill thanked her doctors but bravely told them she would go it alone.

For many months she followed a strict diet based on fresh green vegetables and whole grains. Every day she took a battery of carefully selected food supplements. Jill exercised regularly and joyfully, and set aside an hour a day for guided imagery, picturing, with her mind's eye, the white blood cells of her immune system devouring her cancer. She also recited daily affirmations out loud and silently, with enthusiasm and belief. As she described her program to me, I realized that she had unknowingly adopted the ten Pillars and become positively addicted to herself, to her health and happiness.

"My program was important in regaining my health," she said, "But I also had to learn to remove all the negativity from my life. The doctors, my family and friends all meant well, but they were negative. They kept reminding me of what could go wrong. They were always going on about how my program would be impossible for me to follow. So I got new doctors and dropped some of my friends. I told the rest of my friends and my family to not say anything to me unless it was something I'd be glad to hear. They had to help me be 100 percent positive, I said, if I were going to make it. It may sound strict, but I refused to be around anyone who made me doubt myself in the slightest."

Jill saw her (new) doctor at regular intervals for checkups. He saw no progress at first, but she was determined to stick to her guns. Eventually, there was some sign of success, then slowly but surely the tumor shrank until finally it was no more.

While I do not encourage people to treat themselves, I think we can all learn a lesson from this brave woman. I firmly believe that her steadfast determination to beat the cancer without the surgery was a very strong medicine indeed. Jill adds, "I know I couldn't have done it if I had any doubts."

THE COURAGE TO REACH FOR THE STARS

Lift up thy voice with strength; lift it up, be not afraid.
Is. 40:9

Jill's is an inspiring story of determination, and of courage as well. Where does determination come from? How do we dare to believe in ourselves, against all odds?

Somewhere within you, within all of us, is a seed of great determination. How quickly your seed grows, how strong and tall, depends on the quality of your spirit. How nourishing is the soil of your spirit?

What makes for great determination? Self-esteem, your great belief that you can do it; vision, the mental picture of the thing you want, spurring you on; the courage to persevere. You also need optimism, the belief that good things do happen to you, because you are a deserving person living in a nurturing world, and you need serenity, the ability to let the occasional negatives wash off your back, like water off a duck. Most of all, determination is fueled by burning desire, wanting something so much that you *will* have it–wanting something so much that you redraw all the boundaries of your life, rip up all the limit signs, until you get it.

The Enemy of Determination

We have nothing to fear but fear itself.

F.D.R

Fear, self-doubt, pessimism: These are the enemies of determination. A person whose eyes are glued to the negatives cannot see the positives. I see many such patients. When a new patient comes to my office, after the examination has been completed, the forms filled out, tests taken, and laboratory results confirmed, I carefully review my findings and recommendations with him.

Often when I give them a copy of the laboratory results–32 blood tests–they are sure to spot the one test that is slightly abnormal. "Oh, no!" they say. "My cholesterol is six points too high!" Maybe it's their blood fat that's slightly out of line, or their liver function, white blood cell count, or T_4 count. They invariably find the one test of 32 that is slightly high or low. They're frightened, they want to know what disease they have, how serious it is. Focusing on the negative this way can destroy their confidence and sap their determination.

"All your other tests are excellent," I'll say. "Having only one out of 32 slightly off is pretty good." But no matter how often I point to all the good test results, they think of the bad. To them, one bad test, even if only slightly off, outweighs 31 good tests.

Staring at the negatives will only–will always–weaken your resolve. Look to the positives. Acknowledge the negatives, yes;

understand them, make plans to fix them. But focus on the positives! Tell yourself that your life is a plus, that you have plusses now, and that you will continue living with plusses.

> **Doubt is the enemy of self-esteem and determination. Doubt is a deadly disease that must be fought every step of the way. Focusing on the positive is a powerful medicine to cure the doubts.**

Making Points on the Compass of Life

Be not soon shaken in mind.
2 Thess. 2:2

Every time I urge my patients to stick to it, I add that it is no sin to fail. If we fail because we did not try hard enough or because our heart became faint, if we fail because we did not properly school ourselves, or because our plan was incomplete–whatever the reason, we should look upon our failure as nothing more than a point on a compass. Somehow our compass needle points toward the wrong point today. Not a wrong point exactly, simply a point we did not select today. There are many valid points on the compass, but perhaps we found ourselves a few degrees off. When the explorer realizes that he is off course, he makes a correction left or right. There's no talk of sin or failure. It's a simple course change.

We're all explorers charting the great voyage of life. We need a compass to help us stay on course, but we shouldn't be overly concerned when we stray. Each person's life is unique, unmapped territory full of interesting things and some hazards as well. We may know our eventual destination, but we don't have to adhere to that "perfect" point on the compass without some "give." Every detour presents a rich opportunity to learn and enjoy. Besides, staying on course every step of the way would require devoting our lives to watching the compass. He who keeps his eyes glued to the compass sees nothing else. Life passes by unseen.

The compass is your guide, not your life. As long as you keep your eventual destination in mind, deliberate diversions and accidental detours can spice your journey through the mysteries of life.

The Success of Failure

God hath not given us the spirit of fear; but of power, and of love, and of a sound mind.

2 Tim. 1:7

My patients are often surprised when I tell them that sometimes the greatest thing we can do is fail. "What do you mean?" they ask. "How can failure be great? Doesn't failure write nasty things into our mental gospel? Shouldn't we always strive to succeed?"

Absolutely. We should always aim for success. But it behooves us also to rejoice in our failures. Indeed, I heartily recommend a failure now and then. We should all fail occasionally—for the right reason.

There are two main reasons for failure: (1) We don't give our all, and (2) We bite off more than we can chew. Lack of effort is not a good reason for failure, nor is it a good habit to acquire. But biting off more than we can chew is a worthwhile reason for failure—and an excellent way to nourish our seed of "sticktoitivity."

Some time ago, I met a vice president of a major manufacturing company that built jet airplanes. This man was in charge of long-term forecasting, responsible for figuring out what types of jets will be needed 5, 10, 20 years from today. It takes a long time to design and build a jet so manufacturers must know—or guess—what to build years ahead of time. Will more people be flying, will we need bigger jets? If fuel is expensive in 10 years, won't we want more fuel efficiency? Will the emphasis in 20 years be on customer comfort, or on putting the maximum number of people in one plane? Will the growth of medium-sized cities create a need for short-hop planes? This man has to look at economic trends, demographic figures, the politics of the Middle East, forecasts of materials availability, ecological considerations, breakthroughs in design and construction, and more—a bewildering array of information. From all this, he must decide on the product his company should start working on now, to be ready for the future. It's an incredible task.

I asked this very knowledgeable and friendly man how often he had to be right. "Do your superiors expect you to hit it on the head 80 or 90 percent of the time? What happens if you tell them to build the wrong kind of a plane?"

He smiled as he said, "If I were always right I would probably lose my job. It would mean I wasn't taking chances, wasn't trying hard enough. If we don't take chances, our company will be mediocre in the field. The other companies with more daring will put us out of business. We can only grow and stay ahead of the competition by pushing ourselves, by sticking our neck out occasionally. Sometimes we're right, sometimes we're wrong. That's the nature of the business. I'm paid to take risks, not to play it safe. If I'm not wrong sometimes, I'm not doing something right."

That's a terrific lesson we can all take to heart. If we're not wrong sometimes, it means we're only taking tiny bits of life. We're not pushing ourselves to physical, emotional, intellectual, and spiritual limits; we're content to remain static. *But if we never push against the boundaries of our lives, we will not grow. And when we do not grow, we actually shrink, because we lose what we do not use.* Unused muscles become flabby. Unstretched imagination becomes passive. Unstretched intellect loses its spark. Emotions that are never challenged miss that new source of joy. A neglected spirit becomes brittle and dry.

As babies and children we constantly pushed against the boundaries of our capabilities in life. That's how we grew. Sure, we often fell. But if we hadn't risked falling, we would have crawled forever. Let's make it a point to fail every so often. Not because we didn't try hard enough, but because we dared to reach beyond our grasp.

Every time you dare to stretch the boundaries of your life, you are again a little baby taking your first step—your greatest step.

THE COURAGE TO SUCCEED

There is only one answer to defeat, and that is victory.
Winston Churchill

We cannot succeed unless we are willing to fail. That is the Law of Success. And it's true that most of the great successes failed miserably before achieving greatness.

Winston Churchill, the indomitable British bulldog who led his country through the dark days of World War II, put it bluntly: "Never give in! Never give in! Never, never, in nothing great or small, large or petty–never give in except to convictions of honor and good sense." Except to honor and good sense, never give in!

Abraham Lincoln, one of our greatest presidents, was also a "failure" of almost legendary proportions. In 1832 Lincoln lost his job and ran unsuccessfully for the state legislature. His business failed two years later, and a year after that, his sweetheart died. He had a nervous breakdown in 1836. By this time he was a member of the state legislature, but was defeated when he ran for Speaker in 1838. He ran unsuccessfully for Congress in 1843, couldn't even get nominated for Congress in 1848, and was refused the job of Land Officer in 1848. His campaigns for the Senate in 1854 and 1858 were unsuccessful, and he lost the nomination for vice president in 1856. Luckily, Lincoln didn't have the "good sense" to give up, for he was elected President in 1860.

Babe Ruth, the great home run hitter, is also the strikeout king. Charles Goodyear, the man who invented vulcanized rubber, began his experiments in debtors' prison. Many of our great inventors, actors, writers, politicians, and others were written off as failures before they became successes. *I say they were always successes because they had the determination to persist!*

Some are fueled by incredible confidence, others by nothing more than deep desire. They succeed because they do not know how to surrender!

Persevere in Peace

Follow peace with all men, and holiness without which no man shall see the Lord.

Heb. 12:14

Approach every task in life—life itself—with your mind at peace. Don't allow negativity to enter your mind by arguing with others. No matter what the argument might be, avoid it. Discuss problems and issues, of course, but avoid arguments. Your eyes are turned toward the negatives when you argue, and that diminishes your force.

The Man Who Was Determined to Die

The spirit shall return unto God who gave it.

Eccles. 12:7

The story of determination I am about to tell involves a man who knew that his time on earth was ending. He was ready to go, peacefully, but neither his family, nor the medical system, nor the state was willing to let him do it. Donald was in his late sixties, and his body was devastated by cancer of the prostate which had spread to the bones. He had a terrible anemia due to peptic ulcer disease and stress. His kidneys were failing. He had undergone coronary artery bypass surgery, and, toward the end, he suffered a severe stroke. His body was saying, "Enough. It's time."

Pressured by his wife, children, and doctors, Donald had submitted to every imaginable procedure. Surgeons had removed his prostate and gallbladder. He had undergone coronary artery bypass surgery and was receiving chemotherapy treatment for his cancer. After every surgery, the doctors proudly announced another "success." Yes, Donald's prostate and gallbladder had been successfully removed, his clogged artery properly bypassed. But each "successful" surgery left him worse off than before. I don't know how he withstood the physical pain and emotional agony of these treatments, but he took it all without complaining.

Donald was a friend, not a patient. We had gone to school together in Philadelphia. He often called me during the several years in which all these diseases struck, asking me what his doctors were doing to him. That's how he phrased it: "What are they doing to me, Arn? I've led a good life. I've had my ups and downs, my good times and bad. Now it's time to die, but they won't let me."

I flew to Philadelphia to spend part of his last weeks with Donald, visiting him at home and in the hospital. When I saw him in the hospital, the requisite tubes were sticking out of his body and pain was carved into his face. "Isn't it time?" he asked me. And he told me that he wanted to die at home in his own bed, not in a sterile hospital where machines would take up the space at his bedside where the family ought to be.

One evening, Donald's wife frantically called me. He was fading fast, she said, but he wouldn't go back to the hospital. Could I help?

How much more should he have to endure? I asked myself again and again as I drove out to his house.

When I pulled into the driveway, behind an ambulance, his wife rushed out to meet me. "Make him go to the hospital," she pleaded. "He'll listen to you."

I hurried into the bedroom where Donald lay, skin gray, breathing hard, fighting to remain conscious. I didn't have to touch his skin to know that it was cold, nor did I have to listen to his heart to know that it was barely beating. The man I had known when he was strong and healthy turned his head to look at me through worn-out eyes, and gave me a grunt of recognition. In the giant bedroom he seemed so small.

Though he could barely move and his speech was garbled, he said, "Don't let them take me to the hospital. I don't want to die in the hospital. I've explained it to my family but they're weakening. Give them your strength."

Give them my strength? I thought. If only I could give them yours.

Soon he could not speak at all, and could move only his left arm and hand. His wife called for help. In no time at all, two paramedics came into the room with stethoscopes, syringes, and special emergency equipment at the ready. "We'll take him in," they said.

"Wait a minute. He doesn't want to go," I said. They looked at me suspiciously. "Ask him yourselves."

We all looked to Donald, who was fighting to stay conscious, because he knew that as long as he remained conscious he could refuse treatment–that was his right under the law. Once he lost consciousness, however, his wife or the government, represented by the paramedics, could make the decision for him. And their orders are clear: Keep everyone alive at all costs.

I sat on the edge of the big bed, taking my friend's hand in mine. He squeezed it, just a bit. "Don, it's Arnold. Do you want to go to the hospital?" He didn't answer. He was trying, but he couldn't talk. "Don, squeeze my hand once for yes, twice for no," I instructed. "Do you want to go to the hospital?" He squeezed my hand twice, weakly. "He said no," I told the paramedics. They wanted to feel his negative squeeze themselves. "He said no," one of them said to Donald's wife.

"Take him to the hospital," she commanded the paramedics. "I'm his wife. Take him!" But they couldn't. She pleaded with Donald to go, saying she couldn't live without him, that his children and grandchildren wanted him to live. But he signaled by squeezing my hand twice: No.

In response to the paramedics' call for new instructions, two policemen arrived to take Donald to the hospital. Again I said they should ask the patient, and again Donald signaled by squeezing the policeman's hand twice. The police called in to the precinct for advice.

Donald had to continue fighting to stay conscious, else they would not let him die the way he wanted. As I watched this sad, macabre scene, I thought of the many times Donald's determination had saved the day. Considering the terrible blows his body had taken over the years, it was amazing that he lasted as long as he did. As a physician, I can tell you that he "should have" died a long time before this. Donald's longevity was a tribute to his positive outlook on life, his joy, and especially his courage. I remembered how he had fought so long and hard to clear his good name, unfairly smeared years ago by a business rival. I remembered how he had bravely cashed in his bonds and life insurance, emptied his bank account and mortgaged his house, begged and borrowed every penny he could to finance a new business. Everyone said he was crazy, it couldn't possibly work. Five hard, hungry, frightening times he had fought for life, and now he was fighting to die with the same courage and tenacity.

Donald had often quoted the Bible during his financially tough times: "Oh, God, strengthen my hands," he would say. And, "Fear not, neither be thou discouraged."

"Oh, God, strengthen my hands." What a strange world we live in, where one must be strong and of good courage in order to answer the Creator's call. "Fear not, neither be thou discouraged." Can these great words, which tell us that we have every reason to live, be voiced as a prayer by one who wishes so much to die?

One of Donald's sons and some grandchildren arrived to plead with him. The friend who lived next door and another doctor who had treated Donald were called in. They took turns trying to convince him to go to the hospital. One at a time, in pairs or trios, they tried to sway him with rational arguments or with tears, loudly and softly. As the scene went on, I could swear Donald's eyes grew sharper and more focused, more determined, and, yes, more pained, as he continued to hold his ground. Eventually the family agreed that Donald should be allowed to die at home.

I took my old friend's hand again, saying softly to those determined eyes of his, "Thou takest away their breath, they die, and return to their dust." It seemed his eyes were smiling as he squeezed my hand twice. Then, almost immediately, his eyes closed. Was he dead, or merely unconscious?

As his family cried, as the paramedics began the final preparations, I remembered something I had heard many years ago, as a child, something from the Bible: "Thou shalt be gathered into thy grave in peace."

Finally Donald was at peace. His family had loving reasons for wanting him to live; and the paramedics and the state had their reasons, too. But Donald had his own reasons for wanting to die when it was time for him to die, and he bravely did so.

Rx: Determination

Waters wear the stones.

Job 14:19

Today is Day Eight of Making Miracles, the Day of Determination. This day is devoted to building up your self-esteem, confidence, optimism, fortitude, enthusiasm, and serenity–the elements of determination.

Recite these affirmations throughout the day, today and every day. Be sure to "see" each affirmation as you recite it.

Upon awakening: "Rejoice and Be Glad"
This is the day that the Lord hath made; I shall rejoice and be glad, be gladder than glad. I give myself permission to see all the happiness that is in my world, to think of the happiness, and to speak of the happiness. The Creator has filled the world with unlimited joy that is mine for the taking.

Morning: "It is Good to Give Thanks"
It is good to give thanks unto the Lord for making me the healthy, happy, and successful person I so richly deserve to be. I am open to receiving all the blessings of His abundant universe.

Noon: "Endless Enthusiasm"
The Creator has filled me to the brim with enthusiasm. I gladly and generously pour my unlimited enthusiasm over my every thought and action. Armed with endless enthusiasm, I find excitement and adventure in every day.

Afternoon: "Spiritually Minded"
To be spiritually minded is life and peace. I give myself permission to be as calm and serene as the quiet waters of a beautiful, still lake.

Evening: "A Merry Heart"
A merry heart is a good medicine. My heart and spirit

and the gospel of my mind are filled with joy. I am full of the thoughts and things of health, happiness, and success.

When going to bed: "Put on the New Me"
Today was another successful step toward the new me. With enthusiastic anticipation and absolute certainty that I'll make even more progress tomorrow, and every tomorrow, I'm putting on the new me.

Recite each affirmation out loud, with enthusiasm. Go beyond the minimum and recite the affirmations all day long. You can't overdo it with affirmations!

In addition to your daily diet of affirmations, enter into your mental gospel this special R_X for Determination several times today, with energy and conviction.

Set aside some time today to sit in a quiet room, on a comfortable chair. Tell everyone that you do not want to be disturbed; take the phone off the hook. Close your eyes. With your mind's eye, picture yourself in a garden. It's a beautiful garden, like the Garden of Eden. It's your garden, the garden of your spirit. All the lovely grasses and plants, each of the tall and mighty trees represents an aspect of you. There's your tall tree of self-confidence, a towering tree grown so high it seems to touch the sky. Next to it are your trees of optimism, enthusiasm, serenity, fortitude, and the others.

Right in the middle of the garden of your spirit is your tree of determination. This is the tallest, strongest tree of all. Look up at your tree of determination: It seems to stretch up forever, so high you can hardly see the top. See yourself, the caretaker of your spirit, tending to your garden. With your mind's eye, see yourself planting the seeds of confidence, optimism, enthusiasm, serenity, belief, and forgiveness. With a little spade you carefully turn over the soil, planting the seeds of great spirit.

Look up at your tree of determination again. It's taller and stronger, its branches are stretching out farther, its leaves are greener than ever. Your entire spiritual garden is richer and lusher than ever. Marvel at the beauty of your spirit as you say:

My spirit is rich with self-esteem, with confidence, optimism, enthusiasm, serenity, and forgiveness. I have the determination, skill, and courage to set the boundaries of my life wherever I want them to be. My life is mine to direct, and mine to live in great joy.

DRIVEN BY DETERMINATION

Look also at the ships; although they are large and are driven by fierce winds, they are turned by a very small rudder when ever the pilot desires.

James 3:4

Determination is the rudder on our ship of life. Determination keeps us on course, no matter how the winds of life buffet us about. We may have to turn into the wind at times, or away from the wind, or sideways to the wind, as occasion demands. As long as we are determined, we can steer ourselves back on course.

Fight the good fight. Invoke the Law of Success by daring to fail. Know that with every brave step you are a daring child once more, taking your first step–your greatest step. Nourish your seed of determination with self-esteem, with confidence, optimism, enthusiasm, serenity, belief, and forgiveness–plus plenty of desire. Always keep the picture of the garden of your spirit–with that strong, tall tree of determination in the center–in the forefront of your mind.

As President Calvin Coolidge pointed out, nothing can take the place of determination. Not talent, not genius, not education, not background. There are uncounted talented, bright, educated people who never achieved their dreams. Determination, persistence, perseverance: These are the keys to success.

Day 9

SHOUT FOR JOY!

Shout unto God with the voice of triumph.

Ps. 47:1

I once knew a very old man who was considered a crazy old coot by most people; cute, but kind of a pain in the rear. His name was Arthur, though everyone called him "the Shouter." You see, Arthur believed in shouting and dancing for joy, five minutes at a time, three times a day, every day. I know it sounds bizarre, but no matter where he was, who he was with, or what was happening, he would politely excuse himself and step into another room or outside, where he would actually shout and dance for joy. Then he would calmly return to what he was doing before. Arthur smiled often and easily and always appeared to be enjoying himself, even when not shouting and dancing for joy. Full of enthusiasm and love for life, he constantly encouraged others to put aside their troubling thoughts and be happy.

I still chuckle when I think of that old man: a small guy, the remaining hairs on his head silvery white, always immaculately dressed in a white suit. Soft-spoken and deferential, Arthur was a perfect gentleman, and a scholar as well. Formerly a professor of American history, he had spent the 20 years since his retirement enthusiastically delving into the minutiae of the founding of our country.

Imagine sitting with Arthur in his book-lined study, discussing the Boston Tea Party or the Continental Congress. As you're talking, he checks his watch then politely excuses himself. A few moments later you hear what seems almost a child's voice shouting: "I'm happy! I'm shouting in triumph to God because He created happiness!" You look out the window to see this distinguished old professor hopping from one foot to another shouting about happiness! Soon he breaks into what appears to be an Indian dance, then a European folk dance, some tap steps, and finally a partnerless waltz–all the while shouting and singing for joy.

Or imagine yourself as a doctor trying to examine Arthur in the hospital as I did. Arthur had cracked a few ribs in a fall. At the request of his general practitioner, I stopped by Arthur's room to check him out. While I was listening to his heart, the polite old gentleman asked me to excuse him. He carefully eased himself out of bed, and right there in front of me began dancing and shouting.

At first I didn't know what to make of this, especially when a nurse rushed in to try to quiet Arthur. She imperiously ordered the man to "get in bed and act your age!" Arthur was too wrapped up in his celebration of joy to even notice.

I persuaded the nurse to leave the room and waited until "the Shouter" was finished. I was expecting him to explain his behavior, but he simply returned to bed without a word and without the least bit of embarrassment or concern. Then he politely requested me to continue with the examination.

I still laugh when I think about this distinguished gentleman's dancing around like a kid. "We must be joyful," he told me. "My father taught me that when I was a little boy. No matter what happens, we must be joyful. I remember my father as always being that way. Even when the drought wiped out our little farm and we had nothing to eat, he had us dancing and singing joyfully. He used to say that God gives whatever you thank Him for in advance. That's why he taught us always to thank God with the voice of triumph for creating joy.

"My father isn't the only one who came to this conclusion," Arthur continued. "Abraham Lincoln said that 'Most people are about as happy as they make up their minds to be.' And the German philosopher Immanuel Kant said, 'It is God's will, not merely that we should be happy, but that we should make ourselves happy.' The Bible tells us to 'Shout unto God with the voice of triumph.' I am simply acting according to the collective wisdom of the ages, as taught to me by my father."

Arthur was 85 years old at that time. Except for the one fall that led to the cracked ribs, he was in excellent health. His mind was razor sharp, he walked briskly for 15 minutes every day after dinner, his appetite was healthy, his vision and hearing good. More importantly, his spirit was strong and his cup runneth over with life. He was in his nineties when he moved away and I lost track of him. I wouldn't be surprised, however, if he were still dancing and singing for joy.

We can all learn a lesson from this wise old man. Let's thank God, in advance, for creating joy, and for making us joyful people.

Shout of your joy with triumph, for when you are joyful you are triumphant.

NEVER SURRENDER YOUR JOY!

Let them praise His name in the dance; let them sing praises unto Him with the timbrel and harp.

Ps. 143:9

There's an interesting aspect of joy: Some people can't stand your joy. They're infuriated when others are happy. Some of the doctors and nurses were very upset by Arthur's dances. They said he was upsetting hospital routine. He was annoying the other patients. He wasn't acting his age. I never heard the other patients complain. And I believe there's no such thing as "acting your age"; we act as we are. Besides, who says that only youngsters are allowed to be happy?

One day, while I was examining Arthur, a doctor burst into the room and began lecturing Arthur about his silly and embarrassing behavior. "Your artificial happiness," he told Arthur, "is a desperate attempt to cover up deep sadness. I'm going to prove it!" The doctor's face grew red; he was shouting and shaking his fist in the air. I could see the veins on the doctor's forehead bulging. I knew that his blood pressure must be sky-high and his glands must be pumping out large quantities of adrenaline and other high-voltage chemicals. The tirade went on for several minutes before the doctor ran out of steam and fell silent. Arthur, who had not batted an eye, put his hand on the doctor's shoulder and said, with genuine sincerity, "I hope you feel better soon. Why don't we shout for joy together?"

People whose cups have run dry may try to strangle your joy. They'll tell you you're fooling yourself into thinking you're happy; they'll tell you you're not realistic; they'll tell you you're ignoring the very real problems of this world; they'll tell you you're not acting your age. They'll tell you anything to quash your jubilation. But don't let them get to you. Instead, you tell yourself that joy is one of the Ten Pillars of Spirit. Tell yourself that joy is a medicine for the spirit. Tell yourself that joy is infectious, that others will "catch" your joy. Tell yourself that you are filled with joy. Shout unto God with a voice of triumph and joy!

Your joy is a gift from God, and it is a gift from you to the world. It's yours; let no one take it from you.

WHY OTHERS TRY TO LIMIT YOUR JOY

Why are some people—so many people, it seems—upset when you are joyful? Why were people trying to quiet Arthur "the Shouter"? I remember one woman, at a party, saying that she wished so-and-so were present so he could prove to me that I was unhappy. "He'll tear your happiness to pieces and make you face your real self," she said triumphantly.

We've all experienced this, people telling us to quiet down or giving us disapproving looks when we're joyful. And how many of us have looked at others with the disapproving look? How many times have we felt embarrassed being around someone who was obviously having a great time?

Why does joy upset people? Because joy is by nature expansive. Sorrow, self-pity, depression and the like are inward emotions, black holes that suck you into a world of quiet despair. Joy, on the other hand, radiates outward in every direction.

Joy upsets the joyless. Yes, it does. Joy shakes up their world. Joy is a reminder that they live in a cave of gloom. Joy is movement and energy. Joy is love—love of life and love for others. Joy is everything the miserable person is not. Your joy shows them how much of life they're not living. They're not mad at you or embarrassed by your joyful behavior: They're jealous because you've got what they so desperately want. They're angry at themselves. You're a reminder of what they're not, and they don't like it.

When they tell you to act your age, they're admitting that they've forgotten the joyfulness of their youth. They use age as a convenient excuse for having forgotten.

When they say you're embarrassing yourself, they're confessing their fear. Your joy impinges upon their gloom. Your joy challenges them to crack the cement shoes of their despair. But it's hard for them to do that. It is easier to try to quiet you!

When they tell you how unhappy you "really" are, they're revealing how miserable *they* are. Your joy is actually painful to them, for the sound of your joy echoes in the emptiness of their spirit. Their attempt to quiet you is an indication of their pain. Pray for them that they may feel better, and keep on being the joyful person that you are.

Your joy is celebration of life; your life, and yes, theirs as well. Keep offering the world your joy. You *will* touch people. You *will* change someone's life.

THE MEDICINE CALLED JOY

Rejoice evermore.

1 Thess. 5:16

Joy is happiness, laughter, energy, excitement, enthusiasm, anticipation, love, curiosity, openness, creation, movement, growth, and more. What does joy do for us? Joy colors our mind with health. When we're filled with joy, our joy is projected out onto our world. Our world becomes a joyful place to be. Thoughts of joy fill our mental gospel with the great words that strengthen our health and make us into magnets that attract great things.

How does joy prevent disease? Here's a well-known example. The best-selling drugs in the world are ulcer medications. It's been well established that while ulcers are disturbances of the stomach or intestines, they are born in the mind. When I present my slide talks, I project a large image of an X ray on the screen. The X ray shows a duodenal ulcer, a very common type of ulcer. Then I show an X ray of the brain and say that this is where the ulcer really began, not in the stomach. The popular medicines we give for the ulcer attempt to treat the ulcer in the stomach. But the cure, along with the cause, is usually in our thoughts.

Recent articles in the *New England Journal of Medicine* and other prestigious journals report that certain germs, such as chlamydia, are associated with ulcers. Does this mean that germs cause ulcers?

Unbridled stress floods the body with high-voltage chemicals (especially cortisone), which eat away at the protective lining of the stomach. Excessive stress also prompts an increase in acid in the stomach. The extra acid together with the weakened protective lining can result in anything from mild irritation to a full-blown ulcer.

In addition, continued stress weakens the immune system. With your immune defenses down, germs can gain a foothold in the already-weakened stomach lining–making the problem worse.

Yes, we physicians have medicines for ulcers. For most of us, however, the best medicine is joy. After all, stress and unhappy thoughts are the real culprits, and joy is a powerful antidote to stress.

Aside from ulcers, joy helps prevent elevated cholesterol levels, high blood pressure, heart disease, cancer, and other killers. As an internist and cardiologist who has treated many very ill people in intensive care units and coronary care units, I can tell you that joy has antibacterial and antiviral properties. Joy helps prevent disease.

How does joy bring great things into our lives? Remember that the recipe for joy includes generous portions of energy, enthusiasm, curiosity, openness, creativity, movement, and growth. The unhappy person is a victim of inertia, the tendency of a body at rest to remain at rest. In other words, the unhappy person is like a bump on a log: He's not going anywhere. The joyful person, on the other hand, has the energy and enthusiasm to generate new projects. The joyful person has the curiosity to explore and learn, plus the ability to grow, pushing the boundaries of his or her life farther and farther out. The joyful person is open to and actively seeks out new ideas, people, and things. Imbued with these great qualities, the joyful person is more likely to come across good things, to recognize them, and to take them to heart.

Rejoice forevermore, knowing that joy is a magnet for the great things in life. It's a special kind of magnet, attracting endless new joy into your life.

THE COST OF DOING BUSINESS

I have learned, in whatsoever state I am, therewith to be content.

Phil. 4:11

A well-known movie and television writer–you've probably seen his work–once came to my office complaining of ulcers, high blood pressure, and irregular heartbeats. After taking a complete personal and family medical history, performing a physical examination and the appropriate tests, I sat down with the man in my office. "What do you like about life?" I asked him.

"What?" he replied, surprised.

"What do you feel passionate about in life? What do you want more of?"

"I'll tell you what I don't like," he growled. "I'm one of the top writers in the business, but they've got some 14-year-old baby telling me how to write my scripts!"

"Who's they?"

"The banks. The studios don't back films like they used to–you have to go to a banker. These damn bankers send squirts just out of school, who couldn't write a coherent paragraph if their life depended on it, to tell me how to write my scripts! I could strangle the little squirts!"

"What brings you joy?" I asked.

"The thought of strangling those jerks."

"Well," I said. "What I'm going to tell you is more important than the examination and tests. Your blood pressure is high. I can give you medicines to bring it down. The medicines may or may not work, but they'll certainly have side effects. Depression is a possible side effect. So is impotence. The pharmacy downstairs has all kinds of drugs for your heart and ulcers.

"Your cholesterol level is high. There are also drugs for lowering cholesterol. Or I could put you on a diet of oat bran, complex carbohydrates, and other good things to lower your cholesterol, without drugs. But none of these will help significantly because your stress is responsible in large measure for your high cholesterol."

"Stress does that?" he asked incredulously.

"There have been many studies documenting the relationship between stress and an elevated cholesterol level. If you throw people into cold water, which is a form of stress, their cholesterol level will go up. If you check students just before and during final examinations, you'll see that their cholesterol level is up.

"Anger stresses the body. Anger raises your cholesterol level. The cholesterol level stays up long after you've gotten over your anger. For people who are constantly angry, the cholesterol level never has a chance to come back down.

"And it's not just cholesterol levels. New studies have monitored the heart activity of heart patients during stressful situations such as speaking in public. The tests show that these people suffered irregular heartbeats and dysfunction of the heart muscles during stress.

"If our diseases are caused by stress, anger, and other manifestations of lack of joy, then the medicine we need is joy. Joy is a wonderful medicine. It's free, it works; it has no side effects. Your anger is strangling the joy in your life. It's strangling your life. I can give you a prescription for drugs. It won't work as well as a prescription for joy.

"You have to deal with kids who don't know the first thing about writing. That's unfair. It's also the way it is. Unless you put up the millions of dollars it takes to make a movie, you're going to have to deal with these kids looking over your shoulder. We all have to deal with things like this. I'm a physician with over 30 years experience treating patients. But some bureaucrat who doesn't know anything about medicine is deciding for the insurance company that I'm not treating my patients properly, so they're not going to pay.

"These aggravations are a part of doing business. That's life. No matter what you do, there's a cost of doing business. The bankers interfere with your writing. You can scream all you want, but they'll still be there. Since they're going to be there anyway, why lose your health over them?"

The Bible tells us that there is "a time to weep, and a time to laugh; a time to mourn, and a time to dance." It's OK to gripe a little when things go wrong. But the time to complain comes and goes, replaced by the time to laugh and dance.

When facets of life get you down, just write them off as a cost of doing business, and forget about them. Write yourself a prescription for daily joy.

Worry: Stranglehold On Our Lives

My life has been full of terrible misfortunes, most of which never happened.

Montaigne

Worry is a great enemy of joy. We have a lot to worry about: our relationships, raising our children, money, taxes, our jobs, traffic, pollution, whether there will be a war, and on and on. We can worry forever without worrying about everything there is to worry about.

The word "worry" comes from an old Anglo-Saxon word meaning strangle. I gently touch my hands to my patients' necks to give them a concrete illustration of what worry does to us. Worry strangles our thoughts, our creativity, our health, our very life.

While in a studio to tape a television program, Barry and I met the very friendly Reverend Frank White of the Religious Science Church of El Cajon, California, near San Diego. The Reverend Mr. White gave us a pamphlet he wrote called *Some Things To Remember About Worry*. It's an excellent pamphlet explaining exactly what is wrong with worry. With his permission, we reprint it here. Our comments are in italics.

Worry Doesn't Work

In the entire history of mankind, nothing constructive has ever been accomplished through worry.

Concern is constructive. Concern, an awareness of possible trouble and a desire to correct the situation, does not strangle us like worry does. Concern, thought, planning, and appropriate action–these are the steps to accomplishment. Leave worry out of the equation. Charles Darwin worried that his ideas on evolution would not be received well. He worried for years, only finally publishing because someone else was beating him to it. His worry did not improve his work or the reception it received. It did almost write him out of the history books. Whether we agree with his ideas or not, the point is that worry accomplishes nothing.

Worry Is a Sign of Separation

We worry because we believe, consciously or unconsciously, that God isn't "on the job." For whatever reason, we think we are out of touch with the infinite.

Believing we have lost touch with God makes it extremely difficult for us to hear God calling to us, to recognize the guidance He is sending us. God has filled our world with ideas, approaches, and solutions that are always out there, waiting for us to grasp. When we lose touch with God's world, however, we can no longer see the good that is ours for the taking.

Worry Is Negative Faith

Worry believes that something bad is going to happen–that somehow we are not capable, our means not sufficient, our power usurped by others. Faith in God (good) gives the lie to such ideas.

The worried people have lost faith in themselves. Worried people write "I'm all alone" and "I can't do it" into their mental gospel. These words are prophecies that are bound to come true.

Most of Our Worries Are Not Our Own

We tend to worry for and about others. Worrying for and about others is even less effective than worrying for and about ourselves. **You can't live other people's lives** anymore than they can live yours. Release them to God's care. Know that they are God in action–just as you are.

Worrying for someone else strangles two people–you and the person you are worrying for. Trust in other people's ability to take care of themselves. Help them if you like, or pray for them, but don't worry. Your worry chokes you when they need you most to help.

Worry Keeps Us in the Problem

Focusing on answers takes us out of the problem and into the solution. It takes no more mental and emotion energy and effort. The result is greatly different, however.

When we worry our eyes are focused on the problem. All our mental energy is concentrated on the negatives, and these negatives are written over and over into our mental gospel. The more we worry the more the negatives are written into the gospel of our mind, and the firmer we draw the noose around our own necks. "Lift up thine eyes, and look from the place where thou art." Turn your eyes away from the muck of negativity and gaze upon the golden possibilities.

Don't Worry, Be Happy

Just as two objects cannot occupy the same space, two thoughts cannot occupy the same mind. Deliberately and consciously choose happy thoughts. Abraham Lincoln was right when he said: "Most people are about as happy as they make up their minds to be."

Some of the worst things that happen to us are brought about by our own worry and negative thoughts. I've treated countless patients who made themselves very sick with their unhappy thoughts. Some even died because of their negative thinking.

"Weeping may endure for a night, but joy cometh in the morning," says the Psalm so wisely. "The sun will come up tomorrow," proclaim the lyrics of that great song, "Tomorrow," from the Broadway show *Annie*. The sun always comes up tomorrow. It's fine to be concerned, it's OK to gripe a bit now and then. But keep your eyes firmly focused on the joy in you and in life. You'll be healthier, happier, and more successful in every way.

REJOICING THROUGH SORROW

Let the heavens rejoice, and let the earth be glad; let the sea roar, and the fullness thereof.

Eccles. 9:7

This is a story of great joy, but it's a bittersweet tale, for its heroine who spread joy so freely died young in life, after suffering great pain. Martha was a beautiful woman, a girl-next-door type with a sunny smile that could light up the darkest night. Her life had been the stuff of fairy tales; born to an upper-middle-class family, she was an excellent student and talented athlete, star of her high school debate team, and very popular. She won a full scholarship to an Ivy League university, where she earned a bachelor's and a master's degree before marrying and beginning a family. Martha seemed to be a superwoman, raising two children while running a growing mail-order business out of her home. This young woman was blessed with a spirit rich in joy and love. She always ate the bread and drank the wine of life with a merry heart.

But she was only in her early thirties when I had the sad duty of telling her that she had leukemia, a fatal cancer of the blood. Her parents and husband were devastated, her young children frightened and confused, but Martha was remarkably unperturbed. She told me that she was sorry to have cancer but would not be sad.

"Let the heavens rejoice, and the earth be glad," she said with a smile.

"Do you mean that sarcastically?" I asked. But I knew there was no sarcasm in her voice.

"No. Let the heavens rejoice and the earth always be glad because everyone should always be happy. I'm a happy person, Dr. Fox. Yes, I'm a little sad now. But it'll pass. It's my nature to be happy, no matter what."

I wondered if she wasn't denying to herself the severity of her disease. Usually patients cry when I tell them they have cancer, or they refuse to believe me, or become angry at me. They say they are afraid, they say they don't want to die, they ask who will take care of their family. They don't smile and talk of rejoicing.

"Do you understand what I'm telling you?" I asked, gently. Perhaps she was in shock, I told myself. Perhaps she was so frightened that her subconscious would not allow her to comprehend what was happening.

"A friend's mother died of leukemia, Dr. Fox. I know what's ahead for me. Odds are I'm going to die. What's ahead is ahead, there's nothing I can do about it. What I *can* do is to make sure that I never lose my joy."

She never lost her joy. "Bread and water is a banquet if eaten with joy," she used to say. "Whatever life gives me I'll grab onto with joy."

"You've got a great philosophy," I said to her one day, after several weeks of painful chemotherapy. "Tell me how you can be joyful in the face of. . ." and I faltered.

"In the face of death?" she asked, to complete my sentence.

"Yes. And in the face of your pain. Tell me so I can tell others."

This is what she said:

> I believe that joy is life. When we lose our joy, we die. The body may hang on for another 50 years and we may go through the motions, but we're dead. There are so many living dead people. I won't be one of them! I'm going to be 100 percent alive until the last second! It's important that my children learn how to be joyful when things are going wrong. That's when it's most important to be joyful. My illness will be their teacher.

This poor woman suffered through an incredibly painful and painfully protracted series of chemotherapy treatments. Her hair fell out in chunks. Her youthful skin seemed to age 50 years as it covered over with sores and blisters. Her beautiful figure melted away, leaving behind a bruised skeletal shell. Her eye sockets were dark and deep. Nausea was her constant companion, pain always there to torture her. Deep pain, terrible pain that "comes from my bones, Dr. Fox."

Remembering how my own mother had suffered through chemotherapy before dying of leukemia, I often cried for Martha. We all cried for Martha; me, her husband, her parents, her children, her many friends. The nurses, so accustomed to death, cried for Martha, too.

Everyone cried for Martha—but Martha. She always smiled. God! It was such a beautiful smile, formed by lips that were so weak they could hardly move. We all cried for Martha, the joyful woman who never cried for herself.

Only once, following a long, painful, and draining series of chemotherapy treatments, did she ask, tears in her eyes, "What's going to happen to my children? Why are they being put through this?" Before I could say anything she added, "I don't expect answers."

Eventually Martha's condition improved. She went home, running her household and her mail-order business as best she could. She knew that the remission of her leukemia did not mean she was cured—far from it. The cancer was only being held at bay. Still, she radiated joy and enthusiasm. "I get up each morning to watch the sun rise," she told me. "Every day is a new beginning, another chance to be joyful. If the kids are up, they watch with me. I want them to remember that the sun is always rising if you're happy."

The sun finally set on the beautiful woman that was Martha. Her great joy did not save her, did not revive her immune system, did not crush the cancer. Even her joy was not the magic medicine we all wished she could have.

Her joy was, however, her gift to her children, and to the world. Her joy eased her transition into the next world, for herself and for her family. She died easily, at peace with the world, joyfully anticipating the next life. Joy was life and life was joy for Martha. The heavens will always rejoice for her, with her, and the earth will be forever glad.

A heart full of joy can raise a smile even in the midst of misery.

Six Tips for Being Joyful

How can we be joyful every day, even when dealing with the normal and extraordinary stresses of life? Here are the six tips for being joyful I learned from Martha and other exceptionally strong patients.

1. Know That God Wants You to Be Filled with Joy

> *Thou hast turned my mourning into dancing: Thou has put off my sackcloth, and girded me with gladness.*
>
> Ps. 30:11

God created the heavens and the earth, the stars, moon, and sun, fish and birds and trees and animals. God created man, and He created joy. Joy is one of God's greatest creations, for joy gives life to our life. It is His great wish that we all eat of the tree of joy forever.

We're told to "rejoice, and be exceeding glad. . ." The best way to partake of the joy God has given to us is to be glad in the Lord and all His creations. Like spirit, joy is the touch of our God within us. When we are joyful, we are with God, and He with us.

As it is said: "Joy is the ineffable expression of the presence of God within us." Keep that in mind as you say, out loud:

> Joy is of God and God gives joy. I am with God in my joy, and He with me.

Recite this affirmation for joy all day long, every day for the rest of your life. Remember that with every bit of joy you take into your heart, God takes a corresponding measure into His.

2. Get the Great Wisdom of Joy

> *Happy is the man that findeth wisdom, and the man that getteth understanding.*
>
> Prov. 3:13

The wise man is happy, and the single most important bit of wisdom in the world is that we can choose to be happy. We *can* be happy, once we understand that our world is what we make of it. With the words written in our mental gospel; with the colors of the filter of our mind; with the attitudes we project out onto the world; with our words, thoughts, and attitudes, we create our world.

Write these words of wisdom and understanding into your mental gospel.

> I am exceedingly happy, because that's exactly how God and I want it to be!

Memorize these words of wisdom. Keep repeating them over and over as you write the wisdom of joy into the gospel of your mind.

3. Focus on the Positive

> *The heart of the wise teacheth his mouth and addeth learning to his lips.*
>
> Prov. 16:23

Stop worrying! A wise man said that we shouldn't sweat the little things in life, and we should remember that most things are little. Worry accomplishes absolutely nothing–it only impairs our spirit, our creative facilities, our ability to think the problem through, and our courage.

God placed the potential for unlimited joy into your spirit, into your heart. Let your heart teach you what to say, what to think, and how to behave. Keep joy–the touch of God within you–in the forefront of your mind. Paint the filter of your mind the colors of joy and look at the world through eyes of joy. Say:

> I have the Touch of Joy. Everything I touch fills me with joy.

As you recite this affirmation for joy, use your mind's eye to see yourself with a big smile on your face.

4. Shout for Joy!

> *Make a joyful noise unto the Lord, all the earth: make a loud noise, and rejoice, and sing praise.*
>
> Ps. 98:4

Actions speak louder than words. Actions also write boldly in our mental gospel, very boldly indeed. When "the Shouter" danced and sang of his joy, he was triumphantly writing chapters of joy into his mental book. Each of his actions launched a thousand words.

Make your life one great shout of joy. When you rise up and when you lie down, do so with joy. When you walk, walk with joy. When you talk, talk with a joyful voice. Greet everyone enthusiastically. Accept every task as a marvelous opportunity to demonstrate your talents.

Every day is the day the Lord hath made, rejoice and be happy. God is joy–when we are joyful, we are with God. Look at yourself in the mirror every morning and say:

> I'm shouting for joy, because this is the day the Lord made!

Say it with feeling: "I'm *shouting* for joy, because *this* is the day the *Lord* hath made!"

It feels great to be joyful. Joyful thoughts, words, and actions trigger the release of biosubstances that make us feel great! These substances strengthen our immune system as well, so we're double winners.

We are what we make ourselves. Put the joyful thoughts into your head, even if it seems artificial at first. Your brain doesn't care how the thoughts got there, all it knows is that good thoughts are present. Your brain will respond to the good thoughts you place there by realigning your body chemistry. From thoughts to biochemistry, from thoughts to great joy and vibrant health, the pathway is clear.

5. Give Joy to Others

> *Freely have you received, freely give.*
>
> Matt. 10:8

In giving joy you give a matchless gift. Not only that, you help keep yourself young. You see, when you give to others you show your love for God, and love helps to keep us young. As Emerson said, "Some thoughts always find us young and keep us so. Such a thought is the love of the universal and eternal beauty." Give your joy to everyone, saying as you do:

> My gift of joy to the world is a fountain of youth, for me and for others.

Keep this affirmation bubbling up in your mind.

6. Help the Sun Rise on Tomorrow

> *Weeping may endure for a night, but joy cometh in the morning.*
>
> Ps. 30:5

No matter how dark the night, the sun will rise to lighten the sky. *The sun will always come out tomorrow.* And with God's help, with the spirit of joy He placed in all of us, we can make the miracle of speeding the moon in its flight through the dark of the night, so that the darkness may give way to the light of success. With God's help, Joshua made the sun stand still. With God's help, we can cause the sunlight of joy and health to forever reign in our sky.

Make the miracle of joy. Say:

> With the help of God within me, I have decreed that the sun of joy is always rising on my world.

Recite this affirmation for joy all day long, from sunrise to sunset and beyond.

Review the six tips for being joyful and resolve to incorporate them into your approach to life:

1. Know that God wants you to be filled with joy.
2. Get the great wisdom of joy.
3. Focus on the positive.
4. Shout for joy!
5. Give joy to others.
6. Help the sun rise on tomorrow.

Know, get, focus, shout, give, and help: These are the beginnings of great joy.

Rx: Shout for Joy

He that is of merry heart hath a continual feast.

Prov. 15:15

Today is Day Nine of Making Miracles, the Day of Joy. This day is devoted to shouting for joy.

Recite these affirmations throughout the day, today and every day. Be sure to "see" each affirmation as you recite it.

Upon awakening: "Rejoice and Be Glad"
This is the day that the Lord hath made; I shall rejoice and be glad, be gladder than glad. I give myself permission to see all the happiness that is in my world, to think of the happiness, and to speak of the happiness. The Creator has filled the world with unlimited joy that is mine for the taking.

Morning: "It is Good to Give Thanks"
It is good to give thanks unto the Lord for making me the healthy, happy, and successful person I so richly deserve to be. I am open to receiving all the blessings of His abundant universe.

Noon: "Endless Enthusiasm"
The Creator has filled me to the brim with enthusiasm. I gladly and generously pour my unlimited enthusiasm over my every thought and action. Armed with endless enthusiasm, I find excitement and adventure in every day.

Afternoon: "Spiritually Minded"
To be spiritually minded is life and peace. I give myself permission to be as calm and serene as the quiet waters of a beautiful, still lake.

Evening: "A Merry Heart"
A merry heart is a good medicine. My heart and spirit and the gospel of my mind are filled with joy. I am full of the thoughts and things of health, happiness, and success.

When going to bed: "Put on the New Me"
Today was another successful step toward the new me. With enthusiastic anticipation and absolute certainty that I'll make even more progress tomorrow, and every tomorrow, I'm putting on the new me.

Recite each affirmation out loud, with enthusiasm. This daily menu sets up the daily minimum requirements of glad tidings. But I tell my patients to go beyond the minimum and recite each affirmation all day long: 5, 10, 20 times a day. You can't overdo it with affirmations!

In addition to your daily diet of affirmations, enter into your world this special R_X for Joy several times today, with energy and conviction.

Set aside some time today to sit in a quiet room, on a comfortable chair. Tell everyone that you do not want to be disturbed; take the phone off the hook. Close your eyes. With your mind's eye, picture yourself standing upon a great mountain. This is a mountain so tall it seems to touch the skies. The clouds surround you, the air is sparkling and clear, you're alone and the feeling is exhilarating. As you look up to the heavens, peering through the clouds, you can sense the presence of the Creator. And you know that your joy and the gifts of joy you give to the world have brought you close to Him. As you see yourself standing on the mountaintop, say all your affirmations for joy:

> Joy is of God and God gives joy. I am with God in my joy, and He with me.
>
> I am exceedingly happy, because that's exactly how God and I want it to be!
>
> I have the Touch of Joy. Everything I touch fills me with joy.

> I'm shouting for joy, because this is the day the Lord made!
>
> My gift of joy to the world is a fountain of youth, for me and for others.
>
> With the help of God within me, I have decreed that the sun of joy is always rising on my world.

After you've seen and said your special R_X for Joy, get up and shout for joy! Dance for joy! Whatever kind of dancing you like–waltzing, tap dancing, folk dancing, hopping from foot to foot, or shuffling around–get up and dance for joy. Shout out your joy while you dance. What should you shout? Use your affirmation for joy, sing your favorite song, or make something up. The words are not important; it's that great feeling of joy you are celebrating.

Besides singing and dancing for joy, there's whistling. I'm a whistler myself. I often find myself whistling happy songs, wondering–Wow! where did this song come from? I heard it back in 1939 or 1940, and now it's popping up at just the right time to give me the boost of enthusiasm and joy.

I know a doctor who sings while walking down Wilshire Boulevard in Beverly Hills, oblivious to the onlookers' puzzled stares. People say, "I wonder what's wrong with him? He walks around singing. Doesn't he know how bad things are in the world?"

This same doctor sings with his patients. You want to know who the doctor is? It's me. I admit to this with a little hesitation because some of my colleagues say, "Arnie's a good doctor, but singing is not good scientific medicine." I love to sing joyous songs like "It's a Lovely Day Today," or "Oh What a Beautiful Morning," or "Almost Like Being in Love," and "California Here I Come." I've taught that last song to my two-year-old grandson Andrew, who, by the way, cannot speak yet, but sings along using only one word: "eh." Melanie and Joshua, my other two grandchildren, have learned to sing with me wherever we go. They like "Yankee Doodle Dandy," "Give My Regards to Broadway," and "When the Red Red Robin Goes Bob-Bob-Bobbin' Along" (in honor of their mother, Robin).

I sometimes use singing as medicine for select patients

because music is joyful, and because so many songs are about love, optimism, and joy. My son Steven says I'm always off-key, but that doesn't matter–it's the spirit that really counts. Let me tell you how song helped one patient.

I was out jogging early one morning when my beeper went off. I called my exchange from a pay phone. They told me that the wife of one of my patients had called. When I contacted her, she anxiously reported that her 80-year-old husband, who had a history of an enlarged heart and severe congestive heart failure, was experiencing difficulty in breathing. "I think he should go to the hospital," she said. "Should I call an ambulance?"

I knew that this man, who had terminal heart disease, would be made very miserable at the hospital, surrounded by doctors who had to stick needles in him, inject things in, draw things out, perform this and that test. "Let me come over and see him first," I told her.

Still in my jogging clothes, I drove over to his house. He was indeed very short of breath, and his lips were blue. His greatly enlarged heart was beating rapidly. I helped him out of bed, got him sitting up in a comfortable armchair, and began talking to him. I got him to slow down his breathing. After a while I said, "Your son, who is one of the finest doctors in Beverly Hills, told me that many years ago you would come home early from work and sing with your children. He told me that you taught them the old songs from the twenties, thirties, and forties."

Very intently and seriously he said: "Yes, I did."

"Do you remember any of the songs?" I asked.

He was breathing rapidly as he said, "No."

"Well, I remember some of them. How about 'Tomorrow Is a Lovely Day'?" I sang a few lines from this song of yesterday, then said, "Join in with me." He did, singing breathlessly.

"How about 'Pack Up Your Troubles'? You must know that one," I said. He sure did, because he sang it with me. "Here's one from the fifties," I said. "I bet you know it. 'Put On a Happy Face'."

"Sure, I know that," he said eagerly, beginning to sing before I could.

When we were finished with that one I looked out the window and said, "It's a beautiful morning." The brain, wonderful instrument that it is, immediately seized the song "Oh, What a Beautiful Morning" from my mental files and shoved it into my consciousness. "Let's sing 'Oh, What a Beautiful Morning'."

He was breathing much better as we sang. His wife joined us, no longer looking so worried. As we continued singing, his daughter and her children came in. I was thoroughly enjoying this singing, for singing is joy and joy is a sign of being with God. We sang until I suddenly realized that over two hours had gone by. The man was breathing well and his color had returned. "How are you?" I asked.

"Fine," he answered.

"I've got to go," I said. "Why don't you continue singing?"

I left to shower and get to my office. He did very well for a long time until finally his overburdened heart gave out. He had picked up the idea of song, which he had forgotten about, as a means of bringing joy to himself and to his wonderful family.

Day 10

Forgiveness and Amends

I will forgive their iniquity, and I will remember their sin no more.

Jer. 31:34

I'll never forget my father's last will. Only in his early seventies when felled by a stroke, he had lived a life that was often difficult. He was a man given to quick anger and bitter memories. I remember going with him to the farmers' produce market in Philadelphia when I was a child, where he would purchase fruit and vegetables to sell. On one occasion some men there deliberately cheated him, leaving him with nothing during the hard days of the Depression. Dad was furious; he swore he'd never forgive those so-and-so's. He calmed down as he aged, though as far as I knew, he never forgave those who had hurt him. Dad had a lot to forgive, and a lot to be forgiven for.

The day after he died, my mother gave me his last will and testament. This is how it began:

> My last will: All of them owe me no more–I forgive them–may they forgive me.

I forgive them, and ask that they forgive me: What a perfect formula. For what better way is there to get forgiveness than to give the same? As it says in the Bible: "Forgive, and ye shall be forgiven."

Tending the Garden of Our Spirit

I am tormented in this flame.

Luke 16:24

Why is it so important to forgive? What did it matter if Dad did or did not forgive people for things that happened half a century before?

It's funny: We talk about "nourishing" our anger or "nourishing" a grudge, but these negative thoughts nourish nothing good. In fact, failure to forgive turns your spirit into a barren wasteland. No longer a fertile soil in which to grow joy and courage, the unforgiving spirit is piled high with trash called grudges and embarrassments, anger and rage.

Our spirit should be our Garden of Eden, our very source of life and joy, but failure to forgive strips the garden's soil of life. The trees of joy and courage and of love and belief should grow strong, but they wither in the harsh climate of unforgiveness.

Do we ever need anger? Is anger ever good? Yes. In the right circumstances and proportions, anger is useful. Anger can be a warning, like the whistle of a teapot. That whistle tells you that the water is boiling, it's time to turn down the heat and use the water for a purpose. If directed in a positive way, anger can sometimes be very helpful. Suppose the government is cutting off support money for the poor and elderly. Your anger over this can be a spur to action, getting you steamed up enough to make phone calls, write letters, form committees, raise money, and so on.

But suppose, like a too-hot teapot, you let the hot anger keep whistling. Soon the hot water boils over and ruins your spiritual garden, blisters your health and happiness. We must learn to use only that portion of anger necessary to move us to positive action, and set aside the rest by forgiving those who have harmed us. As you'll learn, however, forgiveness is only the first step.

With anger we banish ourselves from our spiritual Garden of Eden, turning the once-lush source of life, love, and joy into a barren wasteland. Forgiveness, and forgiveness alone, will turn our spiritual garden back into a land of milk and honey, a garden where life and exuberant health grow on every vine.

Forgiveness to Joy: Coming Full Circle

He that is slow to anger is better than the mighty.
Prov. 16:32

"Yes, I've forgiven that tramp who ruined my marriage," Marilyn solemnly assured me. "She'll get her punishment in hell."

Boy, I'm glad I'm not on this 48-year-old nurse's bad list. The "other woman" may or may not face judgment in the next life, but this nurse was certainly torturing herself with anger in this life. She told me she had forgiven: To forgive, as she defined it, is to "not want to throw the person in jail or kill her." That's not real forgiveness. Marilyn had grudgingly spooned a few drops of gall out of the bucket of bitter hatred seething in her spirit. That kind of "forgiveness" will torment Marilyn forever.

Real forgiveness is a deep and deeply spiritual process that begins with words, but goes way beyond. Even if we really mean it, saying "I forgive you" is only the beginning. Setting aside our anger is good, but we must still deal with the unhappy marks that have been made in our spiritual gospel. Joy–great joy–must be written into our book in order for the process of forgiveness to be complete. Why? Because forgiveness has as much to do with you and your health as it does with those who forgive.

True forgiveness envelops the spirit with energizing joy. "You mean I've got to be happy because somebody did me wrong?" an incredulous patient asked. The happiness I'm talking about has nothing to do with the wrong committed. The happiness I'm talking about has everything to do with the great *right* you create by coming full circle from anger to joy.

Forgiveness must come from deep within your spirit if the garden of your spirit is to remain green and healthy.

Saying the Words

It is an honor for a man to cease from strife.
Prov. 20:3

Most people think of forgiveness as a straight line: Someone offends me and I forgive them; you do to me and I do to you. But true forgiveness, the complete forgiveness that leaves your spirit filled with joy, is really a circle that brings you back to the starting point, your spirit stronger than before the hurt. True forgiveness turns a setback into a spiritual victory. Every wrong done to you is an opportunity to strengthen your spirit.

Begin circling from anger to joy by saying the words. Not *simply saying* the words, as Marilyn did, but *saying the words* and *meaning* them. Say "I forgive you." Even if you're mad as can be, even if you'd like to pop the person in the nose, even if he deserves it, say "I forgive you." When's the best time to say "I forgive you"? Right then and there. As soon as the offense is committed, or as soon as you learn about it, forgive him.

Say the words in person, immediately. Say them out loud. Say them with sincerity. "I'll say it but I don't feel it," many patients have replied. That's fine. Pretend you're sincere. Make believe you're a great actor doing the biggest scene of your career, with everything hinging on your believability. Most of all, you want to convince your spirit that you genuinely forgive, so that forgiveness may be written into your mental blueprint. When you feel the steam of anger whistling up and out of you, say:

I forgive you, freely and unconditionally.

Say the words over and over, out loud and to yourself, after the incident. If you didn't say them then, say them now. If 50 years have passed, it is still vital that you say the words. If the person has died, say the words. If you have already "punished" them or taken revenge, *say the words* of forgiveness. Then ask that you might be forgiven.

Said often enough, said with conviction, words eventually become the belief of the spirit. *Say the words* over and over, so that your spirit may come to forgive and progress to joy.

Drop Your "Guard Bones"

Saying the words is a great beginning, for this stops the pen of your mind from writing harmful thoughts into your mental gospel. But perhaps some angry garbage has already been dumped into the garden of your spirit. It must be gathered up and carted away immediately.

I learned a terrific lesson on how to release dangerous thoughts from a five-year-old boy who had been badly frightened in an amusement park horror house. A cute, very articulate little guy, he stood outside the horror house tapping his temples, explaining to his father: "I'm making my guard bones go down so the scary thoughts can get out."

"Guard bones?" his father asked, puzzled.

"They keep my thoughts in my head. I make them go down when there are bad thoughts in my head."

From the mouths of babes! Only five years old, yet he understood the need to get bad thoughts out of his head. It would be nice if all we had to do was let our "guard bones" down, but we haven't any guard bones, so we can't. No, wait a minute, I take that back. We *do* have guard bones that keep our angry thoughts trapped within our heads. What are these guard bones? First among them is pride, the feeling that we're too good to have to put up with things we don't like. Then there's resentment, that feeling of bitterness and indignation. Mixed in with the pride and resentment is embarrassment at having been bested, or made to look small in front of others. These are the "bones" that lock our angry thoughts in our heads.

The young boy had a simple solution: He tapped his temples until the guard bones dropped. Let's take a lesson from the little guy. When you're angry, say:

> I am forever relaxed and peaceful because my guard bones let my angry thoughts escape. I keep only the good thoughts in my head.

Close your eyes and gently stroke your temples with a downward motion, as if pushing your guard bones down. Keep your eyes closed as you recite your affirmations. Imagine those guard bones falling as negative thoughts flee your mind, escaping into the air, where they disappear forever. Encourage every negative thought to fly from your mind immediately.

> **Guard your good thoughts, coax them into your mind and entice them to stay. But let your bad thoughts escape immediately. Open the door, show them the way out.**

Turning Anger to Joy

Bless them which persecute you: bless, and curse not.
Rom. 12:14

I can still picture one patient of mine, a 52-year-old engineer, shaking hands with a man who had publicly criticized his work. As this engineer accepted the man's apology and said, "All is forgiven," he broke into a big smile. Later, I asked him why he had smiled. Was it because he had made the other guy eat crow? "No," the engineer explained. "I smiled because I make it a point to always replace anger with joy. Not being mad isn't enough. I want to be happy."

For a brief moment, just after our anger has fled, there's a tiny gap in our spirit: an opening, a potential. Unfortunately, we tend to replace our anger with, "See, I made you back down," or, "I forgave you but I don't like you," or, "That's the last time you get anything from me," or other such negative feelings. These thoughts are scar tissue forming over the wound of anger. As the scar tissue builds, our spirit loses its natural health and beauty, its elastic smoothness. As the scar tissue builds, we're left with a lumpy and dry spirit, one that has no resilience and has lost much of its beauty and health.

Don't let your spirit scar over. Don't fill the gaps with the "pleasure" of having won the point, for that is a false happiness which will scar your spirit. Fill the gaps immediately with the most joyful thoughts you can generate.

Rejoice in your great ability to forgive others, freely and unconditionally. Rejoice in the fact that you have removed a bit of tension from the world. Rejoice in your love of mankind. Rejoice because by forgiving, you have done a great favor for someone else. Rejoice because you are doing a great thing for yourself. Rejoice for the sake of rejoicing. Envelope your spirit in great happiness, if for no other reason than doing so is one of the greatest gifts you can give yourself. When you forgive, say:

> My spirit is soaring with wings of joy, as the pen of my mind fills my mental gospel with the good tidings of great joy.

Bless them that curse you: Do so, and you'll set a rainbow in the skies above the garden of your spirit.

> ***Say the words,*** **let down your "guard bones," and rejoice: These are the steps to true spiritual forgiveness and joy.**

Is It Ever OK to Be Angry?

> *I am merciful, saith the Lord, and I will not keep anger for ever.*
>
> Jer. 3:12

I tell my patients that there is nothing wrong with getting angry once in a while, for anger is a natural human emotion. Some anger now and then is a normal reaction to the stresses of life. And like pain, anger is a valuable warning sign. Pain tells us that we are injuring body tissue. Anger warns us that we are threatening spiritual tissue, we're coming into a spiritual danger zone. If we heed the warning and back off, then the anger has served its purpose.

"That's nonsense, Dr. Fox," a 53-year-old movie director practically sneered at me. "I'll tell you what anger is. Anger is a 'Damn the torpedoes! Full speed ahead!' response to challenges. Anger is that glorious emotion that ensures people do things the way I want them done. The right way!" he barked, pounding my desk with the palm of his hand.

I recently spoke at a national conference on addictions. While listening to the other speakers, I heard a highly respected psychologist tell the people in the audience that they must hold on to their anger, for anger is strength. Furthermore, she counseled, you should confront the person who offended you, demanding satisfaction. You must make them agree that you're right, she insisted.

Hold on to our anger? Would you hold on to your pain? If your hand were hurting, would it help you feel strong? Would you feel more alive with power if stomach cramps were doubling you over with pain, or if there were a jagged bloody gash on your leg?

Hold on to our anger? How can that help us? Is the spirit that is doubled over by the terrible cramps of rage able to find joy? Is the spirit that is rent almost in two by a bloody gash at peace with the world? What about the spirit covered over with scar tissue? Is this the spirit we want?

I'd rather be healthy than "right." Think about the times you've demanded satisfaction from someone. If you were their parent or boss, or otherwise held power over them, they probably apologized. But did they really mean it? Did your action increase their love for you, or your love for them? Did it bring any joy to the world? Or did the fire of your anger burn red-hot as you "put them in their place"? And how much of your spirit was scarred over as you wrote "Ha ha ha!" and "Boy, did I tell them!" into your mental book? Angry confrontations accomplish nothing except to flaunt your power, or expose your lack of power, over someone else.

> **Anger walls us off from joy and love. Anger saps our strength, starves the muscles of our spirit, and makes us very weak indeed. The strongest person in the world is the one who is happiest, who loves the most, and is loved most by others.**

Develop Your Spiritual Reflexes

God gave us bodies with wonderful built-in reflex mechanisms to help us avoid pain and tissue damage. When the doctor hits your knee with the little rubber hammer, your leg jerks forward automatically. People often laugh when I do this, saying, "Wow! Isn't that wonderful!" When we accidentally touch a hot stove, a reflex instantly jerks our hand away. Unfortunately we don't have spiritual reflexes to protect our spirit. But we can develop them.

When you feel the first pinprick of anger against the skin of your spirit, pull back. Close your eyes. With your mind's eye, picture someone gently touching the palm of your hand with a pin. See your hand pulling away. Again, watch your hand pulling away when the pin touches. It's automatic. Now picture a book, your mental gospel, resting on a table. A pin comes floating down toward your gospel, trying to prick your spirit with anger. Before the pin even touches the book, however, your book gently slides to the side. Again the pin comes down toward your mental book, and again the book slides easily to the side. Your mental gospel cannot be touched by anger. Tell yourself:

> Only positive thoughts are written into my mental gospel, and my mental book is filled with the good.

Write this scene into your mental book by continually seeing it and saying it. Make it the spiritual reflex that will keep you off the horns of anger.

> **Physical reflexes protect our bodies from physical damage. We can give ourselves spiritual reflexes to keep our spirit from pain.**

Can We Always Forgive?

Cease from anger, and forsake wrath.

Ps. 37:8

I don't know how many times people have told me that they absolutely cannot forgive so-and-so, never, and that's all there is to it, end of discussion. I remember one young man who came to me complaining of spastic colitis, chest pains, and headaches.

He threw a fit anytime someone mentioned his estranged wife. "If she did to you what she did to me," he would shout, waving his hands about wildly, "you'd hate her too."

Usually I don't ask, but this time my curiosity got the better of me. "What did she do?"

"I came home and found her in bed with another guy. She confessed that it wasn't the first time. All right, all right, so she liked someone else better, I could live with that. We had our lawyers arrange the exact 50/50 split of everything. I went away on business for two days, when I got back everything was gone. All the furniture, the rugs, the kitchen stuff, her clothes, *my clothes,* the stereo, TV, CD, the records, the videos, the tapes, everything! She took stuff that was of no value to her, like my clothes. She even took my old baseball mitt and my Little League trophy! That stuff wasn't worth anything, but it meant a lot to me. Then I started getting the credit card bills. She and her boyfriend had spent *$10,000 in two weeks!"* he spat out through clenched teeth, grinding fist into hand. Suddenly he clutched his stomach in pain.

We talked about forgiveness for a long time, as I tried to convince him that his pains and colitis were in large part due to his anger. (This was confirmed by my physical examination, review of his family and personal history, and the laboratory studies, which revealed no physical source for his problems.) "There's no way I can forgive her," he insisted. "It's impossible. Do you have an aspirin? My head is killing me."

I gave Brian aspirin for his headache and some medicine for his colitis. But I had no aspirin for his spirit, no pill that would mask his deep pain. Even if I had I would hesitate to use it, for "spiritual aspirin" would not solve the problem. Indeed, by masking the pain it would encourage him to hang on to his anger, to ignore the warning signs as the garden of his spirit withered beneath the emotional rubbish he was piling high.

Because of his colitis and constant diarrhea, blinding headaches, and chest pain, Brian wound up in the hospital. He lost 30 pounds; there were needles and tubes stuck into his arms; he was haggard and depressed. Still, he stubbornly refused to forgive his ex-wife. "There's no way," he insisted.

I was not Brian's primary physician, so I don't know what

eventually happened to this young man. I can only imagine the difficulties that lay ahead of him. And I can only wish that we could forgive as easily as we anger.

What is anger, that we seem to value it so much? It's not food, it's not health, it's not a happy memory, it's not gold. Anger is not pretty to look at, it makes nothing grow. Anger is the negation of everything we hold dear. Why do we hold so strongly to this terrible emotion?

As you'll see later on in this book, many of us are literally addicted to anger, we're hooked on the chemicals that flood our body during anger just as smokers are addicted to nicotine and drinkers to alcohol. We get the quick "rush" that may indeed feel good, but it passes quickly, leaving behind dangerous substances in the body that must be controlled before they harm our immune system, our heart, and the rest of our body. Unfortunately, in many of us, the harm cannot be contained.

"Spirituitis": A Killer Disease

. . . a man of understanding holdeth his peace.

Prov. 11:12

I've seen many patients whose diseases, I am convinced, were primarily caused by their anger. We talk about heart disease, cancer and stroke as being killer diseases. But these and other diseases, even accidents, are often the symptoms of a spirit taken over by anger and rage. The state won't let me put down "40 years of burning hot anger" or "30 years of self-loathing" as the cause of death on a death certificate, but that's what really causes many patients' cholesterol levels to rise so high and stay there; that's what keeps their bloodstream flooded with high-voltage chemicals that constantly shock the heart; that's what prompts the continual release of cortisonelike hormones that eventually wear down the immune system.

Anger, embarrassment, rage, jealousy, the desire for revenge: These terrible spiritual poisons cause a disease I call "spirituitis," the real killer disease in this country. With spirituitis we're predisposed toward heart disease, cancer, stroke, high blood pressure, elevated cholesterol, various and multiple addictions, accidents, and much more. Spirituitis is an epidemic that must be stopped. Forgiveness is the cure.

Spirituitis begins in the spirit but quickly spreads to the body, attacking the heart, lungs, immune system, circulatory system, and more. Caused by burning hot anger and jealousy, spirituitis is only cured by the soothing medicine called forgiveness.

If You Can Only Forgive a Little . . .

Agree with thine adversary quickly, whiles thou are in the way with him.

Matt. 5:25

Many patients tell me that they can't entirely forgive someone. "I can forgive him for this," they say, "but not the other thing he did."

If you can only forgive one little bit, do it. If you can only take the first step to complete forgiveness, that's a start. As a doctor I can tell you that even lancing a small part of an abscess in the body, draining even a little bit of the infection away, is helpful.

Each bit of anger in your spirit acts as a magnet, pulling in embarrassment, frustration, desire for revenge, and other garbage. Anger is the root of much negativity. Rip out the root of anger. Do it all at once if you can; if not, do it weed by weed.

If you have to forgive in steps, take the first step. If you can only rip one weed of anger from your spiritual garden, rip up that first weed. The next ones will be easier.

If You're Not Yet Ready to Forgive. . .

Grace, a 48-year-old mother of two, told me she wasn't ready to forgive her stepmother. "Dr. Fox, I don't care what you say. I agree with you intellectually, but emotionally I just can't forgive her."

Grace's mother had died when she and her two brothers were teenagers; their father remarried a few years later. The new wife, their stepmother, did everything possible to separate father and children. Although proper, she was cold to the children, and she whispered nasty things about them into their father's ear. By the time the children went to college the stepmother had built a wall between children and father. They rarely saw him after they left for college. Occasionally he'd call and they'd have dinner (without the stepmother), and they'd exchange Christmas greetings and birthday cards. That was all that remained of their relationship.

When Grace's father died, she and her brothers attended the funeral but said nothing to their stepmother. Neither did they visit or phone her afterward, or send a card. Grace was wracked with conflicting emotions. On one hand she wanted to send a card or pay a condolence visit to her stepmother. "She loved Dad, I know she's hurting." But on the other hand she was feeling angry and vengeful. "The old witch robbed us of our father. She couldn't have her own children so she wouldn't let Dad have his! Maybe I'll forgive her later, Dr. Fox. Maybe I won't."

If you are in a situation where you are not ready to forgive right away, that's all right. We do get angry, we can't always control our feelings. If we did have absolute control over our feelings, we wouldn't be the spontaneous, sometimes delightfully nutty people that we are. Sometimes our negative emotions get away from us.

If you feel you can't forgive, all I ask is that you don't close that door on forgiveness. Perhaps tomorrow or the next day, next week, next year, you'll be ready to forgive. Don't tell yourself that you'll never forgive, don't write that rigid message into your mental gospel. Instead, make a mental note that you'll think about forgiving later. Keep the doors open, for today's hate often becomes tomorrow's regret, and the next day's acceptance–sometimes even love.

Keep the door to forgiveness open, even if just a crack. Every so often, when passing by, take a look inside. One day all that forgiveness inside of you will look so enticing, you'll let some of it out.

Getting a Little Help

Many people have developed special ways to help themselves forgive. I learned about one of these from the Reverend Daniel Morgan of the Guidance Church of Religious Science in Los Angeles. While speaking about forgiveness, the Reverend Mr. Morgan confessed that he sometimes had trouble giving up the grudge. He told us his secret. He simply says to God: "God, I'm having trouble forgiving this person. But if you forgive them, I'll go along."

This is not a trick, it's a wonderful way of reminding yourself that God forgives everyone. If God does so, then it must be right.

Discount the Wrongdoer

Father, forgive them; for they know not what they do.
Luke 23:34

When angry, we can do things we'll be sorry for later, like punching someone in the nose, storming off the job, or telling a loved one to take a hike. I've found that discounting is a great way to steer clear of anger.

The idea is to discount the person in your mind, so what he or she says or does has no meaning, or, at least, no nasty meaning.

If someone threw a jar of urine on you, no doubt you'd be angry. But suppose you were reading a story to a young child sitting on your lap, when all of a sudden you noticed that warm, wet feeling on your leg. Would you be angry, would you scream at the child? No. You'd understand that you're dealing with someone who has not yet learned control. We don't get angry at those who cannot help themselves: We discount their actions.

Apply this idea to the boss who's screaming at you; to the driver who cut you off and stole your parking space; to the clerk who gives you a rough time; to the IRS agent who treats you like a criminal because your accountant made a minor error. Discount all the people who wrong you. Don't get angry at them, for they don't know what they're doing. They're stuffed full of their own imagined importance; they're under pressure; they're full of hatred, and so on. Don't let *their* problems write negatives into *your* mental gospel, don't let *their* shortcomings stop the sunlight from shining on *your* spiritual garden. Discount them. Think of them as you would a child who has soiled his pants.

> **Anyone who gives you a rough time is acting childishly. They may have power over you, you may have to do what they say, but you don't have to let them upset you. Keep your spiritual garden green by discounting them.**

Forgive the Neediest First

> *If he trespass against thee seven times in a day, and seven times in a day turn again to thee, saying, I repent; thou shalt forgive him.*
>
> Luke 17:4

Forgive everyone who asks forgiveness. Search through the files of your mind, pulling out the names of those whom you have not forgiven, or who have not asked for your forgiveness, and forgive them, too. But first, forgive the one who most needs your forgiveness–you.

When we haven't forgiven ourselves for our past errors, we feel guilty. Our self-esteem is low, perhaps we're embarrassed to face certain people. If not forgiving other people fills our spiritual garden with rubbish, not forgiving ourselves fills the garden of our spirit with a kind of radioactive poison that might linger for a lifetime.

As a physician, I've treated very wealthy jet-setters and movie stars, I've treated poor immigrants, and every type in between. Rich or poor, native-born or newly arrived, young or old, man or woman, we all risk being infected by the germ of guilt.

I see a lot of guilt, especially among my weight-loss patients. We meet regularly in my office, a group of overweight and newly slim people. The image of the jolly fat person is not a true one, for most obese people have a very poor self-image. The stories my group tells are sad, and filled with guilt. Guilt leads many of these people to become obese. Many feel guilty that they are so large. They feel guiltier than ever about the food they ate to assuage their guilt. Their self-esteem is often so low, they doubt their ability ever to do anything right.

One woman was particularly filled with self-doubt. "I've got a new boyfriend," she announced one day. "But I'll probably ruin this relationship in a couple of months like I did all the others."

"Is it always your fault?" another member of the group asked.

"Yes," she replied.

"Isn't it ever the guy's fault? Don't they ever do anything wrong?"

That idea never occurred to her. In her mind, she was a worthless person responsible for everything that went wrong. It was written into her mental gospel that nothing could go right for her. Her subconscious made sure that everything went wrong: She couldn't lose weight, she couldn't maintain a relationship, she was never happy at work. She simply could not imagine herself being happy and successful at anything.

As we dig into stories such as this, we invariably run into giant rocks of guilt. In people's minds, what they have done is the worst sin ever committed. To their minds, they are forever branded by their sin. Until they agree to let go of their guilt and self-hatred, all the diets in the world won't do much good. Not when they're intent on punishing themselves by destroying their bodies.

Earlier I said that failure to forgive others lead to spirituitis, a terrible scourge of mind and body. Failure to forgive yourself also causes spirituitis, even quicker. Forgive everyone, especially yourself. Forgive yourself for your errors and omissions, for the things you said and did, the things you planned. Forgive yourself for your shortcomings. Forgive yourself 70 times 7 times rather than let the garden of your spirit turn to stone.

Guilt is self-hatred; it is the inability to see yourself doing something right; it is the desire to be punished. Guilt is a thick black pen filling our mental gospel with words of self-hatred.

Error Is Not Failure

Though your sins be as scarlet, they shall be white as snow.
Isa. 1:18

I have treated many well-educated, sophisticated professional people who could not shake the feeling that they were terrible people, that they deserved to be punished because of something they did. This horrible feeling they carried around within themselves made them physically ill, destroyed their happiness, and often harmed them professionally as well.

Ted was a well-known actor, respected by his peers as a top-notch performer and a great guy. Ted treated everyone as though each were very special, from the messenger boy to the makeup girl to the director. Somehow he became addicted to cocaine, marijuana, uppers, downers, and more. Although it rarely affected his performance in the beginning, his personal relationships, however, did suffer, and he went through a string of girlfriends, friends, agents, and managers. The public couldn't tell, but Ted's colleagues soon realized that his acting was slipping. Eventually, he wound up in a hospital detox unit.

Ted went to the hospital voluntarily, but checked himself out a few days later. "They're all weirdo addicts there," he told his friends. "I'm not a weirdo."

Two of his friends brought him to my office. "Dr. Fox is going to help you. Do what he says," they ordered. I had seen this intelligent, well-spoken, good-looking man many times on television and in the movies, so I was totally unprepared to see the incoherent, haggard man they practically dragged in. It was obvious that talking to him at that point wouldn't help, so I immediately began treating him nutritionally using intravenous (IV) therapy. He thrashed around, cursed, vomited, but we managed to pull him together, enough so that he could talk coherently. I kept Ted in my office a good part of the day, working on him.

That evening, after the patients, nurses, and secretaries had left, Ted and I sat in my office. He said, "Doc, thanks for helping me. Thanks for not getting mad at me when I called you names. Was I violent?"

"Well, don't worry," I said, rubbing my side where he had accidentally kicked me while thrashing around. "It only hurts when I laugh." We both laughed.

"What do you want me to do, Dr. Fox? I can't go on like this, I'll do anything."

"First you have to admit that you're an addict."

But he couldn't make that admission. "Doc," he protested, "I'm not one of those weirdos. You know me, you've seen my work."

It took several sessions before he said, "Doc, you're right. I've been denying my problem. So has everyone around me. They're trying to protect me. All right, my life is unmanageable. But how come I'm still a good actor?"

"I've treated lots of professionals," I replied. "My observation, and that of other experts in this field, is that your professional skills are often the last thing to go. I've seen doctors perform surgery under the influence, lawyers handle cases, actors act. But eventually it all goes. Eventually all untreated addicts get severe disease, and finally die."

Ted agreed to follow the strong, nutritionally based program I set up for him. He exercised enthusiastically; in fact, every day he had a trainer come out to his home overlooking Beverly Hills. He seemed to be following the spiritual program I outlined for him, and friends said he was looking better and seemed to be happier than he had been in a long time. At the same time, his psychologist and psychiatrist were working to help him. They dredged up material from his childhood; they found out about his mother, his father, his teachers; they learned about his secret dreams, and so on. But every so often he'd slip. He'd go with the program for a month or two, then I'd hear that he'd gone back to the drugs. Soon after that he'd be in my office. "Doc, I need some more IV's," he'd say, even though I explained that they were not the ultimate solution, or "You've got to adjust my diet," or, "Maybe if we changed this part I could stick to the program better. I really want to, but. . ."

After the third or fourth time he had slipped and started using drugs again, I said, "There's something you haven't told me."

"Oh, no. You, of all people, I've told everything. I trust you the most."

"I've been a doctor for a long time. I've seen lots of people act in self-destructive ways. It's often because they have guilt feelings. They've done something they're ashamed of and they can't forgive themselves. So they punish themselves."

Ted insisted he didn't feel guilty about anything, and he wasn't holding back any information. He reviewed his program, made some minor changes, and he left. But he was back again the next week. "Tell me what's bothering you," I said. "I'm not a policeman, I'm not your conscience, I'm your doctor. I'm here to help you, without making judgments."

And then the story came gushing out. It seems that years ago, when he was a struggling actor seemingly on his way to nowhere, Ted had been befriended by an older actor. This older actor encouraged Ted, put a good word in for him with casting directors, helped him get auditions and a good agent, and so on. "He was a father to me. He never asked anything back. Nothing. He just liked to help people."

A few years later, when Ted had become successful, this old actor was having trouble getting work. "I didn't help him," Ted confessed softly, eyes to the ground. "Then he had a stroke, and I only visited him once. He ran out of money, and I didn't help him. I could have. I could have bought a whole hospital for him, but I didn't." Ted cried as he asked, "Why didn't I help him? What's wrong with me?"

I put my arm around him as he sobbed.

"Doc, what am I going to do! I think about this all the time. He's the only person who really put himself out for me, like a father, and I let him down and he died. Maybe if I had helped, he would be alive. What am I going to do?"

"Ted, you need to be forgiven. By God, by this man you wronged, and most of all, by yourself. God forgives them who ask for forgiveness. Go to your church, or your synagogue, or wherever you speak to God, and ask for His forgiveness." Ted agreed. "After you ask God for forgiveness, ask the man you wronged to forgive you."

"But he's dead."

"Do you know where he's buried?"

"Yes."

"Go down to his grave and ask him to forgive you. If he's the great man you described, I'm sure he'll forgive you."

"I can't, I feel so bad."

"Ted, you're a human being, like everyone else. We all make mistakes. You cared too much for yourself, and so you hurt this man. You can't bring him back by killing yourself. That's where you're headed, Ted, right into the grave."

Ted sobbed, "Have you ever heard of someone doing something this bad?"

"The Bible tells us to 'Go, and sin no more.' Ask God for forgiveness. Every religion has special prayers and other methods for forgiveness. Speak directly to God, or Creator, or Special Force, if you like. In any way that's appropriate for you, ask for forgiveness.

"Next, ask the person you've wronged for forgiveness. Don't ask to be let off the hook, let them know that you accept responsibility for what you've done. But ask for forgiveness. Even if you're sure they're not going to grant it, ask.

"Finally, make amends. Try to set the situation right. You can't bring the old actor back. You can't make amends to the dead, but you can do something for the living. Everything you wanted to do for your mentor, do for someone else. Find someone you can help, the way your friend helped you. Make amends to that great man by giving help and hope to someone else.

"It's OK to grieve, my friend, and to feel low. But let it pass. Admit your error, ask God for forgiveness, ask the person for forgiveness, make amends, and then forgive yourself and get on with life."

"Doc, I'll do it!" Ted promised. Two weeks later he was back in my office. "I admitted my error, I asked for forgiveness. You know what? As I stood over the grave asking for forgiveness, I could almost see him standing there in front of me saying, 'I forgive you.' He was a great guy. Then I went to a little theater in Hollywood where I heard there were some talented young actors. They're just like I was ten years ago: hungry. I got them new PR photos, I introduced them around, I got one of them a pretty good audition. I feel better about myself. Now what do I do?"

"Forgive yourself," I replied. "You've done everything possible, and I know you'll keep doing it. Now let go of your guilt. Replace it with awareness of limitations as a human being, and replace it with the joy that comes from helping others."

"Go and sin no more?" he asked, with a little smile.

"Keep helping others. Soon a lot of people will be talking about what a wonderful guy you are."

Ted kept helping others, and not just actors. He gave the gift of education, setting up a college scholarship for promising poor kids from his home town, and he personally taught several disadvantaged children how to read and write. Unfortunately, a little bit of guilt still lingers in him. We can learn to control and live with our unhappy emotions, we can even keep them in perspective, but we can't always banish them. That's the way God made us. We can't change how we are or what we did, but we can always make the best of it.

Error is not failure! Admit your mistake, ask for forgiveness from God and from the person you harmed. Make amends, then forgive yourself and get on with your life.

Make Me Aware, That I May Better Myself

Forgive us our sins.

Luke 11:4

All religions understand the importance of forgiveness and have special prayers and ceremonies for forgiveness. During Yom Kippur, the very holy Jewish Day of Atonement, the entire congregation confesses to its sins. In a remarkable series of prayers, the people ask:

> May it be Thy will, O Lord, our God and God of our fathers, to forgive us all our sins . . .
> For the sin which we have committed before Thee under compulsion or of our own will;
> And for the sin which we have committed before Thee by hardening our hearts;
> For the sin which we have committed before Thee unknowingly;

> And for the sin which we have committed before Thee with utterance of the lips. . .
> And for the sin which we have committed before Thee knowingly and deceitfully;
> And for the sin which we have committed before Thee in speech. . .

And so on. Shortly thereafter, the congregation chants a prayer called the "Ashamna," in which everyone states:

> We have trespassed, we have dealt treacherously, we have robbed, we have spoken slander, we have acted perversely, and we have wrought wickedness; we have been presumptuous, we have done violence, we have framed lies, we have counseled evil, and we have spoken falsely; we have scoffed, we have revolted, we have provoked, we have rebelled, we have committed iniquity, and we have transgressed. . .

"Why should I confess to all these things?" a friend asked when I showed him this prayer. "I haven't done these things." Why indeed? Why does every Jewish person around the world confess to sins most have not committed? I wondered about this, until I realized that in addition to being a prayer of forgiveness, this is a prayer of awareness.

"Make me aware of my sins," prays the congregation, *"so that I may better myself. Let me say that I have trespassed, and let me think on it."* I think most of us will find that we have trespassed—on someone's peace of mind, if not their property.

"Let me say that I have dealt treacherously, and let me think on it." Have we lied to hurt another person in a moment of anger? Have we colored the truth to protect ourself? I went through this remarkable prayer and found that I have committed many many sins, if not breaking the letter of the law, then certainly the spirit.

Why should we be made aware of all our sins, why rehash every little error? Because forgiveness begins with admitting the error. It is equally important, as we go through the list of errors and realize our wrongdoings, to realize that most other people have committed the same errors. We're humans, we're not perfect. Neither are we alone in our errors. The "Ashamna" concludes:

> Incline our hearts to forsake the path of evil, and hasten our salvation. Let the wicked forsake his way, and the unrighteous man his thoughts; let him return unto the Lord, and He will have mercy unto him. . . for He is ever ready to pardon.

We admit our errors, we ask for forgiveness from God, and we know in our hearts that forgiveness is granted–forgiveness from God. We must still make amends to our fellow men.

> **If God can forgive us for our sins, then certainly we can forgive others, and most importantly, forgive ourselves.**

Rx: Forgiveness and Making Amends

Today is Day Ten of Making Miracles, the Day of Forgiveness and Making Amends. This day is devoted to clearing the emotional rubbish from our spiritual garden so that the good may thrive.

Recite these affirmations throughout the day, today and everyday. Be sure to "see" each affirmation as you recite it.

Upon awakening: "Rejoice and Be Glad"
This is the day that the Lord hath made; I shall rejoice and be glad, be gladder than glad. I give myself permission to see all the happiness that is in my world, to think of the happiness, and to speak of the happiness. The Creator has filled the world with unlimited joy that is mine for the taking.

Morning: "It is Good to Give Thanks"
It is good to give thanks unto the Lord for making me the healthy, happy, and successful person I so richly deserve to be. I am open to receiving all the blessings of His abundant universe.

Noon: "Endless Enthusiasm"
The Creator has filled me to the brim with enthusiasm. I gladly and generously pour my unlimited enthusiasm over my every thought and action. Armed with endless enthusiasm, I find excitement and adventure in every day.

Afternoon: "Spiritually Minded"
To be spiritually minded is life and peace. I give myself permission to be as calm and serene as the quiet waters of a beautiful, still lake.

Evening: "A Merry Heart"
A merry heart is a good medicine. My heart and spirit and the gospel of my mind are filled with joy. I am full of the thoughts and things of health, happiness, and success.

When going to bed: "Put on the New Me"
Today was another successful step toward the new me. With enthusiastic anticipation and absolute certainty that I'll make even more progress tomorrow, and every tomorrow, I'm putting on the new me.

Recite each affirmation out loud, with enthusiasm. This daily menu sets up the daily minimum requirements of glad tidings. But I tell my patients to go beyond the minimum and recite their affirmations all day long: 5, 10, 20 times a day. You can't overdo it with affirmations!

In addition to your daily diet of affirmations, enter into the world of this special R_X for Forgiveness and Amends several times today, with energy and conviction.

Set aside some time today to sit in a quiet room, on a comfortable chair. Tell everyone that you do not want to be disturbed; take the phone off the hook. Close your eyes. With your mind's eye, picture a circle painted on the ground. You're standing on the circle. You take a big step along the painted line, saying, as you do:

I forgive you, freely and unconditionally.

As you say this you know that you are forgiving everyone who ever wronged you—and you're forgiving yourself. With your mind's eye, see yourself taking a second step along the circle, saying:

> I am forever relaxed and peaceful because my "guard bones" keep only the good thoughts in my head.

Put your hands gently on your temples as you say this, and see yourself, with your mind's eye, putting your hands on your temples as you stand on the circle. Feel your "guard bones" dropping to allow all the unhappy thoughts in your head to fly into the air and disappear. Now take your third step along the circle. This last step takes you back to where you started. See that big smile on your face as you say:

> My spirit is soaring on wings of joy!

Now see a beautiful book resting on a table: This is your mental gospel. The book is open to a clean white page. A hand—your hand—is writing good tidings of great joy into your mental book as you say:

> The pen of my mind always fills my mental gospel with the good tidings of great joy. Only positive thoughts are written into my mental gospel, and my mental book is filled with the good. Filled with forgiveness, I am joyfully optimistic and enthusiastically open to enjoying all the great things in my world.

Forgiveness is one of the strongest of the Ten Pillars in the Making Miracles program. I can't emphasize enough how important it is to forgive yourself and others freely and unconditionally. When you forgive others you aren't saying that you're wrong, and you aren't saying you agree with what they did. When you forgive, you're telling yourself that you will not allow anyone else to harm your spirit.

One of my patients is an uneducated immigrant who works in a factory somewhere in East Los Angeles. He tells me that the bosses there give everyone a rough time. They especially love to give it to the illegal immigrants, insulting them, giving them the worst possible jobs to do, constantly threatening to turn them over to Immigration.

"I've got to put up with this because I can't get another job," my patient told me in his broken English. "They can push my body around and make me do things, but they cannot make me angry. No matter what they do I forgive them, because otherwise I would make myself sick with my anger. I can't change them, but I can change myself."

"What do you do with your anger?" I asked, wondering if he held it inside, or let it turn to depression and despair.

"I give it to God," he told me. "Every day when I leave work I look up and say, 'Here's my anger, God. I can't keep it. Will you get rid of it for me?' And He does."

We're told that it is good to love our enemies, to bless them that curse us, to do good to those who persecute us. That great forgiving attitude, which the immigrant worker has so much of, is one of the strongest medicines we can give to ourselves.

Day 11

MAKING DREAMS COME TRUE

. . . the dream of yesterday is the hope of today and the reality of tomorrow.

Robert Goddard

As a commissioner for the California State Board of Medical Quality Assurance, it is my periodic pleasure to help administer oral tests to doctors applying for a license to practice medicine here in California. During one of these examinations, I was paired with a professor from the UCLA medical school as a fellow examiner. This man–let's call him Dr. Bart–was very dour, and downright unpleasant to the mostly young doctors taking the tests. He spent the day complaining about, well, about everything. At one point, for example, he said, "I'm required to publish a bunch of worthless papers if I want to retain my professorship, I have to teach a bunch of unappreciative students, and I spend time doing research that has no meaning."

Finally, during the lunch break, I asked him, "What's really bothering you?"

"Existing," he replied.

As we continued to talk I learned that Dr. Bart was unhappy with his job, his wife, and his children. "I don't even know why we had kids. I suppose we had them just because that's what married people are supposed to do. I loved my wife years ago, but that wore off. And I find her friends a bunch of egotistical know-it-alls."

Dr. Bart told me that he had to struggle to get himself up in the morning, and push himself through the day. Then he struggled to "convince myself to go home at night. There's nothing I look forward to, there's no one I want to see, nothing I want to do, no place I want to go."

"Why did you become a doctor?" I said.

"My parents wanted me to."

"How did you manage to become a professor at one of the greatest universities in the United States?"

"It just happened."

"Isn't it exciting to hold such a prestigious position?" He shook his head disdainfully. "Well, surely you get satisfaction from influencing our future doctors?" Again, he shook his head. "What are your dreams?" I asked.

"All I want to do is get through the day," he replied, shrugging. "I had dreams when I was a kid," he said, sounding a little wistful, I thought. "Some things I wanted to do. But that's silly, you can't spend your life dreaming dreams that won't come true. You do what you have to do. I got married, I had kids, I became a doctor, then a professor, I serve on the important committees, I conduct the experiments, and I write the papers–all because I have to. Today I do what I have to do today; tomorrow I'll do what I have to do tomorrow. That's life."

"How can you survive without having dreams?" I asked, amazed.

"Dreams are for fools," he snapped angrily.

"No," I shot back. "Dreams–positive dreams–are for everyone."

After a little more back and forth he said, "Arn, I like the way you talk to people. Not only the people we're testing but everyone. You're positive about everything. I don't like being such a grouch. How can I change?"

"Dream of what might be." He started to protest but I raised my hand. "Hear me out. Start imagining yourself being nice to people. Put a picture of you being nice in your head. Keep it there. Look at it every day. Dream of being a nice person. Dream how great it'll be when you like everyone, and everyone likes you. If you want something, dream it–then do it."

We talked some more, then went back to testing. I see Dr. Bart at the tests every so often. He's definitely changed; he's happier, and he treats everyone nicer than he ever did. Dr. Bart tells me that he still has to churn out papers to keep his professorship, but he accepts that as a fact of life. Meanwhile, he is working on the great paper about something he believes will really help people. Dr. Bart says that teaching is more interesting now, for he looks upon it as an opportunity to do good for the student, and for the world. As the Greek philosopher said: It's more important to write on the hearts of people than on parchment. "Everything's not peaches and cream yet," he remarked. "My relationship with my wife is better, but not as good as I'd like it to be. I've got a long way to go, and I've got to remember to work on my improvement program every day, or I slide back. But it is working, and that's no dream."

Positive Dreams

Dreams–positive dreams–are for everyone. What are these positive dreams? Positive dreams are goals, visions, hopes, and desires born of love and joy. Positive dreams are the exciting things you want to do, the beautiful places you want to go, and the great things you want to be.

Positive dreams are based on the Golden Rule, the Ten Commandments, and other loving writings, so these dreams can never hurt others. In Phil. 4:8 it is written:

> Whatsoever things are true,
> Whatsoever things are honest,
> Whatsoever things are just,
> Whatsoever things are pure,
> Whatsoever things are lovely,
> Whatsoever things are of good report;
> If there be any virtue, and if there be any praise,
> think on these things.

If there be any virtue and if there be any praise, *dream* of these things. That's what positive dreaming is.

Positive dreams are visual statements of our spirit's desires. When we dream of what might be, that's really our spirit talking to us, saying, "Let's go!"

Positive dreams are our spirit's way of showing us how wonderful our future can be.

Positive dreams are our goals; they're the places we want to go, the people we want to see, the things we want to do, and the things we want to be.

Positive dreams are our spirit's way of telling us that everything's going to be great!

Dreams are not just images we "see" while asleep; dreams are our goals, our aims, the things we greatly long for and desire. Dreams are visions of what might be.

People who dream positive dreams have talkative spirits. Are you prepared to hear what they say?

Positive dreams are statements of loving and joyful desire. Positive dreams are motivations to make our lives as great as they possibly can be.

Learn to Be a Great Listener

Dreams are the touchstones of our characters.

Henry David Thoreau

Our word "dream" comes down to us from the ancient roots of the English language. Its meanings include mirth, joy, music, and noise. Positive dreaming is by nature joyful and musical, for when we dream of the great things that might be, we get that great endorphin life, we're filled with happy anticipation, we feel like singing and shouting to the world. Simply *dreaming* that you will be healthy strengthens your immune system, along with the rest of your body, in the fight against disease. Likewise, *dreaming* that you will be happy can also tilt the biochemistry of your body in favor of happiness. How about *dreaming* that you'll be successful? That also works, for positive dreams can be written into your mental gospel just as positive words can be, and with the same results.

Dreams are not idle visions. Properly managed, positive dreams become reality. Like our words, our dreams become our thoughts, our actions, our habits. Listen to a man's dreams; listen, and you'll hear his character speak.

I used to know a guy who was always reaching for the stars. Frank was loaded with dreams; he was going to invent a new kind of car engine, he was going to master French and Italian, he wanted to learn to sail and climb mountains. When he became mired in a mid-level engineering job working for a large defense contractor, he began to dream of opening his own firm–and he did. Worried about the increase in violent crime here in Los Angeles, he dreamed of being able to defend himself–four years later he was awarded a black belt in karate.

"The funny thing is, Arnold, when I dream about something enough, then I know it's going to happen. It's as if my dreams are my cheerleaders, cheering me on to the goal," he explained. "If I can dream something, I know I can do it."

Frank liked to say that his dreams never failed him. "When I was a little kid my parents made me take swimming lessons. God, I was petrified of the water! I cried the whole time. Then I started having a dream at night. I'd see myself swimming underwater, like a fish. There I was swimming around underwater, feeling great. Then I'd come up for air, and go back under. The next day I told my teacher I was going to swim underwater–and I did it! After that, swimming on the surface came easily. Seeing myself comfortable in the water made it come true. Dreaming was my way of telling myself what I wanted to happen. And that's when I first noticed the power of my dreams."

Frank listened carefully to his dreams, for he understood that his dreams were his spirit talking. One day, while he was driving home, his car was hit by a drunk driver. When he woke up in the hospital, he patted his body to make sure everything was still there. It was all there, but he had no feeling below his waist. His doctors said he would spend the rest of his life in a wheelchair.

Frank was devastated. "I seriously considered killing myself," he later confessed. "I knew all the intellectual arguments about how valuable life was, and that because I'm an engineer I don't need my legs to work, and instead of jogging I could do wheelchair races. I knew that, but. . .Christ! I lost my legs!"

Mourning deeply for the loss of his legs, his mobility, his very image of himself, Frank moped about in the hospital, recovering from his injuries very slowly. This once active go-getter who constantly sought out new challenges barely cooperated with the physical therapists and others who tried to help him adjust to the facts.

"My family was very supportive, and I went back to work. Being in a wheelchair didn't hurt business any, we just had to move some furniture around, get me a new desk, and fix up the bathroom. I felt hollow, like there was nothing inside of me for the longest time. My dreams were all negative. I'd see myself sitting alone while everyone else was dancing, or I'd imagine getting mugged in my wheelchair. That one scared me a lot. There are jerks out there who'd love to mug some helpless sap in a wheelchair.

"Then, I don't know, maybe six, seven months later, after I got out of the hospital, I had this crazy dream. I was going over some papers at my desk, and all of a sudden I had this image of myself, alone, wheeling down a dark street at night, and this guy jumps out of nowhere to mug me. He thinks I'm helpless so he gets close and *boom*–I get his arm, twist it around, grab his hair and he's mine.

"I had that dream a couple of times that day and I got to wondering. Is there wheelchair karate? If not, why not? Over the next couple of days I figured out some moves I could do from my chair, then I started to see myself teaching a wheelchair karate class. I got the names of some people in wheelchairs and I called them up. Now I teach three or four people wheelchair karate every weekend. I don't feel so hollow anymore.

"Then I started seeing myself running a wheelchair road race, you know, those 10K's they have on the weekends? I trained, then raced at UCLA. God, those hills are steep! But I did it. And you know, I saw some racers in wheelchairs who were a lot worse off than I was.

"Being in a wheelchair isn't the same as having working legs, but I've still got my dreams–those cheerleaders that cheer me on across the finish line. So I cross the line sitting down. I'm still a winner."

In a sense, dreams are predictions of what could be. Do they come true? That depends largely on you.

Dealing with Negative Dreams

Our positive dreams are visions, they are statements we make to ourselves describing what we want to do and be. What happens when our dreams are negative?

Cynthia was grossly obese at 34, and the owner of a busy restaurant in West Los Angeles. She came to see me hoping I could help her lose weight. She had already tried gastric stapling (surgery to make her stomach smaller), jaw-wiring, total fasts, and "52 diet book diets." She did lose weight on the diets, but quickly gained it back. Wiring her jaw shut was not helpful: She drank milk shakes through a straw. Having her stomach stapled over so she couldn't eat much didn't work well, either: She ate so much, the staples burst.

After performing a thorough physical examination, reviewing her personal and family history, studying the reports her other doctors sent to me, and checking the results of her laboratory studies, I sat down with the woman in my office. Instead of launching into a discussion of my findings and recommendations, I asked her, "What are your dreams?"

She looked at me as though I were speaking Martian. "What?"

"What are your dreams?"

"What has that got to do with anything?"

"It may help explain why you have difficulty remaining trim. Tell me, what do you dream about?"

"At night?"

"Any time. Night dreams, daydreams, long dreams, short dreams, detailed dreams, half-baked ideas flying through your mind, anything."

"I dream I'm not so fat."

"OK," I said, marking it down. "What else?"

She thought and thought. "That's it."

"What do you see when you dream you're not so fat?"

"I see my fat self looking fat in the mirror, not being able to fit into my regular-people's clothes, having to squeeze myself so I can get the door shut in the bathroom stall, people laughing at me. Some dream, huh?"

"Those are some pretty negative dreams. A negative dream is no dream at all, not in the sense that I think of dreams."

"So what do I do?" she asked unhappily.

"Dream positive dreams, and work to make them come true."

"But I've tried every gimmick and I've been on every diet in the world," she protested.

"Without the dream," I answered. "You dieted without the dream. Not the image of how bad it is now, but how good it can be. Without the dream of how great it will be, it's nearly impossible to slim down. When you have no dream, the future does not beckon. When you have no dream, every little step forward seems as difficult as climbing Mount Everest. When you lack the dream, there is little reason to make any effort, because every tomorrow looks as bleak as today."

I leaned forward in my chair, excited by these thoughts pouring out of me. "Your dream is your destination, and it's more. The dream charges you with desire, it gets you going by kicking you in the pants. Your dream gives you the energy and enthusiasm to map out a strategy. Your dream is your cheerleader, waving those pom-poms, jumping up and down, cheering you on to victory. And when the going gets tough, your dream is the shot in the arm that keeps you going.

"Dreams are blueprints to our future. So long as we keep the dream alive, we know what we want to be, and what we must do."

"I know what I've got to do," Cynthia objected. "It's pretty obvious to anyone who looks at me."

"It's obvious to your intellect but not to your heart, not to your spirit. When your spirit catches a dream, it's all but accomplished. But until then, you're acting without spirit. Spiritless action is all but doomed to failure. You'll be very frustrated by your failure. You'll come to consider yourself a failure in life and your self-esteem will shrink. I've seen this happen many times.

"Nondreamers want so much–as we all do–but they can't get it. They lack the dream to tell them where to go, to give them the energy to get there. And so they settle for anger and bitterness, and they take their frustration out on everyone else. The Bible says that where there is no vision, the people shall perish. When we lose our personal visions or dreams, our spirit shrivels. And with every bit of our spirit that shrinks, a bit of us dies.

Luckily, we can always help our spirit to grow again."

Having no dreams, or having negative dreams, invites failure, anger, bitterness, and frustration.

Seeing Is Believing

"Dreams are not cotton candy of the mind. Dreams are very real," I told Cynthia. "We can touch dreams for we are our dreams.

"Put your hand to your chest," I instructed Cynthia. "Do you feel yourself?"

She nodded.

"Do you feel the warmth of your body, do you feel your heart beating?"

She nodded.

"There's your dream, your great, enthusiastic, positive dream of what can be. What *will* be. Inside of you is the beautiful, healthy, trim woman you want to be. It's there, it's always been there, in your spirit. But unless you can see it, it will remain hidden, buried within you."

"Wait a minute," she said. "First you said that my dreams are my spirit telling me what I want, now you're saying that my dreams are in my spirit."

"Your spirit is you," I replied, "and you are your spirit. Everyone, no matter how angry and cynical he might be, has dreams. The spirit is the keeper of our dreams. Some of us can't see within our spirit, can't hear our spirit. Others won't."

"Why not?" she asked.

"Because they're afraid. They've built so many brick walls around themselves, they're desperately afraid of seeing who they really are and what they really want. If they did let those dreams out, all their walls would crumble. They're so used to hiding behind their walls, they wouldn't know what to do without them."

"What about people who can't see their dreams?"

"There are many reasons why some people can't see or hear their spirit. Often it has to do with the way their parents taught them to look at life. Many parents train their children to be 'realistic', to focus too much on the negatives in life, to ignore their 'foolish dreams'."

All of a sudden Cynthia began to cry. I was surprised, for she had seemed so tough, so cynical. But you can never tell when you'll find the thing that touches people's emotions.

"I want to be able to see my dreams, Dr. Fox," she said with a soft voice, wiping her eyes. "I'm not afraid, I just can't see them. How can I see them?"

Rx: Believe

What can we do to help ourselves see our dreams? Begin by realizing that you have dreams. We all dream; that's part of being fully human. No matter how much we ignore it, our spirit is always looking to the future, dreaming of how great it can be. Everybody has a dream. Tell yourself–everyday–that you have a dream! Say:

> I have a dream! There are things I can't wait to do, there are places I can't wait to go! Every time I think about the future, I see a great tomorrow for myself!

Every time you say this to yourself, out loud with energy and enthusiasm, your words are floodlights turned on and illuminating the darkness of your spirit. Your positive words will illuminate your dreams.

Rx: See

> *Lord, I pray Thee, open his eyes, that he may see.*
> 2 Kings 6:17

First, believe. Next, devote time every day to positive dreaming. Set aside some time today to sit in a quiet room, on a comfortable chair. Tell everyone that you do not want to be disturbed; take the phone off the hook. Close your eyes. With your mind's eye, picture your book, your mental gospel, lying closed on a table. It's that thick, leather bound book that contains everything written into your spirit. A hand–your hand–opens the book to a blank page, picks up a glistening golden pen and begins to write. What is your hand writing in the gospel of your mind? Your dreams. All your joyful, happy, enthusiastic, loving dreams.

With your mind's eye, see yourself slim and healthy. There's a big smile on your face as you admire yourself in the mirror. And you're wearing those slim, stylish clothes you've always wanted.

Or with your mind's eye, see yourself standing comfortably in front of a group of people, confidently and forcefully, but pleasantly, explaining your views or delivering a speech. Look at your audience: They're listening carefully, nodding in agreement. They respect and admire you and your views.

Picture yourself as your boss tells you that you're getting a promotion. And listen as the boss tells you that he's got a lot of faith in you, that he knows you can do it.

With your mind's eye, watch what happens when someone tries to take advantage of you. Firmly yet politely, you stand your ground, confident in the knowledge that you can always stand up for yourself.

See yourself studying for the big test. There you are at your desk, easily going through your material, taking notes. See yourself again at your desk, studying. Two hours have passed and you're still at your desk, concentrating, taking it all in. Now see yourself in the test room, confidently writing out the answers. Then see yourself later, when you get the results. See that big smile spread across your face when you learn that you passed with flying colors!

See yourself with your loved one, sitting close as you say the things you've always wished you could say. See your loved one's face: He or she understands, and loves you more than ever.

See yourself climbing the mountain or hitting the ball, see yourself doing all the great things you've always wanted to do, having the terrific things you want to have, being the best possible person you can be.

As you see the great thing you desire happening, say:

All my dreams are coming true! Whatever I can see and believe, I can achieve!

With your mind's eye, see your hand writing in your mental book. Your hand has just finished writing your dreams into your mental gospel. See the pages and pages of dreams written there. Your spirit is filled with dreams.

Rx: LISTEN

A wise man will hear. . .

Prov. 1:5

Believe that you have dreams, and practice seeing them; now listen carefully to your spirit. In those unguarded moments, when a little glimmer of a dream peeks out, speaks out, look at it, listen to it! Don't turn away to think of "real" things, focus on your dreams. Rather, don't focus, for it can be difficult to force a dream. Relax, and let your spirit speak to you.

Remember: Positive dreaming is not wasting time. Positive dreaming is a conversation between you and your spirit. A conversation? Absolutely! Feel free to talk back to your spirit. When you can easily positively dream, change the dreams around, invent your own, fantasize. When we fantasize, we're often working a problem out, trying something on for size.

If you dream that you've climbed most of the way up a mountain, but you feel you should go higher, change the script. See yourself climbing all the way up. See yourself standing on the top of the mountain, above the clouds, in the cool, clear air. Converse with your spirit. Rewrite your dreams: change the lines, make your character smarter, more talented, more articulate, better looking, whatever you like. They're your dreams, your life. Write your dreams exactly the way you want them to be. See those dreams over and over again, for as you do, you're rehearsing the way you want to be, feel, think, walk, talk, and act. That mental rehearsal is very, very important. As you listen to your spirit, as you write your life's script exactly the way you want it to be, say:

> My conversations with my spirit give me direction and drive. When my spirit catches hold of a dream, I'm unbeatable!

Rx: Act

> *Be rich in good works.*
>
> 1 Tim. 6:18

Believe, see, listen; now act. Dreaming is your spirit's way of helping to see what you want. Now that you know, make it a reality. To dream is to desire, and desire is half of accomplishment–more than half, much more. They say that necessity is the mother of invention. I say that desire is the parent of achievement. Want something enough, want it so bad that you can almost taste it. That great desire will focus your energies and spur you to action. So, when you feel the great desire for something good, act! Say to yourself, out loud and with conviction:

> Energized with the power of spirit, every day I work to achieve my great, good goals. Every day is a giant step forward, another celebration of the unlimited power of my spirit.

Believe, see, listen, and act. Dream, and make all your great dreams come true.

The Greatest Dream

> *. . . if one advances confidently in the direction of his dreams, and endeavors to live the life which he has imagined, he will meet with a success unexpected in common hours.*
>
> Henry David Thoreau

When I ask my patients what their dreams are, I get every kind of reaction, from stunned silence to eager statements about wanting to save the world. People ask me which dreams are worthwhile. I tell them that every great dream is worthwhile, from the grandest to the most modest.

Your dreams may be about things that concern you: Losing weight, going back to school, learning to play golf, joining a social organization, getting a new job, moving to your own home, finding that someone special, learning to like yourself, winning the Nobel prize.

Your dreams may involve a bigger universe: Work to pressure the government to clean up the environment, work for world peace.

Your dreams may be immediate: Lose ten pounds by summer, do well at next month's job review, give the beggar five dollars tomorrow morning, stand up to that so-and-so at work next time, help the children with their homework every day, be able to run a mile by next month.

Your dreams may be long-term: Teach your children strong values, become president of the firm in 15 years, get your candidate elected next time around, read 20 books a year for the next 50 years, run 100 marathons, visit X number of countries in the 1990s, keep your marriage intact and loving until your golden anniversary.

Your dreams may be large scale: Raise $1 billion to feed America's hungry, climb Mount Everest, design an automobile engine that gets 150 miles to the gallon.

Your dreams may be of a smaller scale: Help one child to succeed by teaching him or her how to read.

Your dreams may be grandiose: Win the $50 million lottery and marry your favorite movie star, or be discovered and become a movie star yourself.

Your dreams may seem more realistic: Work hard to improve your relationships, help one person get a job, take two strokes off your golf game.

We do best when we have all kinds of dreams: short and long term, realistic and "far out," very personal and worldwide in scope. Usually, one or more of our dreams call to us loudly, while the others speak more quietly. Heed them all. Keep those difficult, long-term goals in sight, even as you achieve the short-term and easier ones. Those long-term goals help keep you on track through life.

Any positive dream that gives you something to look forward to, something to work for, is a great dream. While all our positive dreams make us happy, I've found that doing for others makes us feel great. That's why I tell my patients that some of their dreams should be "outer-directed," that is, dreams of helping others. There's nothing like a warm smile of thanks for righting an injustice to get our endorphins flowing and make us feel great about ourselves.

But the greatest dream of all is simply this: To be the best person you possibly can be, to be happy, and to give the next generation the gift of love and joy.

Long-term or immediate, personal or all-inclusive, realistic or "far out," all positive dreams are great.

Rx: Dreams

The eyes of the blind shall be opened, and the ears of the deaf shall be unstopped.

Is. 35:5

Today is Day Eleven of Making Miracles, the Day of Dreaming and Doing. This day is devoted to listening carefully to our spirit, then making our dreams come true. You've already been given your special Rx for Dreaming and Doing. Enter into the world of your Rx often today, learn to dream and do throughout your life.

In addition, recite these affirmations throughout the day, today and every day. Be sure to "see" each affirmation as you recite it.

Upon awakening: "Rejoice and Be Glad"
This is the day that the Lord hath made; I shall rejoice and be glad, be gladder than glad. I give myself permission to see all the happiness that is in my world, to think of the happiness, and to speak of the happiness. The Creator has filled the world with unlimited joy that is mine for the taking.

Morning: "It is Good to Give Thanks"
It is good to give thanks unto the Lord for making me the healthy, happy, and successful person I so richly deserve to be. I am open to receiving all the blessings of His abundant universe.

Noon: "Endless Enthusiasm"
The Creator has filled me to the brim with enthusiasm. I gladly and generously pour my unlimited enthusiasm over my every thought and action. Armed with endless enthusiasm, I find excitement and adventure in every day.

Afternoon: "Spiritually Minded"
To be spiritually minded is life and peace. I give myself permission to be as calm and serene as the quiet waters of a beautiful, still lake.

Evening: "A Merry Heart"
A merry heart is a good medicine. My heart and spirit and the gospel of my mind are filled with joy. I am full of the thoughts and things of health, happiness, and success.

Recite each affirmation out loud, with enthusiasm. This daily menu sets up the daily minimum requirements of glad tidings. But I tell my patients to go beyond the minimum and recite their affirmations all day long: 5, 10, 20 times a day. You can't overdo it with affirmations!

DARE TO DREAM

I like the dreams of the future better than the history of the past.

Thomas Jefferson

Martin Luther King, Jr. had a dream. So had all the great people of history: philosophers, inventors, kings, rebels, lovers, writers, athletes, explorers, teachers, scientists. Our country was founded by dreamers who risked everything to come across an ocean, then later challenged the mighty British Empire. And parents—parents are dreamers, perhaps the greatest dreamers of all.

Dare to dream—way beyond your reach. It's not foolhardy, it's your spirit's way of telling you that you want to extend the boundaries of your world. We're all much more talented, stronger, and more creative than we allow ourselves to believe we are. Dreams help us take the handcuffs off our talents so that we might reach for the stars. Were the Wright brothers foolhardy because they dreamed man could fly? Was Thomas Edison foolish for dreaming that he could light the night? Was Harry S. Truman a foolish dreamer, "wasting" his time campaigning against Thomas E. Dewey? Most of our "impossibles" are possible, at the right time, given the right preparation, the correct approach, and maybe even a dash of luck. But if we never try. . .

Dare to dream! You know what I dream about? One of my dreams is that someday I'll be in a book like this. And it'll say, "Was Edison a foolish dreamer? Were the Wright brothers foolish dreamers? Was Truman a foolish dreamer? Was Arnold Fox a foolish dreamer for believing that everyone had the potential to be enthusiastically joyful, vibrantly healthy, and very successful?"

Dare to dream! Many people don't dream because they're afraid to fail. Is it smart to hide safely in a little dark shell? Rough Rider President Teddy Roosevelt didn't think so. One of his favorite poems expresses his philosophy:

> Far better it is to dare mighty things
> To win glorious triumphs
> Even though checked by failures
> Than to take rank with those poor spirits
> Who neither enjoy much
> Nor suffer much
> Because they live in the grey twilight
> That knows not victory or defeat.

Dare to dream! Be part of a crusade, reach for the stars. Take spirit in your dreams, and remember that you belong to everyone and everyone belongs to you.

Dare to dream. The dream is the impetus, the seed planted in the garden of your spirit. Water the seed with action, and you're on your way!

As Eleanor Roosevelt said, "The future belongs to those who believe in the beauty of their dreams."

Day 12

"I Shall Please": The Medicine of Belief

There is one thing stronger than all the armies in the world, and that is an idea whose time has come.

Victor Hugo

When I was a premed student at the University of Pennsylvania and newly married, my wife, Hannah, and I lived in a tiny house in South Philadelphia. It was so small you could hardly turn around in it. One day I was suddenly struck by a flaming pain in my side that doubled me over in agony. One after another the pains shot up and down my side, as though I were being whipped by a razor-tipped cat-o'-nine-tails. Hannah helped me upstairs and into bed, then called our doctor.

Dr. Cooper had been my family's physician ever since I can remember. He was a very kindly man who spent long hours walking up and down the streets of South Philly, visiting the patients too ill to go to his office, sitting by their bedsides, listening to their hearts beating, taking their pulse and temperature, administering medicines, holding their hands, reassuring them. Dr. Cooper was wise and kind. He cared so much, he was a part of every family. He gave the same compassionate care to everyone, even to those who could not pay him in those Depression days. To us, he was an angel sent by God to be His presence in our little neighborhood. I named my son Barry for Dr. Cooper, and I'm sure many others named their children for him as well.

As we waited for the doctor to come that day, I lay in bed clutching my side, wondering what terrible disease I had, my every thought interrupted by a fresh stab of pain. Hannah held my hand, my breathing was rapid and shallow. It seemed hours before we heard the doorbell ring, though the clock said only 30 minutes had passed. The pain was so terrible I wanted to cry. I couldn't wait for him to climb the 13 steps up to our second story bedroom and take my pain away. And I counted his steps: One, a whiplike pain lashed me back to front. Two, 3, 4, the comforting footsteps announcing impending relief from my pain. Five, 6, 7, again a pain whipped into me, a smaller pain, without the sting of its predecessor. Eight, 9 steps, only 4 more to go. I noticed that my breathing was slower and deeper, more normal, not the rapid-fire shallow gasping it had been. Ten, 11, I could feel the pain subsiding with each of his steps. Twelve, 13, and a few more steps to bring the doctor through our tiny hallway and into the bedroom. As I watched him stride to my bedside, so confident, warm, I wondered what had happened to the pain. Where had it gone? Once again, the presence of the man we loved and trusted so–his mere presence–was a medicine of its own.

A Lesson Never to Be Forgotten

It turned out that I was suffering from a kidney stone, one that I quickly passed. The stone was soon forgotten, but I learned a great lesson in healing that day. I learned that the medicine of the mind is as powerful as the medicines of man. I forgot that same lesson as the years passed, dazzled as I was by the wonders of medical science we medical students, interns, and residents came to master. It's a funny thing: We doctors proudly proclaim ourselves the originators, interpreters, and applicators of medical science. We can tell you that our minds are open to everything that might spur healing, but in truth we are wedded to our own very narrow definitions of science and medicine and healing. We insist that we are absolutely objective and willing to change as we learn, but the fact is we have our biases and prejudices just like anyone else. We like our position atop the health-care heap, so we're reluctant to accept ideas not born among our own ranks. As a result our horizons remain limited, our ideas inbred and rapidly being bled of vigor.

As an aspiring healer I learned a lesson that should have immediately been crossbred with the most robust of contemporary medical theories to produce a new generation of healing techniques–the idea that a doctor could heal by simply walking into the patients' presence. The concept was mocked; it was not "scientific," it was imaginary, it was quackery. The critics were locked into an outdated approach to healing.

In a certain sense, I believe modern drug-based medicine has come to the end of its intellectual line. Oh, don't get me wrong, modern medicine can defeat deadly germs and regulate the heartbeat. Using magnetic resonance imaging (MRI) and other techniques we can "see" into patients' bodies; we can transplant hearts and other organs from person to person; we have machines that will cleanse your blood and breathe for you; we can even reattach severed limbs. As far as technology goes, modern medicine is thriving.

As far as healing goes, however, modern medicine is desperately in need of new ideas. Though it can do many things, it cannot give us vibrant health, nor produce joy, courage, peace of mind, love or any of the other ingredients for true health, the vibrant health and exuberant happiness we all deserve. So long as medicine chooses to ignore the potential hidden within the human mind, it will not be able to give us true health.

"I Shall Please"

That day of Dr. Cooper's visit, I learned what a profound influence our thoughts have on our health and happiness. It was my confidence in Dr. Cooper, my unshakable feeling that everything would be all right once he arrived, that eased my pain. The pain vanished before he even said, "Hello, Arnie," before he sat down on the edge of the bed to probe my side and listen to my heart. Somehow, my very real, very physical pain had been bested by the medicine of my mind. That's a scientific fact.

The most widely used medicine in the world today is the one I gave myself that day. We all use that medicine, physician and patient alike, though many physicians angrily deny that they do. They dismiss this medical measure as voodoo, the doctor who uses it as a charlatan, and the patient who receives it as deceived. But this medicine *does* work. There are stacks of scientific studies testifying to its effectiveness, studies performed by distinguished scientists at the most reputable hospitals and research facilities worldwide. This medicine is called placebo.

Placebo: A fitting word that comes to us from the Latin, meaning "I shall please." Modern medicine defines the placebo as a medically inert (useless, having no medicinal effect) substance that somehow makes people feel better. It's effective 30 to 40 percent of the time. Placebos are used in clinical tests of new drugs and procedures, and are often given to relieve patients who demand a pill or an injection for pain.

Modern medical science grants a very limited role to the placebo. It's primarily used for testing new medicines. During the tests, one group of patients receives the "real thing," another group the placebo. (Neither patients nor doctors know who is getting what, until the study is completed and the secret list is read.) If those receiving the new drug fared better than those taking the placebo, the medicine is pronounced a success. If not, the medicine is discarded.

The medicine is either a hit or a flop. But what of the placebo? What of this "sugar pill" that *sometimes achieves an effectiveness rate of over 60 percent–better than that of most drugs in tests*? What of the placebo, which boasts a healing rate of 30 to 40 percent, in thousands of studies for countless signs, symptoms, and diseases? The placebo is tossed back onto the shelf, dismissed and forgotten until the next "wonder drug" comes along to be tested.

Medicine is any substance, procedure or idea which promotes health and healing. Some of our drug medications are only slightly effective, some very effective.

Placebos are things (thoughts, pills, injections, procedures, surgeries) which promote physical, emotional, and spiritual well-being. Therefore, the placebo is a medicine, sometimes very successful, sometimes not so successful.

Health is defined as a profound state of physical, emotional, and spiritual well-being. Used properly, placebos can help heal the wounded body, the anguished mind, and the broken spirit. Therefore, the placebo promotes health.

Placebos teach us a great deal about the human mind-body connection. They lead us to general conclusions about the way the body works, if we're willing to look at the overwhelming evidence. Placebos affect the human mind, body, and spirit. Oftentimes we can measure these effects (for example, when placebos cause endorphin levels in the body to rise). Sometimes, however, we can't make the measurement, for our instruments are not precise enough. Placebos are concerned with things that go wrong with the body, and how to make the body well. Therefore, the placebo is scientific.

If We Think We Feel Better, Do We?

Placebos are every bit as scientific as aspirin and coronary artery bypass surgery. "Nonsense," some say. "Placebos only make people think they feel better, they don't really work."

Now there's an interesting idea: Placebos only make people *think* they feel better. Do placebos somehow fool us? How can we tell if we really feel better?

The signs and symptoms of pain and illness are either objective or subjective. Objective signs and symptoms are things we can measure. A temperature of 102° F is an objective sign. So is a count of 800 in a test for T_4, the immune system cell damaged by AIDS. A 30 percent blockage in a coronary artery is an objective sign. Thirty hiccups per minute is very objective. We doctors love objective signs and symptoms. Numbers crystallize the problems and solutions, numbers are easy to grasp. If the numbers are too high, bring them down. If the numbers are too low, bring them up.

The subjective is much more difficult for us doctors to deal with. For example, the patient says he is in "great pain": How much pain is "great pain"? Or the patient explains that he doesn't feel as bad as he did last time: How bad is bad, how much is "not as bad as last time"? Two people, same age, same sex, same general background and body build, may suffer from the same illness. One is crying in pain, while the other chats with visitors, asking only for an occasional aspirin. How do we deal with the subjective?

Deciding whether placebos are effective against the objective is simple: Give the placebo and see if the numbers change. *Many studies show that placebos do indeed change the numbers.*

Placebos have changed the endorphin numbers, increasing the levels of these beneficial hormones in patients' bodies. Placebos have changed the stomach acid numbers, the blood pressure numbers, the temperature numbers, and more.

As for the subjective, that's harder to deal with because we can't translate it into numbers. But we do know that countless people have reported feeling better after taking placebos. Were they fooling themselves? Well, we know that there's never a *thought* in the mind that does not produce a corresponding *thing* in the body. Our thoughts produce hormones, peptides, neurotransmitters, which carry the flavor of our thoughts throughout the body. If we *think* we will feel better, we *will* feel better, for thinking always alters our body chemistry.

Are we fooling ourselves into thinking we feel better? Do we deceive ourselves by pretending the placebo is medicine? Ah, but the placebo *is* medicine. Remember, medicine is anything that promotes health and healing. Medicine need not be packaged in little round pills or tube-shaped capsules; neither need medicine be delivered through the point of a needle. The things we get that way are medicines, but not the only medicines. Those medicines come from outside our body: The medicine the placebo provides comes from within.

Can thoughts really change the body? Yes. Using biofeedback methods, we can easily measure the changes in skin temperature, heartbeat, and so on, that occur as a person thinks about making the changes. I've used biofeedback to help teach patients how to slow the heart rate and normalize blood pressure. It can be done—the mind is very powerful.

A New Definition

The little paperback dictionary I keep on my desk defines placebo as "an inert medication used for its psychological effect or for purposes of comparison in an experiment." In other words, placebos are only good for nutty people who "think" they're sick, and as something for comparison against "real" drugs. By definition, the placebo is made to look insignificant.

I propose a new definition, one that will elevate the placebo to the high rank it deserves: A placebo is a process by which a person transforms the biochemistry of mind and/or body so as to achieve a desired result. In this case, good health.

Placebo is a process, not a substance. Placebo is a process that begins with our belief, continues through the transformation of our biochemistry, and ends in the very real, physical, often measurable, desired result.

If I were stranded on a deserted island with only one medicine, I would want it to be the placebo. As far as I'm concerned, the placebo is the most powerful and versatile medicine in my black bag. I've seen it work countless times–I know it works! Let's stop denigrating the placebo and recognize it as the wonderful tool it is. Instead of a year's worth of pharmacology, I propose that all medical students spend four years learning about the placebo. Instead of spending billions of dollars to test drugs–many of which don't work, all of which have side effects, sometimes terrible side effects–I suggest that we have our best scientists discover everything there is to know about the placebo. Rather than allow ourselves to be filled full of dangerous medicines and submit to risky surgeries, I propose that we, the people, demand that our doctors teach us how to use the placebo. And rather than reach for the medicine chest with each ache or bout with the blues, I beg you to reach within your spirit for the best medicine you'll ever have: Your great belief in yourself.

Symbol, Belief, Relief

How can we harness the healing power of the placebo? Let's look at its elements. First is the symbol–the "sugar pill." Don't laugh at the sugar pill, for it represents the healing powers of the human spirit. And as the physical representation of our belief, it is a very important part of the process.

Next is belief, the picture in our mind of what will be. We see ourselves free of pain, we see our temperature dropping, we see our endorphin levels rising: We believe something great will happen.

Now comes relief as the biochemical changes occur within

the body. Endorphin levels rise to strike down the pain; the sympathetic nervous system signals the stomach to calm down; the heart slows to a normal rate, the blood pressure moderates, the pH changes.

PLACEBO IS BELIEF

Symbol, belief, relief: The process of placebo. The symbol is very important to placebo, but belief is the key. Belief is confidence, trust, faith. So is placebo. Placebo is belief, and belief is placebo, there is no difference. Belief is an honored word but we snicker at placebo, yet the two words are two ways of expressing the same concept. "I shall please myself," we say when we believe in ourselves. "I shall please myself with my belief, I shall please myself by making the great picture of what can be reality for me."

Placebo is the belief-based process of altering your internal environment (thoughts, biochemistry) so as to achieve a desired result. Every time we say or think "I believe I will feel better," we set in motion within us the biochemical events that turn our belief into reality. Whether we feel slightly better, much better, or something in-between depends on the strength of our belief. We give ourselves placebos–we unleash our belief–many times a day, every day for a lifetime.

The affirmations and R_X's I've been giving you are placebos–and they work. In telling yourself that good things are occurring, in picturing these good things with your mind's eye, you are calling upon belief.

The only difference between the placebo process in a medical setting and the placebo process we undergo everyday is that in the medical setting, we're given a symbol (the sugar pill) to help us focus our belief.

That symbol is very powerful, which is one reason why the placebo process often works so well in a medical setting. The symbol carries with it the full weight of medical authority, and we believe in our medical system. It's fascinating: A little pill, less than an ounce in weight, or an injection, less than a thimbleful of salt water, musters our belief. This does not mean we are gullible, that we're easily fooled or led astray. No. It means that we have a tremendous ability to focus our belief. Just give us something to start with, and we can bring to bear incredible amounts of belief. The pill or shot is like a seed, from which grows a forest of belief. Let's stop scoffing at the placebo and ask ourselves how we can use this marvelous tool in our everyday life. What can we invent, what can we use to make ourselves believe, make ourselves believe so strongly that we unleash the full power of our spirit?

Prayer is what we can use, and do use, as the symbol of our belief.

Prayer Is Placebo

The prayer of faith shall save the sick.

James 5:15

Placebo is a prayer, a prayer which, with the help of God and the wonderful spirit He gave us, we answer for ourselves when we are able. "I shall please," we pray. "Let me please myself by healing my wound." And so we appeal to our spirit, to that part of God within us, for relief.

"Let me be well," we pray. "I believe I shall be well. I call upon my spirit to prompt the necessary changes in body chemistry, to release endorphins, to strengthen my immune system, to do whatever is necessary to incline me toward health." Is our prayer answered? That depends on the strength of our belief. Is our prayer always answered exactly as we would have it be answered? Well, sometimes God has already made His decision. But our prayer of belief always bring us *the best possible health we are capable of having. Our prayer of health always gathers all our resources, opens our eyes as wide as they will go, focuses our thoughts as much as is possible, puts all our strength into our effort.*

Prayer, be it prayer to God or prayer to the Spirit within us, stirs up our potential. That is why it is written: "Whatsoever things you desire, when you pray, believe that you receive them, and you shall have them." Prayer is strengthened by belief, and belief is a form of prayer. In some respects, belief is prayer, and prayer the belief put into words.

Unfortunately, sometimes we invoke the harmful powers of our spirit without realizing it. Our spirit responds to our unhappy wishes as emphatically as it does to our happy ones. "I shall not please," we unwittingly say when we believe bad things will happen to us. "Let me be ill." We don't realize that our negative thoughts are prayers to the devils within us, but they are; and they are answered with a force that matches our belief in impending doom.

Why do we do this? Because we have been taught since childhood to focus in on the symbols of negativity, on the aches and pains, the temporary setbacks, the occasional heartbreaks that are in a normal part of life. When we repeat "I'm feeling terrible" over and over, when we say "nothing every goes right for me" time after time, we are invoking the negative forces within us; we are calling upon our belief to muster our worst expectations, we are giving ourselves a dangerous antiplacebo.

We wouldn't pray to God for bad things to happen to us. Neither, then, should we believe bad things will happen to us, for belief is a prayer of our spirit. And so we must turn our eyes away from the negative symbols in our lives. Be aware of the negatives, yes; acknowledge them, deal with them, but never focus on them, for such focus is to pray against that touch of God within us.

PUT YOUR FOCUS ON THE BEST

Focus on the positive symbols in your life. Let this focus be your placebo, your belief, your prayer for great things to happen.

When something hurts, concentrate on the rest of your body, where everything functions smoothly.

When something goes wrong, think about all the things that went right, the little and big things, the significant, the not-so-important.

When something bad happens today, ask yourself what great things might take you by surprise.

When someone annoys you, think about all the people you like; the one who tells funny jokes, the one who helped you, the one you work with, the one you exercise with, the one you share lunch with, the friend of a friend you had a nice talk with.

Even when illness strikes hard and the outlook is grim, remember with joy all your years of good health.

"Oh, that's simplistic wishful thinking," a patient scoffed. "Wishful thinking doesn't do anything."

But it does. We're constantly wishfully thinking. It's so much a part of living that we don't recognize it, don't realize that we're doing it. Our every thought is a wishful thought.

Wishful thinking is focus. Focus is the beginning of belief, and belief is prayer. Let us focus, then, on only the best. Let us believe in the best, and let us pray for the best. Let us do this, and the best is all but inevitable.

Rx: "I Shall Please"

According to your faith be it unto you.

Matt. 9:22

Today is Day Twelve of Making Miracles, the Day of Pleasing. This day is devoted to the pleasing prayer of belief in your own healing powers.

Recite these affirmations throughout the day, today and every day. Be sure to "see" each affirmation as you recite it.

Upon awakening: "Rejoice and Be Glad"
This is the day that the Lord hath made; I shall rejoice and be glad, be gladder than glad. I give myself permission to see all the happiness that is in my world, to think of the happiness, and to speak of the happiness. The Creator has filled the world with unlimited joy that is mine for the taking.

Morning: "It is Good to Give Thanks"
It is good to give thanks unto the Lord for making me the healthy, happy, and successful person I so richly deserve to be. I am open to receiving all the blessings of His abundant universe.

Noon: "Endless Enthusiasm"
The Creator has filled me to the brim with enthusiasm. I gladly and generously pour my unlimited enthusiasm over my every thought and action. Armed with endless enthusiasm, I find excitement and adventure in every day.

Afternoon: "Spiritually Minded"
To be spiritually minded is life and peace. I give myself permission to be as calm and serene as the quiet waters of a beautiful, still lake.

Evening: "A Merry Heart"
A merry heart is a good medicine. My heart and spirit and the gospel of my mind are filled with joy. I am full of the thoughts and things of health, happiness, and success.

When going to bed: "Put on the New Me"
Today was another successful step toward the new me. With enthusiastic anticipation and absolute certainty that I'll make even more progress tomorrow, and every tomorrow, I'm putting on the new me.

Recite each affirmation out loud, with enthusiasm. This daily menu sets up the daily minimum requirements of glad tidings. But I tell my patients to go beyond the minimum and recite their affirmations all day long: 5, 10, 20 times a day. You can't overdo it with affirmations!

In addition to your daily diet of affirmations, enter into the world of this special R_X for Pleasing several times today, with energy and conviction.

Set aside some time today to sit in a quiet room, on a comfortable chair. Tell everyone that you do not want to be disturbed; take the phone off the hook. Close your eyes. With your mind's eye, picture a little pill bottle. The label says "I Shall Please." A hand–your hand–takes a pill from the bottle. Look at the little pill. It's round, white. In the middle, a large *P* is stamped. With your mind's eye, see yourself focusing all your thoughts on that pill as you say:

> I shall please myself with the tremendous power of my great belief. I am focusing all of my healing powers, using my powers as a medicine to keep me bursting with health, alive with joy, and flushed with success.

Focus on the Great Things You Desire

> *In his diseases he sought not to the Lord, but to the physicians.*
>
> 2 Chron. 16:12

We doctors can do some pretty amazing things. I've injected adrenaline right into people's hearts. I've cut holes into their windpipes to save lives, and I've pushed tubes attached to pacemakers into hearts. But I've never been able to "make" anyone happy. They don't teach us how to do that in medical school, because it can't be done. No, health and happiness abide in the person with a robust spirit, a cup that always runneth over, and the ability to focus his or her own God-given powers. Focusing and believing: These are the greatest medicines.

Day 13

PAY: POSITIVE ADDICTION TO YOURSELF

A thorn in the flesh . . .

2 Cor. 12:7

"I can't stop, Dr. Fox. I know it's not good for me, but I can't stop. I have to have it."

I don't know how many times patients have said this, or something very much like it, to me. "I can't stop. I have to have it." Have what? It doesn't matter. If you *have* to have it, if you can't stop, you're headed for trouble.

Why *must* they have it, whatever "it" may be? There may be many reasons. We all have our weaknesses: sugar, coffee, cigarettes, food, Valium and other tranquilizers, drugs. Maybe it's alcohol, the cheapest and most easily obtained drug. Do you have a craving, a compulsion, an addiction?

"No, not an addiction, I'm not addicted," the addict adamantly says. "I can stop any time I want. I'm *not* addicted!"

Most families have their quiet secrets: Teenager Bob is on drugs, Dad drinks; Sis is anorexic; Mom is a compulsive overeater; cousin Alex is depressed and suicidal; cousin Ben is a compulsive gambler. I remember, as a child, listening to my aunts and uncles whispering about a relative of ours who would wash a glass 10 or 12 times before using it. His was a relatively harmless compulsion. My father's addiction was not so harmless: He was an alcoholic.

LIKE PUSHING BACK THE OCEAN WAVES

When I came to the Los Angeles County Hospital in 1958 as a resident in internal medicine, eager to save the world, I was amazed at the incredible number of people who were in the hospital because of their addictions. I was shocked to find entire floors of the hospital given over to alcoholics who lay in their beds, tied down, confused, hallucinating, shaking so much the beds rattled. I passed by row after row of yellow-tinged, bloated-bellied people. Nighttime was especially eerie. The huge wards were lit by only a few bulbs hanging by their cords from high ceilings, and there was a cacophony of muted sounds, shadows, and cries of delirium tremens. It was something even the most avant-garde Swedish film director couldn't imagine.

Back in those days, the standard line was that delirium tremens–the d.t.'s–represented the most severe type of alcohol withdrawal. The terrible symptoms came about because of the hyper excitability and irritation of both the cerebral cortex as well as the brain stem. More than 20 percent of the patients who had the d.t.'s died from it. Today we also know that the d.t.'s are the direct effect of alcohol on the brain, they're an extreme example of what addiction can do to a person.

Back then, this was an exciting challenge. Picture it: You're a young doctor mesmerized by knowledge you've been stuffing into your head for so many years, by the thought that you can save lives, by the drugs and other tools at your disposal. You're standing by the metal bed late at night, shadows from the swaying light bulb dancing across the room. The patient is disoriented and wildly hallucinating; agitated, shaking, dripping wet with perspiration. His heart beats rapidly in his chest; you can hear it through your stethoscope and feel it in his pulse. His breathing is rapid and shallow, his temperature is high, he's nauseous and vomits. And there are many more just like him.

You rush around all night, treating first this one, then that, and after 36 hours of this you collapse into sleep. One day blurs into the next. Soon you realize that there's a whole new group of alcoholics in these beds, with their yellow puffy faces, their arms and legs so thin against those giant bellies; bellies puffed by all that liquid trapped in there, and by their gigantic livers. (We called those puff-bellied bodies "spider bodies" because the swollen torso was so enormous and the shrunken limbs so small.)

Many of them went back out on the streets, but most of them died here.

Still you never give up. Time and time again, you save some, lose some, dry them out, teach, preach, cajole. They promise never to drink again but pretty soon they're right back in the hospital, sick as ever. After a while, after months of nights like this, you have to admit it's a little like trying to stop the ocean from making waves. What an incredible hold their addiction has on them.

You know so well what their addiction has done to their brains, their nerves, heart, blood, esophagus, stomach, pancreas, and liver, to their lives, their families, their dreams. They know, too, but they can't stop.

Spiritual Cavity

Avoid it, pass not by it, turn from it, and pass away.
Prov. 4:15

I still work with addicts. My enthusiasm hasn't dampened in the 30-some years that have passed since I began. Only now I want to begin working with people sooner, long before they're so far gone. It's never too late to try, but it's better to start soon. Not just with alcoholism, but with all the addictions.

Our word "addiction" comes from the Latin *addicere*, meaning to surrender oneself to something obsessively. The key word is *surrender*. We feel powerless to resist the obsession that has come over us, so we surrender. Where did the irresistible obsession come from? The obsession is born of our desperate desire to change what we perceive to be a painful life. We give in to our addiction in a futile attempt to change our reality and take away the pain.

Why are we in such pain? Because our spirit is being eaten away by the cancer of negativity, of loneliness, of the terrible feeling that we're all alone in life, that we're not going to reach the stars. That terrible ache we feel comes from the cavity being eaten into our spirit. It's this cavity that we try to fill with our addiction.

Giving in to our addiction, we self-medicate–no, "drug" ourselves. We either drug ourselves with the substance we abuse, or with the thoughts that release certain biosubstances we've become addicted to. Many are addicted to the adrenaline high that comes with anger, for example. We turn on the adrenaline like a caged rat pressing the lever to earn a food pellet. The rat's obsessive behavior–pressing the lever to get food–is learned. So is our behavior–becoming angry to get the adrenaline rush. Riding the adrenaline wave, we feel strong, invincible, explosively powerful. But every breaker crashes, leaving behind desolation. The waves of adrenaline don't fill our cavity; instead, the waves rip into us making the hole in our spirit bigger.

There is tremendous pleasure involved in many addictions. That is why we surrender so willingly. But it's a false pleasure, a pleasure that brings us no joy, only erodes more deeply the cavity in our spirit.

> **When the spirit is not whole, we are in pain. We surrender to addiction in an attempt to heal the cavity of our spirit. But addiction tears at the wound within us, making worse our pain and our need.**

The Sadness of Addiction, The Addiction to Sadness

> *A merry heart doeth good like a medicine; but a broken spirit drieth the bones.*
>
> Prove. 17:22

How many addictions are there, and what are there names? Some people say we've become a society of addicts. Others say no, the problem is that we throw the label "addict" around too easily. Regardless of who is right about this, we know that professional clinics and self-help programs for the addicted have proliferated all across the country. There are self-help groups for alcoholics, the families of alcoholics, child abusers, overeaters, gamblers, drug abusers, smokers, and more. Some critics even charge that people have become addicted to self-help groups.

We are at the same time touched, frightened, and angered by this terrible scourge. What is it that drives so many of us to these unhealthy habits? The experts' guesses range from genetics to advertising. A major contributor that is seldom named, and one that we doctors often see in our patients, is unhappiness. Remember, if happiness is the ultimate good in life, then unhappiness is the greatest evil. No wonder people are willing to do almost anything to find happiness.

Unfortunately, most of us are confused about what we're looking for. We've been taught that happiness is having lots of money, a big house, expensive cars and clothes, prestige, rooms full of new costly possessions, going to all the "in" spots, living the high life. We've been taught wrong. I was raised in the economically depressed South Philadelphia of the 1930s; now I practice medicine in posh Beverly Hills. I've been money-rich and money-poor. Many of my patients and friends are very, very wealthy. Many can afford to fly in from the Caribbean, the Middle East, the South Pacific, or Europe just to see me. It's obvious that their money doesn't make them happy.

Happiness is a state of mind, a word written into your mental gospel, a bright color on your mental filter, a strong spirit. Happiness comes from being in touch with yourself, body, mind and spirit. Happiness comes from your strong belief that you are a worthwhile person. Happiness is a full spirit.

Though happiness is a precious commodity, it is so easy to come by—if you know where to look. Where? Inside yourself. It's when we lose touch with ourselves, when we allow past problems to intrude unhappily on the present and to become the future, when we look outside ourselves for gratification, that we flirt with unhappiness. Then the stage is set for addiction.

Addiction is born of emptiness; it lives and grows strong in the cavity of our spirit.

THE TERRIBLE TRIAD: OBSESSION, ACTION, AND REACTION

. . . so a fool returneth to his folly.

Prov. 26:11

Addiction begins with an obsession or craving, the first of the three phases in the terrible triad of addiction. We crave happiness, satisfaction, inner peace. We need something to fill the hole in our spirit, some cement to make us whole again. We are compelled to grasp for things to make us happy. We become addicted to possessions, status, eating, alcohol, gambling, cigarettes, tranquilizers, pain, sickness, cocaine, what-have-you. We search desperately for happiness everywhere except inside, where it is and always will be.

We usually don't understand that our spirit is hurting. No, we think we're missing some special something that will make us happy. Thoughts of that special something take over our mind, we think of it obsessively, and we pin all our hopes on it. "When I get it," we tell ourselves, "the pain will go away." Or, "If only I could have it, everything would be great!"

Obsession turns to action as we act out the ritual: We light up the cigarette, pour the drink and bring glass to lips, throw down our money on the craps table, abuse our spouse. Now we feel good, like a well-oiled machine. Everything's in gear. Biochemical changes occur in the body and it feels energized. We become inebriated, we smoke a pack, we shoot up, we scream or take a swing at someone, we take the dice in hand. It feels great!

We don't notice the ache in our spiritual cavity. We've pushed it into the background, numbed our mind to its pain. But then comes the crushing reaction. It's inevitable: Obsession, action, reaction. The reaction is guilt and anger over another failure, fear that we will be found out, and frustration at the pain that still persists. And the consequences, the terrible consequences of our drinking, drugging, gambling. Who besides ourselves have we hurt, physically, emotionally, spiritually, monetarily? How badly have we hurt them?

We've indulged ourselves with cigarettes, drugs, gambling, abusive behavior, anger, sex, but none of these things is the medicine that will heal the hole in our spirit. These things can't heal us anymore than stuffing tobacco into a cut on our hand will heal the wound. It will only make matters worse. And we know it, deep down we know it well.

So we punish ourselves mentally for our behavior; some of us punish ourselves physically, as well. The filter of our mind becomes darker than ever, the words in our mental gospel are written with pain and tears. If our mind weren't filled with negative thoughts before, it certainly is now. Now the cavity of our spirit is bigger than ever. Now we think more obsessively than ever about that special something we think will make us happy. So we act again, feeling good again for just a little while before feeling worse than ever. The step we think takes us forward, upward, only prepares us to take two steps backward, downward into mental misery. Obsession, action, the inevitable reaction. Only this reaction is not the equal one Newton promised; it's twice as bad.

Obsession, action, reaction: the terrible triad. Happiness, which is nothing more than a full spirit, is the medicine for our terrible ache.

The #1 Addiction

What this all boils down to is addiction to negative thinking, the single addiction that causes, worsens, or is caused by the other addictions. It has no self-help group, no media attention, but plenty of victims. Addiction to negative thinking is the real issue we're examining in this book. It seems that subconsciously we prefer to write horror stories into our mental gospel, then read them over and over, producing sequel after terrible sequel. It's as though we were taught from early childhood to savor our anger, to relish our unforgiveness, to salivate at the thought of "teaching him a lesson," to revel in our self-pity. With these early lessons written into our mental book, it's no wonder so many of us are addicted to negative thinking. This popular malady has many manifestations: addiction to pain, to sickness, to losing, and more.

In one very important sense all addictions are rooted in the addiction to negative thinking, the drive to fill that spiritual cavity. Our terrible negative thought/addiction/–negative thought/addiction cycle must be broken. The spirit must be made whole again.

Addiction to negative thinking: the number one addiction. It's the "umbrella" addiction that causes or worsens every other addiction. Here is where the cure for most addictions must begin.

YOUR PERSONAL ADDICTION CHECKLIST

All our addictions are related to the wound in our spirit. Is your spirit whole? Are you addicted to negative thoughts? Check the questions that get a yes answer.

❑ Do negative thoughts seem comfortable to you?

❑ Do you savor thoughts of revenge?

❑ Do you feel you don't deserve compliments?

❑ Do you feel strong when you're angry?

❑ Do you feel it's very important to set people straight?

❑ Do you carry long-term grudges–days, weeks, months, years?

❑ Do you wish everyone would leave you alone?

❑ Do you wonder how all those "idiots" got ahead of you at work?

❑ Do you think people enjoy giving you a rough time?

❑ Do you like to throw your weight around, so people will know you're someone to be reckoned with?

❑ Are you afraid to stand up for yourself?

❑ Do you often find it necessary to stand up for yourself?

❑ Do you think you were destined to be unhappy?

❑ Does trying to improve your life seem like a hopeless proposition?

❑ Do you wish that people would pay some attention to you?

❑ Do you wonder if anyone would notice if you suddenly disappeared?

❏ Would you like to go somewhere else and start all over again?

❏ Do you wish you had never been born?

Checking even a few of these can indicate that you are hooked on negative thoughts.

Addiction to Pain

The heart knoweth his own bitterness.

Prov. 14:10

I have seen many patients who were addicted to pain. One in particular stands out in my mind, perhaps because I learned such a valuable lesson about pain addiction from another doctor who was called in on the case. This woman–I'll call her Mrs. Holly–was sent to me by her general practitioner. Mrs. Holly had severe, often incapacitating pain in her back. Every couple of months the pain was so bad she took to her bed, unable to move. Surgeons, orthopedists, neurologists, gynecologists, kidney specialists, and other physicians had tried to help this woman, to no avail. My examination found no organic problem that would explain her pain. While talking to her, however, I came to feel that this seemingly very cheerful woman either was really depressed, or was holding onto a big chunk of unresolved, unrecognized anger. I felt that this was causing her back pain, so I sent her to a psychiatrist.

About a week later I received a call from Dr. Joel, the psychiatrist. He was a giant of a man, with big bushy eyebrows, red cheeks, and a walrus mustache. Twenty years later, I can still hear him bellowing into the phone, "Arn! What do you want me to do with this woman?"

"Fix her up," I replied. "Take away her pain."

"Don't you understand? If I take away her pain she'll have nothing! Her pain gives her her identity. Her pain gives her a cross to bear. Her pain gives her position in her family–she's "the invalid." Her pain is what she's built her life around. I can't take it away from her. She won't have anything left!"

Mrs. Holly was a very "successful" negative thinking addict.

She had built a life around her addiction. Every time she had an attack the whole family took care of her. Schedules were rearranged to suit her needs. People did things for her. Every time she had surgery there was a whirlwind of activity, all centered around her.

Hers was a dangerous addiction, as dangerous as that to alcohol, drugs, or anger. Alcohol and drugs can kill you outright, and anger kills by filling the body with chemicals that can ruin your health. Mrs. Holly's addiction hurt her in more insidious ways: The doctors had taken out every part of her body that could be removed. The surgeries alone could have killed her.

> **Many of us convert our spiritual pain into physical pain. Then, at least, our pain seems "real." But we're no closer to the cure.**

The Sickness Circle

My sighs are many, and my heart is faint.
Lam. 1:22

One night my wife, Hannah and I were at one of our favorite restaurants in Century City, which is right next door to Beverly Hills. Century City is built on what used to be the huge Twentieth Century Fox studio back lot. Giant skyscrapers and plush hotels now sit where cowboys and Indians once chased each other for the cameras.

Ten middle-aged people were sitting at the large round table next to ours, celebrating someone's birthday. They were such a boisterous bunch, we couldn't help but overhear their conversations. The lady in the red dress was recounting the story of her knee troubles. The gray-haired man described his bypass surgery in detail.

Tuning in on conversation after conversation, Hannah and I listened to one recital of sickness after another. The birthday boy showed the man next to him a couple of pill bottles. "The latest from my doc," he said. "A brilliant cardiologist. The best in the state."

Across the table a heavyset woman had been reciting her ailments: back pain, headaches, poor vision, failing hearing, heart palpitations, esophagitis. She stopped when she heard the birthday boy bragging about his physician.

"A boy right out of medical school," she scoffed. "My doctor is chairman of the medical board and a professor."

"Big deal. My doctor had two fellowships, he's a genius. Five doctors didn't know what my problem was, he figured it out immediately!"

Hannah looked at me and said, "They're obsessed with their illnesses and their doctors. It's the Sickness Circle."

She was right. These people were addicted to their illnesses, they were trapped in the Sickness Circle, an unofficial club that meets regularly so that the members can revel in their problems, rehash all the terrible details, brag about their doctors and surgical scars, share and increase their misery. It's one-upmanship, with points given for the most number of pills taken, the most surgeries, the most rushed trips to the emergency room, the longest surgical meeting of this Sickness Circle, the members write into their mental gospel things such as: "I'm sick, I've always been sick, I'm only getting worse." "I'm proud to be sicker than they are." "Being sick gives me status."

One of my close relatives has a Sickness Circle all her own. Recently, my wife told this woman that she had had the flu. "You have the flu," our relative replied. "I was so sick last week, I passed out and cracked my head on the floor. I almost had to have stitches!"

Perhaps the Sickness Circle should be called the Sickness Cycle, for once you've started it's hard to stop. Every time you tell others how sick you are, you tell yourself, as well. What we tell ourselves is always a prophecy: Told enough times, it can't help but come true.

The emptiness in our spirit can literally make us sick. But the drugs doctors have to give cannot heal the sickness. Only by mending the spirit can we cure the disease.

Are You a Member of the Club?

Are you addicted to pain and/or sickness? Are your spiritual ills manifested as physical ailments? Do you:

- ❑ Find yourself thinking about your physical problems a lot?
- ❑ Like to tell people about your aches and pains, ills and pills?
- ❑ Tend to be with people who are constantly talking about their diseases, doctors, and surgeries?
- ❑ Talk all about your problems, but don't take the active steps necessary to regain health?
- ❑ Say that your knee or back hurts because you're overweight, but don't bother shedding the excess pounds?
- ❑ Take medicines for your high blood pressure, but ignore your doctor's advice to lose weight and lower your salt intake?
- ❑ Tell people how high your cholesterol is, even as you eat foods full of cholesterol and fat.
- ❑ Bemoan your loss of youthful energy while slumped in front of the TV?
- ❑ Figure that you'll be sick and have to take pills as you age because that's just the way it is?

If you checked even one of the above, you may be Sickness Circling. A Sickness Circle can be large or small, obvious or subtle. Whatever its form, the deadly Circle has you writing chapters of disease into your mental gospel, painting the filter of your mind with the colors of disease and failure.

Loving to Lose

I remember a very beautiful woman named Connie, a 40-year-old executive with a large investment firm here in Beverly Hills. Suffering simultaneously from a disastrous divorce and a banking crisis, she turned to the one thing that always made her feel good–food, especially those big chocolate chip cookies that she gobbled up by the bagful. She filled her stomach to allay her apprehension, adding another 10 pounds to the 160 she already carried on her five feet four inch frame. Sitting slumped in a chair in my office, eyes down, voice filled with dejection, she said, "I've had three bad relationships and a terrible marriage, right in a row, and I've had two bad reviews at work, my last two. I'm a loser on a losing streak and I don't see any end. I'm supposed to be a hot-shot businesswoman. I was listed as one of the top 100 women in America to watch. Yes. Watch me eat myself to death."

"What do you mean, you're a loser?" I asked. "You made it through college and graduate school, you're an executive, you're considered one of the top 100 up-and-coming women. It sounds like you've achieved quite a lot."

"School's no big deal. You just have to learn how to B.S. on the tests. Affirmative action got me my job–they had to have women. And I've never been able to sustain a relationship. My whole life has been a losing streak. The only thing I do well is eat."

There were plenty of positives in Connie's life, but she only had eyes for the negatives. The filter of her mind colored all her achievements with the colors of failure. In her mental book were written all the explanations for failure. It was written that she was solely responsible for her failed relationships. It was written that she was only promoted because she was a woman. The bad was written in big black letters, with a bold hand. The good was written in cramped little letters, shoved down into the footnotes, ignored. So she stuffed the void in her spirit with food. The food never filled the hole, of course, but it gave her a certain small pleasure.

Being a loser was comforting to Connie. It gave her an identity. It also gave her a ready excuse for the failures we all face in life. Labeling herself a loser gave Connie reason to feel sorry for herself, and invited others to pity her as well. Being pitied is perhaps not as nice as being admired, but it's something; at least people notice you.

Connie was a very interesting person. Although she declared herself to be a loser, she had completed a very tough course of business study at one of the top universities in the country, then landed a very prestigious and high-paying job in

Beverly Hills. As we talked more about her personal and medical history, I learned that her weight problem had begun in earnest during graduate school, when it was clear that she was on the success track. I couldn't help but wonder if putting on all the extra weight at that time wasn't a way to counterbalance the success that was coming her way. Something good was entering her life, it had to be "beaten back" with something bad. Putting on pounds is a great way to make sure you're a loser, given the strong prejudice against the obese, given the well-known health hazards associated with excess fat. She could feel those pounds, see them. Everyone saw her fat, snickered at it.

Overeating is just one of the ways we compensate for our failure addiction, or prove that we are indeed failures. Forty-five million Americans are obese (more than 20 percent over their ideal body weight). Millions more are on their way to becoming obese. Doctors usually hand the overweight patient a sheet with a 1000-calorie diet–which usually doesn't work because it does not address the real problem. We use food to make ourselves feel good, to make up for the lack of love in our lives, to compensate for the depression, anxiety, loneliness, and lack of self-esteem, to fill up the void within us.

I wondered about Connie. Would taking away her obesity hurt her, as taking away Mrs. Holly's pain would have harmed her? Connie's obesity was dangerous, for obesity can literally make us sick–it increases our risk of having heart disease, cancer, stroke and many other serious illnesses.

A famous old-time stage star also used fat to "prove" he was a failure. He had been on every diet you can name, never losing much weight or keeping it off for long. It was always the doctor's fault; he would bellow at them as his waistline grew and his arteries narrowed. I examined him, performed the appropriate tests, reviewed his medical records, then put him on a special high complex-carbohydrate diet. He didn't lose weight, although he claimed to be sticking to the diet. His wife told me, however, that he had a couple of corned beef sandwiches every day at Nate and Al's deli in Beverly Hills. In fact, he had a regular delicatessens route where he met his friends to assuage his addiction, filling up his belly and blocking the arteries in his heart and head, trying to push away the pain of a childhood that left the child in him extremely vulnerable and needy.

I wish I could say that I was successful here, but this very talented and funny man died from his addiction. He made a lot of people happy but was never able to shake the feeling that he was a loser, destined for the worst life has to offer. This man was adored by millions, he had won all the awards there were to win, had made plenty of money, then earned even more love and respect by donating much to worthy causes. He was tremendously successful in every way but one: He couldn't break his addiction to the feeling that he was a loser. Could I or someone else have taken away his addiction? What would have happened if he lost his addiction?

> **Pain, sickness, losing: Your anguish can take many forms. The root is where the cure is: Your spirit. Your thoughts. Your mental gospel. With your thoughts you can begin cutting away the roots of your horrible addictions.**

Are You "Stuffing the Void"?

Is your addiction to negative thoughts manifested as an obsession with food? Do you:

- ❑ Eat when you're unhappy?
- ❑ Eat when you're angry?
- ❑ Eat when you're stressed?
- ❑ Eat even when you're not hungry, because it feels good?
- ❑ Eat when your team is winning–or losing?
- ❑ Eat before making a big decision–or after making one?
- ❑ Eat while watching TV or a movie, not because you're hungry, but because you always eat while watching TV or a movie?
- ❑ Eat more today because you're starting on a diet tomorrow?
- ❑ Eat for most any reason at all?

If you've checked more than one of the items above, you may be trying to use food as aspirin for your spirit. Many people "medicate" themselves with food. Food abuse is not a medicine, it is a serious disease.

The Wrong Approach

There are many cures for our addictions. Most fail, however, because they don't deal with the underlying problem, our distorted mental filter and pain-filled mental gospel.

Obesity, for example, has spawned a whole industry. There are weight-loss clinics, foods, powders, pills, medicines, books, diets, lifestyles, and surgeries. The vicious cycle–pain, eating, feeling good, gaining weight, more pain–often begins in earnest at about age 25. By age 35, the person may be 100 pounds heavier. Extreme case, you say? Maybe, but give or take some pounds, the pattern is all too common.

Hope springs eternal; the next diet is going to do the trick. Most of the quick-fix fad diets are harmful, causing physical problems, plus the psychological upset of having failed again.

Don't underestimate the power of addiction. Some patients who have resorted to surgery to stop eating have been defeated by their addiction to eating frequent, small, high-calorie meals after they had their stomach stapled smaller, or drinking ice cream through their wired-shut jaws. Addiction is a powerful force. That's why we must deal with it at the source, in our minds.

The best medicine for our addiction is the one that heals the spirit.

People Helping People

There is no vaccine for this addiction to self-destructive thinking, no "magic bullet" to cure this terrible problem. Still, there must be some way to fill the cavity in our spirit. How can we help people at least to control their addiction, help them to rewrite at least a part of their mental gospel? The only help–not cure–is to start changing the way the addict lives, behaves, thinks, talks, acts, and reacts.

Medicine itself is not nearly enough. As a young physician, I often detoxified alcoholics in the hospital, treated their d.t.'s and upper gastrointestinal bleeding, but did nothing for the addiction. I was practicing Band-Aid medicine, not curing anything. As soon as they were discharged from the hospital, the patients often headed right for the nearest bar. One of my wealthy Beverly Hills patients had been to several medically supervised detox programs in southern California. Each time, she had her chauffeur meet her when she checked out, ordering him to take her right into her favorite club for a drink.

What do they do when they leave the hospital, what do they do when they are faced with the underlying stresses and strains that prompted their addictions in the first place? What do they do with their mental gospels? That's the key.

I've seen terrific results when people help people. Through the years, I've been impressed at the work done by Alcoholics Anonymous (AA) and other such groups. For many, AA becomes the accepting family they feel they've never had, the place where they are accepted and loved without reservation. Love and acceptance: These are two powerful medicines against self-loathing. I have sent many of my patients to AA or AA-type meetings–and I go with them, too.

One patient, a successful builder, insisted that he absolutely did not want to go to Cocaine Anonymous (CA). "They're weirdos," he said. "I'm all right. I'm working full time, I'm running my company."

"Your life is out of control," I told him. "You're addicted to several substances. I'll meet you there at 8:00 P.M." At 8:00 P.M. I found him, standing by the door.

"Let's go in."

"There are no seats."

We found two seats.

Most of the people at CA are young; beautiful children and young adults. In my late fifties, I was the oldest one at this meeting.

A 12-year-old girl got up to get her 30-day chip. Standing on her tiptoes, this child announced that she had been on drugs since age 8. It took her a year of going to CA before she managed 30 consecutive drug-free days. Everyone cheered. She was trying.

A 34-year-old man told how he had finally, after four years of trying, gotten 30 consecutive drug-free days. "This morning I couldn't resist anymore. So I went to the Sunset Strip to get some crack. I had the money out of my wallet, I was all set. Then I said no, today's my thirtieth day. I didn't buy the crack. Instead, I gave the money to a bum."

You could see the enthusiasm in his eyes, hear it in his voice. He had beaten the beast, at least for today. He knew there was no cure, only day-by-day control, but he had taken a great step forward. Many patients ask me about this. They want to know "When will I be cured?" I tell them that although an addiction may never be cured, we can work—often successfully—to keep the addiction under control.

After it was all over, my patient said, "Doc, what do you want me to do?" I told him to start attending the meetings, and to work with me on the Ten Pillars. He's taking it one day at a time. That's all I ask of him—or of myself.

Why are AA and similar groups so effective for many addicts? Because it's people helping people, and there's no doctor so good as someone who has felt your pain. Because it's people telling you that God loves and accepts you, and so do all the people in the room with you. Because they tell you that you are a good person, no matter what your past misdeeds. Because they tell you that you have the power to change your life, with God's help. These words, written into your mental gospel, *can* change your life.

Most of all, because they understand that treatment begins where the wound is worst: in the spirit.

The cure lies where the germ resides: in the spirit.

My Own Realization

Give me understanding, and I shall live.

Ps. 119:144

I was at an AA meeting with a patient when suddenly I realized that I had never used the word alcoholic in connection with my father. I had never admitted to myself that my father had been an alcoholic, sometimes a dark and dangerous one. He had died over 20 years before, yet I still had not admitted to myself that my father had been an addict. All of a sudden I could say it. It didn't change the love and affection I felt for my father, it didn't make him any better or worse than he had been. It did, however, make me wonder. If it's so hard for me to admit that my father had a failing, how much harder, more painful, is it for the addict to admit it to himself? If my spirit is wounded, how horribly is the addict's hurting?

What a relief. I could say the A-word without feeling shamed or guilty. It didn't diminish my father. It explained his condition, and, what's more, helped me to understand myself, my own behavior, a little better. I had counseled thousands of people over the years. I knew the behavior patterns that may occur in adult children of alcoholics. But I had never measured myself by that yardstick. I also know that people do grow and learn, but there are always some hangovers from the past.

Dysfunction Need Not Be a Disaster

Along with most Americans, I was raised in what is known as a dysfunctional family. Dysfunctional families are simply families that do not function according to what is perceived as the ideal. In a perfect family the mother and the father are open and expressive, they give and take love easily, they're happy, they express their joy, yet they know how to handle anger and disappointments, they're free and open about sexual matters, they give and take criticism in a kindly and well-intentioned manner. This idealized mother and father will then have perfect children, whom they will never criticize, never be overtly disappointed with, never get angry at. Mother and father will never snap at or strike their children in anger, never feel tired, depressed, and unhappy in front of their children, and never, in an unguarded moment, say, "You're such a pain!" The family will have no addictions and no secrets (unhappy families have the most secrets, lots of things to hide). The children will learn to be happy and loving, to be open and frank with their parents, siblings, friends. They'll grow to be perfect people.

This is a highly idealized picture, one which we mere mortals often fail to live up to. That is why I say, in my estimation, that about 90 percent of all families are dysfunctional.

Dysfunctional families are families that do not live up to our ideals. There may be alcoholism or it may be another addiction. If so, there will be a certain amount of shame, the neighbors or relatives shouldn't find out. There is an addict and a codependent, someone who covers up for the addict. The addict may be the greatest person in the world, but at certain times, when under the influence, he's not so great. The father may be abusive, he may be absent, physically or emotionally, due to the alcohol. As the codependent, the mother may be so busy covering up for the father that she has no time or energy for the children. Perhaps Mother is the alcoholic, or the Valium addict. She may be taking Halcion, the most popular sleeping pill, or Xanax for her anxiety. She's as addicted to her drugs as street addicts are to theirs. She hasn't got the energy for her children. They may find her sound asleep when they come home from school. They have to cover up for her. There may be other problems, sexual abuse, addictions to unhappiness, to depression, to fears or guilt.

Happy families are happy in the same way; unhappy families are unhappy in different ways. Families are as sick and dysfunctional as the heaviness of the secrets they have to keep–the secrets of the various addictions.

A lot has been written about dysfunctional families. Many researchers blame our addictions and other problems on dysfunctional families: If only the mother had done this, or if the father hadn't been that, they say, the children would have been all right.

I remember how surprised I was to find that a high school principal, a scholar, a highly respected man, made life hell for his children. He didn't mean to, of course, he was only trying to mold them to perfection. His technique included withholding approval unless they were perfect. One son was perfect; a scholar, an athlete, he "topped" his father by becoming president of a university. He was so full of anger, unfortunately, that he beat his wife and children. Another son never measured up in his father's eyes. He dropped out of high school to bum around, an unhappy hobo who didn't like himself because his father never liked him. It wasn't until his father died that this son held a steady job and began accepting responsibility for his life. While the father was alive, he "knew" he was a failure. The terrible message was always there, in his father's eyes and words. Only after his father died could he begin to like himself.

Perfectly healthy families are few and far between. We're only human, we carry our imperfections with us wherever we go. Most families are dysfunctional in some way.

Don't let the experts tell you, as some are fond of doing, that being raised in a dysfunctional family dooms us to a life of pain and misery. I was raised in a severely dysfunctional family. My mother didn't know how to handle my alcoholic father. Sadly, she sometimes bore the brunt of his pain.

Experts tell us that dysfunctional families have three main rules: Don't trust. Don't talk. Don't feel. They say you *can't* trust, because you've been hurt too many times. I know many adults raised in dysfunctional families who do trust others. Some are very trusting, some have only average measures of trust, some have none at all. I know some who trust everyone, even when that trust is patently not warranted. Perhaps they're overcompensating.

They say you learn quickly not to talk, especially about your feelings. That's interesting. I know many adults who were raised in dysfunctional families who talk quite a lot. Some talk of their experiences in a detached way, some with great anger, some calmly, as a means to teaching others. I talked about my family a lot, but I never talked about my father's alcoholism. Neither did I bring my school friends home.

Analysts say that children in dysfunctional families shut off their emotions, for the pain is too great. I've seen some incredible outpourings of feeling in the regular weight-loss group that meets in my office. Perhaps you suppress your feelings, but they're always there in you, ready to help or hurt you. We are by nature feeling beings. We can't discard our feelings anymore than we can shuck our skin.

I've seen generational charts detailing how dysfunction and pain is carried, inexorably, from generation to generation. I'm always suspicious when experts tell us we're doomed to do this or statistics tell us we're going to be that way. As a physician, I have seen many, many people beat the odds. The odds refer to large numbers of people: They say absolutely nothing about *you*.

If you do come from a dysfunctional family, like most of us you've grown through various experiences since you left the family or formed your own family. We've all had the opportunity to grow or should have grown. True, some of us don't grow, and those are the people who need help.

The point is, we are what we make ourselves. Yes, our families have a profound impact on us, especially in our early years. Yes, we have different physical and mental limitations. Yes, we can be hurt, badly, and we may pull our shell over our head. But nothing is written in stone. We can turn the page of our mental book, we can make a new beginning. Perhaps our new beginning is a bold leap forward. Maybe it's a tentative step. We might even fall flat on our face. That's OK. We can turn the pages of our mental gospel once again, we can find a clean new sheet and begin again. We can always begin again. It's never too late to begin making ourselves exactly what we want to be. That is our God-given power, and no one can take it away from us.

The experts will tell you it's impossible. But I've seen plenty of people turn their lives around, people who suffered more pain than you or I can imagine. Tell yourself that you *can* do it. Write that great thought into your spirit and hold it dear.

THE PAY PROGRAM

Behold, how great a matter a little fire kindleth!

James 3:5

A little fire, the fire of even a single good thought, can brighten the great blackness of negativity. A little fire will shine brightly in the darkness, will warm you and sustain you through your journey to spiritual health.

All addictions are strong and dangerous, especially our addiction to negative thinking. Let's make use of the power of addiction, the same power that can rearrange our body chemistry. But let's choose our addiction carefully, find one that will give us all the good things we need while protecting us against the bad. There's one addiction that fights the others head-on, one that puts us on the road to vibrant health. And that's *P*ositive *A*ddiction to *Y*ourself (PAY), positive addiction to your health and happiness.

To be *P*ositively *A*ddicted to *Y*ourself means filling your mental book with this simple message: I like myself. I may not be perfect, I've done some things I'm not proud of, but I like myself. My world is a loving, joyful, accepting world.

There is outside intervention available for various addictions, but I want you to go beyond that. Use Positive Addiction to Yourself to become as healthy and happy as you can possibly be. The program is called PAY, but there is no cost. You'll be replacing your negative thoughts with positive thoughts. You'll be scraping the dark colors of negativity from your mental filter, replacing them with the rainbow colors of joy and love. You'll be closing the book on anger and other destructive thoughts, and writing of happiness and success instead.

Whether the problem is with food, alcohol, cigarettes, or anything else, this 10-step Positive Addiction to Yourself program (adapted from the 12-step program used by many self-help groups) will be helpful:

1. *You must want help.* If you don't want help, nothing else matters. I don't know how many patients I've seen go through years of psychiatric or psychological counseling, be locked up or voluntarily go to rehabilitation centers, who were not ready to be helped. All the theories and experts and treatments and drugs and talks and sessions were useless, because the patient was not ready to be helped.

A young man, about 23, told me he had been in and out of rehabilitation centers for years, experiencing every approach you can imagine, from the most traditional to the very far out. "It doesn't matter what they do," he told me, "if you don't want to be helped."

I've seen others who, when they were ready, picked themselves up out of the gutter and got on with life. They simply decided it was time.

When is a person ready to be helped? They know. How do

you make a person ready? I don't know. I've dealt with uncounted addicts over the years. Many were patients whose names and faces have faded far from memory. Others are forever etched in my mind. Some were friends and relatives, very close to me. I didn't know how to make them ready. I do know that we must keep the door open, even if only a little, so that when they are ready, they can come to us for help.

For the addicts themselves, I've found that many are suddenly ready because something touches them. Some reach bottom and realize that they have little time left. Some finally hear their loved ones' pleas. Something touches them. If only we knew how to reach all of them!

Want to recover. Find the good thought somewhere within you that will be the spark to get the littlest fire going, and you're on your way.

2. *Acknowledge the problem.* Admit that part of your life has become unmanageable and uncontrollable. No, don't tell yourself that you're a horrible person, that you've harmed everyone else and don't deserve to live. Don't tell yourself that you've ruined everything, or that you can never look anyone in the eye again. Don't tell yourself that everything's OK, either. Don't say that you're no worse than anyone else, or that you can stop anytime you want. Just tell yourself that you have a problem.

3. *Accept responsibility.* Don't blame everyone else. Don't blame anyone else. Don't point your finger at society, at your job, or at your spouse. Most of us are from dysfunctional families, we've all experienced life's ups and downs. Turn that finger around, point it directly at yourself. You are the one with a problem to overcome. You are the one flirting with disease. You are the one who must rediscover happiness within as the first step toward recovering your health.

4. *Now give thanks.* Thank God for making you exactly as you are. Thank Him for giving you life. Thank Him for giving you all the tools you need to become the great person you want to be!

"Give thanks?" some patients ask me incredulously. "Give thanks for being an addict? What good will that do?"

It will put you in the positive frame of mind. It will strike that little match that will grow into your guiding light. When you give thanks for being exactly as you are, you are telling yourself that the way you are, whatever it is, is OK. You're telling yourself that you accept yourself, that you like yourself. Giving thanks doesn't excuse you from the work that must be done. It just tells you that you believe you're OK.

5. *Share your problem with your Higher Power, and at least one other person.* Come clean. Strip away the pretenses. This person can be a close friend or relative, or you can tell members of a support group. Tell God and someone else how you went wrong, and what you intend to do about it.

6. *Write the great news into your mental gospel.* Practice all the special R_X's and affirmations I have given you in this book. With your mind's eye, see yourself as the happy, healthy, successful person you deserve to be. Picture yourself as you will be when you put your addiction and unhappiness behind you. Imagine all the good that will come to you, especially all the happiness that is already within you. Hold that image in your mind at all times. See, feel, act, behave, walk, talk, and think like the happy and healthy winner you deserve to be. Write all this goodness into your mental gospel.

7. *Make amends, wherever possible, to all those people you harmed through your addiction (unless making amends would cause harm to you or them).* Do it for their sake, yes, but more important, for your sake. Earning their forgiveness is important. So is regaining your self-respect. Show yourself that you can do good, as well as harm.

8. *Stay busy!* Get involved in a great cause. Become a foster parent or a Big Brother/Sister. Teach a disabled child to read, help out at the old folks' home. Work to achieve world peace, to end hunger, to clean up the environment. Pick up litter, gather food for the hungry, get an initiative on the next ballot. Help others; that's a great way to help yourself.

9. *Associate with winners.* Seek out those who have found their happiness within, those whose cups truly runneth over with health, happiness, success, and love. Study the way they walk, talk, handle themselves. Imitate the way they walk with confidence. Practice talking the way they do, with that feeling of inner peace, that great contentment you can hear in their voice. Adopt their calm demeanor.

10. *Continue practicing good nutrition, exercise, meditation,*

relaxation, and all the other positive health habits I've described. Make a commitment to yourself. Make your recovery your number one priority. Why? Because nothing in life is as important as your health and happiness. Not money, not prestige, not power. There is nothing as precious as health and happiness.

Let's see if I can boil the 10 steps down to a few words:

Want
Acknowledge
Accept
Give thanks
Share
Write
Amend
Get involved
Associate and
Practice, Practice, Practice!

Ten steps to *PAY*: Want, acknowledge, accept, give thanks, share, write, amend, get involved, associate, and practice, practice, practice! To this you can add one more very important step: Believe. Believe you can do it. Believe it with all your heart.

Each of us is a special, worthwhile person with the tools we need to build health and happiness. If you acknowledge that you're good, tell yourself that you're good, and work to enhance the goodness that is yours, you've lit that first little fire, set that first twig ablaze. You've taken the first, the most important step.

Want, acknowledge, accept, give thanks, share, write, amend, get involved, associate, and practice, practice, practice! This is the easy price for *PAY*.

Rx: Positive Living

Today is Day Thirteen of Making Miracles, the Day of Positive Living. This day is devoted to developing Positive Addiction to Yourself; this is the day when we bring the threads of the Making Miracles Program together.

Recite these affirmations throughout the day, today and everyday. Be sure to "see" each affirmation as you recite it.

Upon awakening: "Rejoice and Be Glad"
This is the day that the Lord hath made; I shall rejoice and be glad, be gladder than glad. I give myself permission to see all the happiness that is in my world, to think of the happiness, and to speak of the happiness. The Creator has filled the world with unlimited joy that is mine for the taking.

Morning: "It is Good to Give Thanks"
It is good to give thanks unto the Lord for making me the healthy, happy, and successful person I so richly deserve to be. I am open to receiving all the blessings of His abundant universe.

Noon: "Endless Enthusiasm"
The Creator has filled me to the brim with enthusiasm. I gladly and generously pour my unlimited enthusiasm over my every thought and action. Armed with endless enthusiasm, I find excitement and adventure in every day.

Afternoon: "Spiritually Minded"
To be spiritually minded is life and peace. I give myself permission to be as calm and serene as the quiet waters of a beautiful, still lake.

Evening: "A Merry Heart"
A merry heart is a good medicine. My heart and spirit and the gospel of my mind are filled with joy. I am full of the thoughts and things of health, happiness, and success.

When going to bed: "Put on the New Me"
Today was another successful step toward the new me. With enthusiastic anticipation and absolute certainty that I'll make even more progress tomorrow, and every tomorrow, I'm putting on the new me.

Recite each affirmation out loud, with enthusiasm. This daily menu sets up the daily minimum requirements of glad tidings. But I tell my patients to go beyond the minimum and recite their affirmations all day long: 5, 10, 20 times a day. You can't overdo it with affirmations!

In addition to your daily diet of affirmations, enter into the world of this special R_X for Positive Living several times today, with energy and conviction.

Set aside some time today to sit in a quiet room, on a comfortable chair. Tell everyone that you do not want to be disturbed; take the phone off the hook. Close your eyes. With your mind's eye, picture total blackness. There's nothing, nothing but the blackness of the darkest night. You know there's pain in the darkness, along with loneliness and fear. The pain, loneliness, and fear are not with you, however, for you've got a single good thought in your head. That single good thought is your shield. The good thought is in your head, and your spirit is whole.

There's a torch in your hand, unlit. With your mind's eye, see yourself focusing on that torch. Like a lightning bolt, the good thought suddenly leaps out of your head and ignites the torch, and the torch is burning brightly. Your torch is like the burning bush; it burns, but is not consumed. Indeed, it seems to grow stronger as it burns.

You're standing in front of a big circular object, like a disk; it's a little taller than you are. This is the filter of your mind. Your filter is covered with the rust and refuse of negativity, the sharp edges and ragged punctures of anger and fear. See yourself holding your flame of positiveness up to your mental filter. The flame leaps from your torch onto the filter, engulfing the filter in a cleansing fire. See the dark colors of rage and hurt melting away. See the jagged edges of the ragged punctures burning away. Now the flame is gone from the filter. Touch your mental filter. Feel it: It's warm, smooth. See it. The colors of hurt and pain have burned away, leaving the beautiful colors of joy and love that were always there, underneath. Now that love and joy are back in view, your view of the world will always be loving and joyful.

The darkness is lit by your flame of positivity, your filter is purified. Now see yourself, with your mind's eye, seated at a table. On the table, open to a brand-new page, is your mental gospel. By the light of your torch, the torch lit by your single good thought, you begin writing in your mental book. All that you write is of love and joy, courage and sharing, forgiveness and friendship. As you write, your torch burns brighter than ever. As you write, say:

> The fire of my spirit is a blazing sun of positiveness. My spirit is whole, my mind is at peace. Everywhere I look, I see love and joy.

The Best Medicine: Spirit!

Addictions come in different varieties. We can easily measure how much a person drinks, smokes, eats, or uses drugs. Thanks to various laboratory tests, we can generally watch the damage accumulate in the body. Other addictions, such as perfectionism and depression, are hard to quantify. We can't measure depression the way we do fat in the blood, but I can tell you that depression rips through your health with the ease of a hot knife slicing through butter.

We all have our compulsions and addictions; some amusing and harmless, others dangerous. In a sense, many addictions—from binge eating to depression to alcoholism—are a way to avoid the present or the future. The addiction, harmful though it may be, is comforting because it is familiar, it is satisfying on a certain level. Addictions are a way of sticking your head in the sand of the past so you don't have to look at the painful present or future. Negative addictions put a part of our life on hold. Tomorrow we'll take care of the problems plaguing us, we tell ourselves. We'll deal with the addiction tomorrow. For most of us, of course, tomorrow never comes.

Whatever your harmful craving, compulsion, or addiction, stop procrastinating. Read the ten steps to *PAY* again. Copy them down, carry them in your pocket. Make copies to hang on your bathroom mirror, on the refrigerator, by your desk. Procrastination only increases self-doubt, making your task that much more difficult. There's no better time to begin recovering good health, happiness, success.

Does *PAY* really work? Can we really make miracles? It sounds so simple, simplistic in fact. Just say some words every day, put some pictures in your head, tell yourself that you see love. It sounds almost airy-fairy. If it's so easy, if it works so well, how come we aren't all doing it?

Modern medicine is caught in what we call the molecular model of medicine. The human body is viewed as a machine made up of many parts. If the machine is broken, according to this reasoning, all the doctor has to do is identify the broken part, fix or replace it, and everything will be fine.

This approach might work if we were toasters or microwave ovens, but we're not. *We're human beings with a body, a mind, and spirit.* We're people with joys, sorrows, hopes and fears. We're more than a body that responds correctly or incorrectly to certain mechanical laws, much more.

Too many physicians treat us as machines. We're becoming patient machines that can be plugged into diagnostic machines like EKGs and CAT scans, then into the treatment machines. Perhaps the hospital of the future won't need doctors at all–a technician will plug all the machines into each other. Imagine a sterile room, monitors and buttons covering the walls and ceiling. Lots of tubes and hoses coming out of the walls and ceiling. In the center of the room, a single bed in which lies the patient machine, hooked by many tubes to the machines hidden in the walls and ceiling. Lasers constantly scan the patient machine, recording every change in body chemistry, temperature, position. Somewhere in the walls is the head machine, the doctor machine that integrates all the information and gives orders for treatment.

But what machine can measure the spirit? What machine can keep tabs on our thoughts, those thoughts that determine, to a large extent, what our body chemistry will be, how strong our immune system will be, how surely and steadily our heart will beat?

Modern medicine has much to be proud of. But we doctors must admit that we have overlooked the incredible power of the human spirit, that intangible something, that touch of God within us that gives us all the power to be our own best doctor. Slowly but surely, medicine is coming to acknowledge that our greatest medicine lies within us.

Become *P*ositively *A*ddicted to *Y*ourself. Use the incredible power of your spirit to ensure that your cup always runneth over.

THE BEGINNING

Being planted, shall it prosper?
Ezek. 17:10

I've given you a program, some guidance and ideas. The seed has been planted: Will it grow?

Can it grow? Yes, it can! I've seen the barren spirit turn into a land of milk and honey, filled with joy and love and courage and dreams and all the other great thoughts and rewards of life.

"Dr. Fox," some patients complain, "you're a nice guy, but you're just talking about words. Words aren't really medicine, words can't make my immune system stronger or protect my heart. You need real medicine for that. Sure, it's nice to be happy, but, come on, this word stuff is nonsense."

Words. Of what value are words? Can words, these vibrations of the air we all throw around so carelessly, do anything, have they any power? We can't touch them, we can't feel them, we can't see them unless they are written down. What gives words their power?

Words are the audible form of ideas. There lies their strength, for ideas are the most powerful entities in the universe.

"NO ONE DIES ON THIS WARD"

Neither man nor nation can exist without a sublime idea.
Fyodor Dostoyevski

There was a fellow name Doc Wiley who knew all about the power of words. He showed how simple words can save lives.

By most accounts, Doc was no one special. Most accounts, however, were wrong. Doc was not a distinguished physician, not any kind of doctor at all. He was a Western Union messenger boy. But he was different from the other messengers, for he believed it was his purpose in life to deliver a little bit of joy and optimism to everyone. He used to carry a pocketful of little pieces of paper, on which he had written slogans: words. Words like "Today is a great day!" and "Keep your chin up!" and "Pack up your troubles!" Each time he delivered a message, he reached into his pocket and gave the person one of his slogans. Some people thought he was nutty. Doc thought that every day was a great day, for it was another chance to spread joy.

When World War II broke out, Doc wanted to fight for his country. He tried to enlist, but they told him to go away, he was too old to be in the Army. Doc was upset; he really wanted to help. So he volunteered to work in a veterans' hospital. And work he did, carrying bedpans around, wheeling disabled soldiers up and down the hallways, doing whatever he could. The hours were long and the work was hard but Doc didn't mind: He was serving his country.

Doc hurt, however, every time he had to roll another soldier off a bed, onto a gurney, and down the hall to the morgue. Every time he wheeled out another dead man, he wanted to cry. Doc hated the thought of seeing another soldier die, but what could he do? He wasn't a doctor, he had no special skills, no knowledge, no training, no nothing. He was just a delivery boy who now delivered bodies as well as messages.

That's it! The messages! That's what Doc Wiley did best, and that's what he could do for the soldiers. He decided to go with his strength.

The next morning, when the soldiers on Doc's ward awoke, they saw a message painted on the wall. In big letters it said: *No One Dies on This Ward*. Six little words, *No One Dies on This Ward*. When the hospital administrators found out about this "message mural," they were furious, they wanted to fire the "old kook." (That's the way administrators are, they want everything to be done by the book.) But the doctors and nurses said, "Wait a minute, don't fire him. It sounds strange, but all these sick and wounded soldiers are sitting up in bed. They're laughing about it, they're making bets as to who will live the longest. They look better. Leave it up!"

Those six words remained: *No One Dies on This Ward*. You

know what? No one died. There was a magic to those words. Every new soldier brought into the ward was made to understand that he couldn't die–*he couldn't, else he'd break the magic spell.*

What began as a joke to most people became very serious. Everybody knew they must believe, they must make those words come true. And they did. The death rate in that ward plummeted. The soldiers came in with the same kinds of problems as before, yet they stayed alive.

It was nothing; it was words, it was paint on a wall, but it was everything: *It was an idea. An idea that every sick and wounded man on the ward took to heart. The doctors and nurses took it to heart as well. Their attitudes about the patients changed–improved. With everyone believing the best would happen, the best was all but assured.* The idea was written into their mental gospel. The seed was planted. And the seed prospered.

Eventually someone died. Doc's words–his great idea–couldn't save all the soldiers' lives but his words were still magic. Protected by Doc's great idea, patients were always healthier on his ward.

Thought Nutrition

Behold, how great a matter a little fire kindleth!

James 3:5

Are words that important? Well, every word we speak or think is written into our mental gospel. So is every word we take in through our ears or eyes. Written into our mental books, our words become our thoughts, and as such, our biochemistry.

In fact, words, like food, provide nutrition for the body. Food nutrients help keep us strong and healthy in various ways. Some of them are converted into other substances: Fructose is transformed into glucose; amino acids are used to manufacture proteins. Certain nutrients are neither transformed nor used to manufacture anything; instead, they serve as "spark plugs" to keep the body's chemistry humming. Some nutrients help the body absorb or utilize other nutrients.

Our words, or more specifically, the words written into our mental gospels, are like nutrients, also with far-ranging roles to play. Sometimes these thought nutrients touch the body gently, sometimes harshly; sometimes with a clear effect, sometimes with an ambiguous one; sometimes they touch lovingly, sometimes painfully. Always, however, even the gentlest touch sets up vibrations which spread throughout the body, affecting everything everywhere. That's the way the body is; there are no isolated "islands" in the body where events can pass unnoticed. Everything that happens is communicated to every other place in the body in some way.

What kind of nutrition do your words and thoughts provide for your body? Are you a "junk thought junkie" mouthing or gobbling down harmful thoughts that will harden your attitudes as surely as junk foods can harden the arteries?

Sixty-Six Words That Changed the World

How much thought nutrition do we need? Are the affirmations and special Rxs I gave you enough to nourish you? The more thought nutrition you get, the better, and there's no need to worry about overdosing. But remember: The actual number of words or thoughts you take in is irrelevant. What counts is the greatness of the ideas they represent.

Great ideas often come in small, simple packages. The Lord's Prayer is only 66 words long. The Twenty-third Psalm is made up of 118 words. Lincoln's Gettysburg Address contains 226 words. The entire Ten Commandments are spelled out in just about 300 words.

The U.S Department of Agriculture directive on pricing cabbage is 15,629 words long! If length were the criterion, this document would be a storehouse of nutrition for mind and spirit.

Despite their brevity, The Lord's Prayer, the Twenty-third Psalm, and the Gettysburg Address are rich in thought nutrition. In less than a page, the Ten Commandments set out a code for living, a marvelous ethical bible. And the brief affirmations and special Rxs I gave you can help change your life in the same positive way.

"I Believe"

He who believes is strong; he who doubts is weak. Strong convictions precede great actions.

J.F. Clarke

What are the most nutritious ideas? As far as making miracles with your spirit is concerned, they can be summed up in this brief credo I give to my patients:

I believe in miracles,
The miracles of my mind.
My thoughts shape and make my world
Filling it with loving joy, courage, peace, beautiful dreams.

I believe that God loves me,
That He wants me to succeed.
I believe I can and am succeeding
For I am imbued with spirit, the Divine touch within.

My cup runneth over,
A never-ending flow.
Strength and inspiration,
Enthusiasm, energy, and excitement; the stuff of life.

I believe my thoughts are written
In the gospel of my mind.
Pages, chapters, and volumes
Every thought making me, mind and body, as great as can be.

I believe in me
All the great things I can be.
I can touch the stars, I can ride the rainbow.
I can make the grade, I can set the standard.
I can win and when I don't,
I'll come back again, better than ever.
If I can see it, I can believe it,
When I believe it, I can be it.
I believe in me.

This is only the beginning
Of the great things that will be.
I believe in my future,
An unending journey.

I believe in miracles,
And I believe in me.
I'm a winner!
I'm a winner!
I'm a winner!

They're only words. But as a physician, I can tell you that if you repeat these words, and all the words in the affirmations and R_Xs I've given you in this book, some great ideas will take hold of your spirit.

Oliver Wendell Holmes said that "Man's mind, once stretched by a new idea, never regains its original dimensions." Stretch your mind–and your spirit–with belief in yourself.

THE ULTIMATE QUESTION

Far away there in the sunshine are my highest aspirations. I may not reach them, but I can look up and see their beauty, believe in them, and try to follow where they lead.

Louisa May Alcott

We can talk endlessly about theories and philosophy, but it all comes down to this: Are you happy? Every other question is ultimately irrelevant, for everything is nothing compared to happiness.

I've been rich, and I've been poor. I've lived on both coasts, and in-between. I've been young, and now, well, I'll always be young in spirit. I've watched my children being born, and I've laid one to rest forever. As a doctor, I've saved people's lives, and I've held others in my arms as they died. Some of my dreams have come true, some have not–not yet.

Through it all, through the ups and downs, the joys and the sorrows, the loves and the heartbreaks, the dreams come true and the dreams slipped away, the only question that really needs to be asked is: Are we happy?

Are you happy? My answer is yes, I am happy. For that reason, and that reason alone, I count myself a success in life.

What is Success?

One of my favorite philosophers, Ralph Waldo Emerson, gave this beautiful definition of success:

> How do you measure success?
> To laugh often and much;
> To win the respect of intelligent people
> And the affection of children;
> To earn the appreciation of honest critics
> And endure the betrayal of false friends;
> To appreciate beauty;
> To find the best in others;
> To leave the world a bit better,
> whether by a healthy child,
> a garden patch,
> a redeemed social condition,
> or a job well done;
> To know even one other life has breathed easier
> because you have lived–this is to have succeeded.

In other words, a success is someone who lived with love and laughter. That's all there is to it.

Having money does not make you a success. I practice medicine in wealthy Beverly Hills, California. My children went to the Beverly Hills schools with the children of movie stars, producers, directors, socialites, bankers, singers, attorneys, and other physicians. My children and I can tell you that money is nice to have, but it adds absolutely no happiness to your life. Not a bit.

If money equals happiness, how come there are so many psychologists and psychiatrists in Beverly Hills? My offices used to be on Bedford Drive in the "Golden Triangle" of Beverly Hills.

Bedford Drive is known as Shrinks' Row because there are so many couches for the unhappy wealthy residents to lie on as they seek peace of mind through hours with busy psychiatrists. Unhappy people are not successes.

Being powerful has nothing to do with happiness. Some of the most powerful people I know are miserable. I don't know what the statistics are, but I'll bet that Beverly Hills takes more medicines, per capita, for ulcers, colitis, headaches, depression, and high blood pressure, than any other area. People whose unhappy thoughts produce physical disease are not successful in life.

A great education and sterling family background have nothing to do with happiness. Education and background can help you become wealthy and powerful, yes, but wealth and power are not the formula for happiness.

There was a 53-year-old physician; wealthy, educated and respected. He wanted to be chief of his department at the hospital, but due to hospital politics, someone else was chosen over him. Several days later, when he saw the new chief sitting in what would have been his office, he became so angry he collapsed. The electrocardiogram showed irregular heart beats and he died. He had it all–all but happiness. This man was anything but a success.

THE WORLD IS WHAT YOU MAKE OF IT

Unto the pure all things are pure.

Titus 1:15

How does one become successful? It's a matter of writing success–that is, *happiness*–into your mental gospel. It's a matter of walking, talking, acting, thinking, and being happy. I know that's easier said than done. But it can be done. It *must* be done.

Barry was recently interviewed by the highly respected Morgan Williams of KBIG-FM radio here in Los Angeles. While waiting for the program to begin, Barry and Ms. Williams chatted about the effects our thoughts have on our bodies, indeed, on our entire lives. Ms. Williams agreed that our thoughts have a profound influence on us, but she wondered how we can keep our thoughts positive in these troubling times. She began the interview by stating:

"I find, from my own experience, as well as the experiences of some of my friends, that [keeping our thoughts positive is] really not easy to do. We all want to. We all want to live good lives, we all want to be happy, we all want peace, not just for ourselves but for the world. But, Barry, the state of the world as it is today is so overwhelming in so many ways that it's really hard to get . . . to where you and your dad say we must."

In his reply, Barry emphasized that while we often can't do anything about the world, we can do everything about our reaction to events. As Shakespeare said in his *Hamlet*: ". . . there is nothing either good or bad, but thinking makes it so."

I don't mean to say that gang violence, pollution, political shenanigans, the threat of nuclear war, racial tension, traffic, and other features of modern life are not bad. They're terrible. *But we must not allow unhappy thoughts of these things to poison our spirit.* The bad things are there. Some, like pollution, harm us from the outside. *We must never allow them to harm us from within.*

We shouldn't tell ourselves that gang violence is good, for it is not. Instead, we should acknowledge that the problem exists, and that it must be dealt with. Some anger or indignation or compassion to stir us into action is good. But keep the "badness" of the situation outside your body. Never invite it in by becoming excessively angry about the problem. That solves absolutely nothing. It only adds to the problem by making *you* sick.

We can't always change the world, but we can change our thoughts. That's why I say that the world is what you (mentally) make of it.

"What do you mean the world is what I make of it?" a man snarled at me after I gave a speech at a large convention. "I don't *make* war, I don't *make* gangs, I don't *make* crooked politicians, I don't *make* millions of people starve all over the world." And each "*make*" was spat out with resentment. "I'm a victim," he proclaimed, "just like everybody else."

We are never victims! Not where our thoughts are concerned. That's the one place where we have absolute control. Remember:

Yours is the only pen writing in your mental gospel. Nothing is written, no thoughts are planted in your spirit, without your permission. That's what makes you so powerful. That's what gives you control over your life. That's what allows you to make the world a pleasing, positive place for *you* to live.

"Unto the pure, all things are pure." If your spirit is pure, your world will be pure.

We are as small as our fears, and as great as our desires. Desire happiness. Want it so much that you're willing to spend time every day working on this program, making the Ten Pillars part of your life, filling your mental gospel with pages and pages of loving joy. Want it: You'll get it. You can be every bit as great as your greatest desire.

William Jennings Bryan said that "destiny is not a matter of chance, it is a matter of choice; it is not a thing to be waited for, it is a thing to be achieved."

Choose to be happy!

THIS IS THE BEGINNING

Be rich in good works.

1 Tim. 6:18

Today is the beginning of your miraculous new life. You're on your way to making your dreams come true. Now, don't put this book down and forget about it; *Making Miracles* is not something to be intellectually understood and then forgotten. *Making Miracles* is not a fact to be memorized, it is a way of thinking, talking, living, and being. As such, it takes constant practice. Practice the program, think about it, work through it. Keep at it until it's automatic, until it's completely written into your mental gospel and has become your way of life.

It may be difficult at first to give up the harsh thoughts we've grown accustomed to. There are habits to unlearn; we must examine ourselves, admit our mistakes. That can be disconcerting at first, but many things are hard for the first time around. After a little practice, however, they become easy.

That great football coach Vincent Lombardi said, "The

quality of a person's life is in direct proportion to his commitment to excellence. . ." Commit yourself to turning your life into a never-ending stream of excellence. You have inside of you enough talent to conquer the world: Make the commitment!

Today is the beginning. How far can you go? How far do you *want* to go?

Keep working at the program, go through the 14 days over and over again. Do them in order, or, if you're having a particular problem, turn right to the chapter that deals with your difficulty. Recite your daily affirmations every day, with energy and enthusiasm. Make the nutritious ideas in the affirmations part of your every thought. Set aside time every day for the special R_X's. Practice seeing, with your mind's eye, the scenes I have described. In no time at all, you'll be able to enter right into the world of your special R_X's.

Somerset Maugham said, "It is a funny thing about life; if you refuse to accept anything but the best, you very often get it." Be rich in good works, good thoughts, and good deeds. Expect the best from yourself. Why? Because you deserve the best!

R_X: BEGINNING

According to your faith be it unto you.

Matt. 9:29

Today is Day Fourteen of Making Miracles, the Day of Beginning. This day is devoted to beginning anew, armed with indomitable spirit! Today is just the beginning of a great life!

Recite these affirmations throughout the day, today and every day. Be sure to "see" each affirmation as you recite it.

Upon awakening: "Rejoice and Be Glad"
This is the day that the Lord hath made; I shall rejoice and be glad, be gladder than glad. I give myself permission to see all the happiness that is in my world, to think of the happiness, and to speak of the happiness. The Creator has filled the world with unlimited joy that is mine for the taking.

Morning: "It is Good to Give Thanks"
It is good to give thanks unto the Lord for making me the healthy, happy, and successful person I so richly deserve to be. I am open to receiving all the blessings of His abundant universe.

Noon: "Endless Enthusiasm"
The Creator has filled me to the brim with enthusiasm. I gladly and generously pour my unlimited enthusiasm over my every thought and action. Armed with endless enthusiasm, I find excitement and adventure in every day.

Afternoon: "Spiritually Minded"
To be spiritually minded is life and peace. I give myself permission to be as calm and serene as the quiet waters of a beautiful, still lake.

Evening: "A Merry Heart"
A merry heart is a good medicine. My heart and spirit and the gospel of my mind are filled with joy. I am full of the thoughts and things of health, happiness, and success.

When going to bed: "Put on the New Me"
Today was another successful step toward the new me. With enthusiastic anticipation and absolute certainty that I'll make even more progress tomorrow, and every tomorrow, I'm putting on the new me.

Recite each affirmation out loud, with enthusiasm. This daily menu sets up the daily minimum requirements of glad tidings. But I tell my patients to go beyond the minimum and recite their affirmations all day long: 5, 10, 20 times a day. You can't overdo it with affirmations!

In addition to your daily diet of affirmations, enter into the world of this special R_X for Beginning several times today, with energy and conviction.

Set aside some time today to sit in a quiet room, on a comfortable chair. Tell everyone that you do not want to be disturbed; take the phone off the hook. Close your eyes. With your mind's eye, picture yourself sitting in a chair. You're holding a book. This is your mental gospel. See yourself opening the book, somewhere in the middle, a clean white page. This is your new beginning. There's a smile on your face, for you know that this is a great beginning. See that smile on your face. Know in your heart that this is the beginning of a new life for you–the life you've always wanted. As you see this, recite your credo with enthusiastic belief:

> I believe in miracles
> The miracles of my mind.
> My thoughts shape and make my world
> Filling it with loving joy, courage, peace, beautiful dreams.
>
> I believe that God loves me,
> That He wants me to succeed.
> I believe I can, and am,
> For I am imbued with spirit, the Divine touch within.
>
> My cup runneth over,
> A never-ending flow.
> Strength and inspiration,
> Enthusiasm, energy, and excitement; the stuff of life.
>
> I believe my thoughts are written
> In the gospel of my mind.
> Pages, chapters, and volumes
> Every thought making me, mind and body, as great as can be.
>
> I believe in me,
> All the great things I can be.
> I can touch the stars, I can ride the rainbow,
> I can make the grade, I can set the standard.
> I can win and when I don't,
> I'll come back again, better than ever.
> If I can see it I can believe it,
> When I believe it I can be it.
> I believe in me.

This is only the beginning
Of the great things that will be.
I believe in my future,
An unending journey.

I believe in miracles,
And I believe in me.
I'm a winner!
I'm a winner!
I'm a winner!

Don't just say it. Say it with joy. Give a shout for joy, shout out the last verse: *"I'm a Winner! I'm a Winner! I'm a Winner!"* Get out of your chair and dance around, jump up and down, get your endorphins flowing. Associate these great words with movement, energy, excitement.

CAN YOU MAKE MIRACLES? YOU BET YOU CAN!

Grace be with you, mercy and peace.

2 John 3

Can you do what I've described? Can you make miracles? You bet you can! Great desire unleashes great potential. Great desire musters your talents and creates opportunities. You can be what you want to be, what you believe you can be. You can live to your fullest potential.

God spoke, and it was done. You have the same power, within your world. Speak, think, act great things: And they will be done. Not by might, not by power, but by the incredible strength of your spirit.

Shout for joy, paint your mental filter with the colors of success, dream of the great things you can be. Make miracles. And always remember: God believes in you, and you believe in yourself. And with good reason, for you're a winner!